CONSCIOUSNESS AND LANGUAGE

One of the most important and influential philosophers of the last thirty years, John Searle has been concerned throughout his career with a single overarching question: How can we have a unified and theoretically satisfactory account of ourselves and of our relations to other people and to the natural world? In other words, how can we reconcile our common-sense conception of ourselves as conscious, free, mindful, rational agents in a world that we believe comprises brute, unconscious, mindless, meaningless, mute physical particles in fields of force? A cluster of individual questions that have preoccupied him – What is a speech act? What is intentionality? What is consciousness? What is rationality? – are all part of the larger problematic.

The essays in this collection are all related to the broad overarching issue that unites the diverse strands of Searle's work. The first five essays address the issue of how to situate consciousness in particular, and intentional phenomena in general, within a scientific conception of the world. The essays that follow discuss the implications of Searle's approach to the mind for psychology and the other social sciences, explore various ramifications of the theory of speech acts, and defend a version of mental realism by challenging the different forms of skepticism espoused by Quine and Kripke.

Gathering in an accessible manner essays otherwise available in relatively obscure books and journals, this collection will be of particular value to professionals and upper-level students in philosophy, as well as to Searle's more extended audience in such neighboring fields as pyschology and linguistics.

John R. Searle is Mills Professor of Philosophy at the University of California, Berkeley. His previous Cambridge books are *Speech Acts* (1969), *Expression and Meaning* (1979), and *Intentionality* (1983).

CONSCIOUSNESS AND LANGUAGE

JOHN R. SEARLE

University of California, Berkeley

PUBLISHED BY THE PRESS SYNDICATE OF THE UNIVERSITY OF CAMBRIDGE
The Pitt Building, Trumpington Street, Cambridge, United Kingdom

CAMBRIDGE UNIVERSITY PRESS
The Edinburgh Building, Cambridge CB2 2RU, UK
40 West 20th Street, New York, NY 10011-4211, USA
477 Williamstown Road, Port Melbourne, VIC 3207, Australia
Ruiz de Alarcón 13, 28014 Madrid, Spain
Dock House, The Waterfront, Cape Town 8001, South Africa

http://www.cambridge.org

First published 2002

Printed in the United States of America

Typeface Baskerville 10/13 pt. *System* LaTeX 2_ε [TB]

A catalog record for this book is available from the British Library.

Library of Congress Cataloging in Publication Data
Searle, John R.
Consciousness and language / John R. Searle.
p. cm.
Includes bibliographical references and index.
ISBN 0-521-59237-2 – ISBN 0-521-59744-7 (pb.)
1. Consciousness. 2. Intentionality (Philosophy) 3. Language and languages – Philosophy. I. Title.
B1649 .S263 C66 2002
126 – dc21

2001043890

ISBN 0 521 59237 2 hardback
ISBN 0 521 59744 7 paperback

For Grace

CONTENTS

INTRODUCTION

The essays collected in this volume were written over a period of two decades. They deal with a wide range of subjects and were intended for a variety of audiences. Despite the variety, there are certain unifying principles that underlie this collection; indeed, I have tried to make a selection that will exhibit a natural progression, as the topics move from consciousness to intentionality to society to language, and finally conclude with several debates about the issues that have preceded. In this introduction I want to try to state some of these unifying principles and offer a brief description (and note I say "description" rather than "summary" or "abstract") of the essays.

There is a single overarching problem that has preoccupied me since I first began work in philosophy almost a half-century ago: How can we have a unified and theoretically satisfactory account of ourselves and of our relations to other people and to the natural world? How can we reconcile our common-sense conception of ourselves as conscious, free, mindful, speech-act performing, rational agents in a world that we believe consists entirely of brute, unconscious, mindless, meaningless, mute physical particles in fields of force? How, in short, can we make our conception of ourselves fully consistent and coherent with the account of the world that we have acquired from the natural sciences, especially physics, chemistry, and biology? The questions that have most preoccupied me – What is a speech act? What is consciousness? What is intentionality? What is society? What is rationality? – have all in one way or another been addressed to this larger problematic. I think this problem – or set of problems – is the most important problem in philosophy, and indeed there is a sense in which, in our particular epoch, it is the only major problem in philosophy.

If one accepts this characterization of my philosophical project then certain other features of my approach to these problems will become apparent, features that are by no means universally shared in the profession. First, philosophical problems of the kind we are dealing with should have clearly stated and definite solutions. There has to be a definite answer to such questions as "What exactly is consciousness and how does it fit in with the rest of the world?"; otherwise we are not making any progress with our task. Though philosophical problems have definite solutions, the solutions can seldom be given as direct answers to philosophical questions. The way I try to proceed is first to analyze the question. Indeed, this is the great lesson of twentieth-century linguistic philosophy: Do not take the questions for granted. Analyze the question before attempting to answer it. I like to proceed by analyzing the question to see whether it rests on a false presupposition, or whether it assimilates the problem at issue to an inappropriate set of paradigms, or whether the terms used in the question are systematically ambiguous. I find that in one way or another, philosophical problems characteristically require dismantling and reconstructing before they can be solved. Once clarity is achieved about exactly what questions are being asked, the answers, or at least the philosophical part of the answers, are often quite clear and simple.

Let me illustrate these points with some examples. Consider the famous "mind-body problem." What exactly is the relationship between consciousness and brain processes? To tackle this question we have to go behind the problem as posed and ask: What presuppositions does this formulation of the problem rest on? This problem resists solution as long as we continue to acept the traditional seventeenth-century vocabulary which presupposes that mental phenomena, naively construed, are in a completely different and separate ontological realm than physical phenomena, naively construed. Once we abandon this vocabulary, and the presuppositions on which it rests, the philosophical problem has a rather simple solution. Once we see that consciousness, with all its inner, qualitative, subjective, touchy-feely qualities, is just an ordinary property of the brain in the way that digestion is a property of the stomach, then the philosophical part of the problem is fairly easy to resolve. But there remains a terribly difficult scientific problem about how it actually works in the brain. I have something to say about both these issues, the philosophical and the neurobiological, in the course of these essays.

This is one pattern of addressing philosophical problems. A clarification of the problem will leave us with residual issues, but these are amenable to solution by scientific, mathematical, or other well-established means. What

I just said about the mind-body problem also applies, for instance, to the free will problem.

If one thinks of the primary task of philosophical analysis as giving a true, complete, and unifying account of the relations of humans and nature, then another distinction between this approach and that of much mainstream philosophy immediately appears. I find that I, personally, cannot take traditional skeptical worries very seriously. I think we made a mistake in taking so seriously, through the twentieth century, the line of skeptical argument and response that was begun by Descartes. I think in the seventeenth century it was reasonable to consider the existence of knowledge as problematic, and to feel that it required a secure foundation. Now it seems to me absurd to try to treat the existence of knowledge as problematic. If one thing is clear about the present intellectual situation it is that knowledge grows daily. The existence of knowledge is not in doubt. But you would be surprised at how much the persistence of skeptical worries, and the consequent epistemic stance, continue to have deleterious effects in philosophy. So, for example, Quine's famous indeterminacy argument, and indeed the whole project to examine meaning using the method of radical translation, is a matter of adopting an epistemic stance where I think it is inappropriate.

The first five essays – "The Problem of Consciousness," "How to Study Consciousness Scientifically," "Consciousness," "Animal Minds," and "Intentionality and Its Place in Nature" – are all concerned in one way or another with situating consciousness in particular, and intentional phenomena in general, within a scientific conception of how the world works. I think of consciousness and intentionality as biological phenomena on all fours with digestion or photosynthesis. If you think of mental phenomena in this way, you will not be tempted to think, for example, that a computational simulation of the mental phenomena is somehow itself a mental phenomenon. Computational simulations of the mind stand to the real mind the way computational simulations of the stomach stand to the real stomach. You can do a simulation of digestion, but your simulation doesn't thereby digest. You can do a simulation of thinking, but your simulation doesn't thereby think.

When I say that consciousness is a biological phenomenon, many people understand that claim to imply that you could not create consciousness artificially by building a machine. But that is exactly the opposite of the implication that I intend. The brain is a machine, and there is no reason in principle why we could not build an artificial brain that thinks and has other mental processes in the way that our brain does. Indeed, there is no reason in principle why we couldn't build an artificial brain out of completely nonbiological materials. If you can build an artificial heart that pumps blood, why not build an artificial brain that is conscious? However, note that in order to actually produce consciousness, you would have to duplicate the relevant threshold causal powers that the brain has to do it. That is like saying that if you want to build an airplane that can fly, you don't necessarily have to have feathers and flapping wings, but you do have to duplicate the threshold causal powers that birds have to overcome the force of gravity in the earth's atmosphere. These are obvious points, but you would be surprised at how much difficulty I have had at getting them across to the philosophical and cognitive science community over the past two decades.

The first three essays are concerned explicitly with the problem of consciousness. They are arranged in chronological order and exhibit a certain level of development in my thinking about consciousness, together with increasing sophistication in neurobiology about the problem of consciousness. The first essay tries to state exactly what the problem of consciousness is by listing the main features that a theory of consciousness would need to explain. The second essay lists a number of mistakes that we need to avoid if we are to get a scientific account of consciousness, and the third essay reviews some features of the current project of explaining consciousness in neurobiology. In this last and most recent essay, I try to identify the prospects as well as the limitations of current research on consciousness. I distinguish between what I call the "building block model" and the "unified field" conception of consciousness, and make an argument that the unified field conception is more likely to succeed as a neurobiological research project.

This approach to the mind has important implications for the explanatory apparatus to be used in explaining cognitive phenomena. These issues are discussed in the next three essays. The first of these, "Animal Minds," defends the common sense view that animals have minds just as we do – with consciousness, beliefs, and desires, as well as pains and pleasures – but that their mental contents are restricted because animals do not have a language. "Collective Intentions and Actions" extends the account of Intentionality from the individual cases "I think," "I believe," "I intend" to the collective cases "We think," "We believe," "We intend." There is a nontrivial problem about getting the formulation of the conditions of satisfaction right for collective intentionality and much of that essay is devoted to that question. How exactly do we represent the content of my intention to do something, where I have the intention, as an individual, only as a part of our having the intention to do something as a collective? I am playing the violin part of Beethoven's Ninth Symphony and thus making my contribution to our collective activity of playing Beethoven's Ninth Symphony. You are, let us suppose, singing the soprano part and thus making your contribution to our collective activity. How exactly do we represent the conditions of satisfaction of the individual and the collective intentions, and their relation to each other? I don't know if anybody else cares about that question, but it gave me a lot of headaches, and this essay is an attempt to characterize those relations in a way that recognizes both the irreducibility of collective intentionality and the fact that individual intentionality will be necessary to move my body even in cases where I move my body as part of a collective activity. I am definitely not trying to reduce the collective intentionality to individual intentionality, even though I recognize that all human intentionality is in the brains of human individuals.

The next two essays, 7 and 8, discuss the implications of my overall approach to the mind for psychology and other social sciences. In "The Explanation of Cognition," I explore in detail what I think is the correct explanatory apparatus for a sophisticated cognitive science to use, and in "Intentionalistic Explanations in the Social Sciences," I discuss the implications of my overall account of the mind for the traditional disputes between empiricist and interpretivist approaches to the problem of explanation in the social sciences.

The next two essays, 9 and 10, are concerned with extending my earlier work on speech acts in light of my researches in the philosophy of mind. A nagging dispute in the theory of speech acts is between those authors like Grice who take the individual intentionality of the speaker as the essential analytic device, and those like Austin and Wittgenstein who emphasize the role of convention and social practice. These appear to be inconsistent approaches, but I argue in "Individual Intentionality and Social Phenomena in the Theory of Speech Acts" that it is possible to reconcile these two approaches. Properly construed they are not competing answers to the same question, but noncompeting answers to two different and related questions. Essay number 10, "How Performatives Work," attempts to explain a phenomenon that originally gave rise to the whole subject of speech acts but which, oddly enough, seems to me not to have been satisfactorily explained. Namely, how is it possible that we can perform the act of promising or ordering, or christening, or blessing, and so forth, just by saying that we are doing it? The paradox here is that the whole subject of speech acts grew out of Austin's discovery of performative utterances and his ultimate rejection of the distinction between constatives and performatives. If you reject the distinction between constatives and performatives, as I do, and as Austin did – and without this rejection there is no such thing as a theory of speech acts – then you are still left with a problem. How do you explain the original existence of performative utterances? Essay 10 attempts to answer that question.

"Conversation" is about the possibility of extending my account of speech acts to larger stretches of discourse involving two or more people, to conversations. I reach a somewhat pessimistic conclusion. We will not get an account of conversation comparable in explanatory power to the theory of speech acts.

The last three essays are more argumentative than the earlier material. "Analytic Philosophy and Mental Phenomena" attempts to explain and overcome the puzzling tendency that many analytic philosophers have had to reject mental phenomena, naively construed. There has always been a tradition in analytic philosophy that attempts to get rid of consciousness and intentionality in favor of behaviorism, functionalism, computationalism, or some other version of "materialism." I diagnose and answer what I think are some of the most flagrant versions of this error.

Finally, the last two essays. In my work in both the theory of speech acts and the theory of intentionality I presuppose a form of mental realism. I assume we really do have beliefs and desires and other intentional states, and that we really do mean things by the words that we utter. Our mental states have a more or less definite content, and our utterances have a more or less definite meaning. When I began work on intentionality there were two forms of skepticism that seemed to challenge these assumptions: Quine's skepticism about the indeterminacy of translation and meaning, and Kripke's version of Wittgenstein's private language argument. If Quine's argument were correct, it would apply not only to linguistic meaning but to intentionality generally. Similarly with Kripke's skeptical interpretation of Wittgenstein's famous argument: If there is no definite ascertainable fact of the matter about whether or not I am using a word correctly, then it seems there is nothing for a theory of meaning and intentionality to be about. I could not proceed with my work on meaning and intentionality before I answered these two skeptical arguments, at least to my own satisfaction. I try to answer Quine's indeterminacy argument and to show that it is best construed as a reductio ad absurdum of the behaviorist premises from which it proceeds. In answering the Kripkean form of skepticism I distinguish two lines of argument in his book, and I claim that only the second of these is used by Wittgenstein. In any case I try to deal with both. This last chapter, by the way, has not been previously published because, frankly, I thought too much had been published about this issue already. I wrote it at the time of Kripke's publication but did not attempt to publish it. However, it does seem to fit neatly into the context of the present book, so I have included it, even though it is the only previously unpublished article in the collection.

1

THE PROBLEM OF CONSCIOUSNESS

I. What Is Consciousness?

Like most words, 'consciousness' does not admit of a definition in terms of genus and differentia or necessary and sufficient conditions. Nonetheless, it is important to say exactly what we are talking about because the phenomenon of consciousness that we are interested in needs to be distinguished from certain other phenomena such as attention, knowledge, and self-consciousness. By 'consciousness' I simply mean those subjective states of sentience or awareness that begin when one awakes in the morning from a dreamless sleep and continue throughout the day until one goes to sleep at night, or falls into a coma, or dies, or otherwise becomes, as one would say, 'unconscious'.

Above all, consciousness is a biological phenomenon. We should think of consciousness as part of our ordinary biological history, along with digestion, growth, mitosis and meiosis. However, though consciousness is a biological phenomenon, it has some important features that other biological phenomena do not have. The most important of these is what I have called its 'subjectivity'. There is a sense in which each person's consciousness is private to that person, a sense in which he is related to his pains, tickles, itches, thoughts and feelings in a way that is quite unlike the way that others are related to those pains, tickles, itches, thoughts and feelings. This phenomenon

This essay was originally published in *Experimental and Theoretical Studies of Consciousness*, CIBA Foundation Symposium 174 (Wiley, Chichester, 1993), pp. 61–80, copyright © 1993 John Wiley & Sons Limited. It is reprinted here with the kind permission of the CIBA Foundation and of John Wiley & Sons Limited. The theses advanced in this paper are presented in more detail and with more supporting argument in John Searle (1992).

can be described in various ways. It is sometimes described as that feature of consciousness by way of which there is something that it's like or something that it feels like to be in a certain conscious state. If somebody asks me what it feels like to give a lecture in front of a large audience, I can answer that question. But if somebody asks what it feels like to be a shingle or a stone, there is no answer to that question because shingles and stones are not conscious. The point is also put by saying that conscious states have a certain qualitative character; the states in question are sometimes described as 'qualia'.

In spite of its etymology, consciousness should not be confused with knowledge, it should not be confused with attention, and it should not be confused with self-consciousness. I will consider each of these confusions in turn.

Many states of consciousness have little or nothing to do with knowledge. Conscious states of undirected anxiety or nervousness, for example, have no essential connection with knowledge. Consciousness should not be confused with attention. Within one's field of consciousness there are certain elements that are at the focus of one's attention and certain others that are at the periphery of consciousness. It is important to emphasize this distinction because 'to be conscious of' is sometimes used to mean 'to pay attention to'. But the sense of consciousness that we are discussing here allows for the possibility that there are many things on the periphery of one's consciousness – for example, a slight headache I now feel or the feeling of the shirt collar against my neck – which are not at the centre of one's attention. I will have more to say about the distinction between the center and the periphery of consciousness in Section III.

Finally, consciousness should not be confused with self-consciousness. There are indeed certain types of animals, such as humans, that are capable of extremely complicated forms of self-referential consciousness which would normally be described as self-consciousness. For example, I think conscious feelings of shame require that the agent be conscious of himself or herself. But seeing an object or hearing a sound, for example, does not require self-consciousness. And it is not generally the case that all conscious states are also self-conscious.

II. What Are the Relations Between Consciousness and the Brain?

This question is the famous 'mind-body problem'. Though it has a long and sordid history in both philosophy and science, I think, in broad outline at least, it has a rather simple solution. Here it is: Conscious states are caused by lower level neurobiological processes in the brain and are themselves higher level features of the brain. The key notions here are those of *cause* and *feature.* As far as we know anything about how the world works, variable rates of neuron firings in different neuronal architectures cause all the enormous variety of our conscious life. All the stimuli we receive from the external world are converted by the nervous system into one medium, namely, variable rates of neuron firings at synapses. And equally remarkably, these variable rates of neuron firings cause all of the colour and variety of our conscious life. The smell of the flower, the sound of the symphony, the thoughts of theorems in Euclidian geometry – all are caused by lower level biological processes in the brain; and as far as we know, the crucial functional elements are neurons and synapses.

Of course, like any causal hypothesis this one is tentative. It might turn out that we have overestimated the importance of the neuron and the synapse. Perhaps the functional unit is a column or a whole array of neurons, but the crucial point I am trying to make now is that we are looking for causal relationships. The first step in the solution of the mind-body problem is: brain processes *cause* conscious processes.

This leaves us with the question, what is the ontology, what is the form of existence, of these conscious processes? More pointedly, does the claim that there is a causal relation between brain and consciousness commit us to a dualism of 'physical' things and 'mental' things? The answer is a definite no. Brain processes cause consciousness but the consciousness they cause is not some extra substance or entity. It is just a higher level feature of the whole system. The two crucial relationships between consciousness and the brain, then, can be summarized as follows: lower level neuronal processes in the brain cause consciousness, and consciousness is simply a higher level feature of the system that is made up of the lower level neuronal elements.

There are many examples in nature where a higher level feature of a system is caused by lower level elements of that system, even though the feature is a feature of the system made up of those elements. Think of the liquidity of water or the transparency of glass or the solidity of a table, for example. Of course, like all analogies these analogies are imperfect and inadequate in various ways. But the important thing that I am trying to get across is this: there is no metaphysical obstacle, no logical obstacle, to claiming that the relationship between brain and consciousness is one of causation and at the same time claiming that consciousness is just a feature of the brain. Lower level elements of a system can cause higher level features of that system, even though those features are features of a system made up of the lower level elements. Notice, for example, that just as one cannot reach into a glass of water and pick out a molecule and say 'This one is wet', so, one cannot point to a single synapse or neuron in the brain and say 'This one is thinking about my grandmother'. As far as we know anything about it, thoughts about grandmothers occur at a much higher level than that of the single neuron or synapse, just as liquidity occurs at a much higher level than that of single molecules.

Of all the theses that I am advancing in this article, this one arouses the most opposition. I am puzzled as to why there should be so much opposition, so I want to clarify a bit further what the issues are: First, I want to argue that we simply know as a matter of fact that brain processes cause conscious states. We don't know the details about how it works and it may well be a long time before we understand the details involved. Furthermore, it seems to me an understanding of how exactly brain processes cause conscious states may require a revolution in neurobiology. Given our present explanatory apparatus, it is not at all obvious how, within that apparatus, we can account for the causal character of the relation between neuron firings and conscious states. But, at present, from the fact that we do not know *how* it occurs, it does not follow that we do not know *that* it occurs. Many people who object to my solution (or dissolution) of the mind-body problem, object on the grounds that we have no idea how neurobiological processes could cause conscious phenomena. But that does not seem to me a conceptual or logical problem. That is an empirical/theoretical issue for the biological sciences. The problem is to figure out exactly how the system works to produce consciousness, and since we know that in fact it does produce consciousness, we have good reason to suppose that there are specific neurobiological mechanisms by way of which it works.

There are certain philosophical moods we sometimes get into when it seems absolutely astounding that consciousness could be produced by electrobiochemical processes, and it seems almost impossible that we would ever be able to explain it in neurobiological terms. Whenever we get in such moods, however, it is important to remind ourselves that similar mysteries have occurred before in science. A century ago it seemed extremely mysterious, puzzling, and to some people metaphysically impossible that life should be accounted for in terms of mechanical, biological, chemical processes. But now we know that we can give such an account, and the problem of how life arises from biochemistry has been solved to the point that we find it difficult to recover, difficult to understand, why it seemed such an impossibility at one time. Earlier still, electromagnetism seemed mysterious. On a Newtonian conception of the universe there seemed to be no place for the phenomenon of electromagnetism. But with the development of the theory of electromagnetism, the metaphysical worry dissolved. I believe that we are having a similar problem about consciousness now. But once we recognize the fact that conscious states are caused by neurobiological processes, we automatically convert the issue into one for theoretical scientific investigation. We have removed it from the realm of philosophical or metaphysical impossibility.

III. Some Features of Consciousness

The next step in our discussion is to list some (not all) of the essential features of consciousness which an empirical theory of the brain should be able to explain.

Subjectivity

As I mentioned earlier, this is the most important feature. A theory of consciousness needs to explain how a set of neurobiological processes can cause a system to be in a subjective state of sentience or awareness. This phenomenon is unlike anything else in biology, and in a sense it is one of the most amazing features of nature. We resist accepting subjectivity as a ground floor, irreducible phenomenon of nature because, since the seventeenth century, we have come to believe that science must be objective. But this involves a pun on the notion of objectivity. We are confusing the *epistemic* objectivity of scientific investigation with the *ontological* objectivity of the typical subject matter in science in disciplines such as physics and chemistry. Since science aims at objectivity in the epistemic sense that we seek truths that are not dependent on the particular point of view of this or that investigator, it has been tempting to conclude that the reality investigated by science must be objective in the sense of existing independently of the experiences in the human individual. But this last feature, ontological objectivity, is not an essential trait of science. If science is supposed to give an account of how the world works and if subjective states of consciousness are part of the world, then we should seek an (epistemically) objective account of an (ontologically) subjective reality, the reality of subjective states of consciousness. What I am arguing here is that we can have an epistemically objective science of a domain that is ontologically subjective.

Unity

It is important to recognize that in non-pathological forms of consciousness we never just have, for example, a pain in the elbow, a feeling of warmth, or an experience of seeing something red, but we have them all occurring simultaneously as part of one unified conscious experience. Kant called this feature 'the transcendental unity of apperception'. Recently, in neurobiology it has been called 'the binding problem'. There are at least two aspects to this unity that require special mention. First, at any given instant all of our experiences are unified into a single conscious field. Second, the organization of our consciousness extends over more than simple instants. So, for example, if I begin speaking a sentence, I have to maintain in some sense at least an iconic memory of the beginning of the sentence so that I know what I am saying by the time I get to the end of the sentence.

Intentionality

'Intentionality' is the name that philosophers and psychologists give to that feature of many of our mental states by which they are directed at, or about states of affairs in the world. If I have a belief or a desire or a fear, there must always be some content to my belief, desire or fear. It must be about something even if the something it is about does not exist or is a hallucination. Even in cases when I am radically mistaken, there must be some mental content which purports to make reference to the world. Not all conscious states have intentionality in this sense. For example, there are states of anxiety or depression where one is not anxious or depressed about anything in particular but just is in a bad mood. That is not an intentional state. But if one is depressed about a forthcoming event, that is an intentional state because it is directed at something beyond itself.

There is a conceptual connection between consciousness and intentionality in the following respect. Though many, indeed most, of our intentional states at any given point are unconscious, nonetheless, in order for an unconscious intentional state to be genuinely an intentional state it must be accessible in principle to consciousness. It must be the sort of thing that could be conscious even if it, in fact, is blocked by repression, brain lesion, or sheer forgetfulness.

The Distinction Between the Center and the Periphery of Consciousness

At any given moment of non-pathological consciousness I have what might be called a field of consciousness. Within that field I normally pay attention to some things and not to others. So, for example, right now I am paying attention to the problem of describing consciousness but very little attention to the feeling of the shirt on my back or the tightness of my shoes. It is sometimes said that I am unconscious of these. But that is a mistake. The proof that they are a part of my conscious field is that I can at any moment shift my attention to them. But in order for me to shift my attention to them, there must be something there which I was previously not paying attention to which I am now paying attention to.

The Gestalt Structure of Conscious Experience

Within the field of consciousness our experiences are characteristically structured in a way that goes beyond the structure of the actual stimulus. This was one of the most profound discoveries of the Gestalt psychologists. It is most obvious in the case of vision, but the phenomenon is quite general and extends beyond vision. For example, the sketchy lines drawn in Figure 1 do not physically resemble a human face.

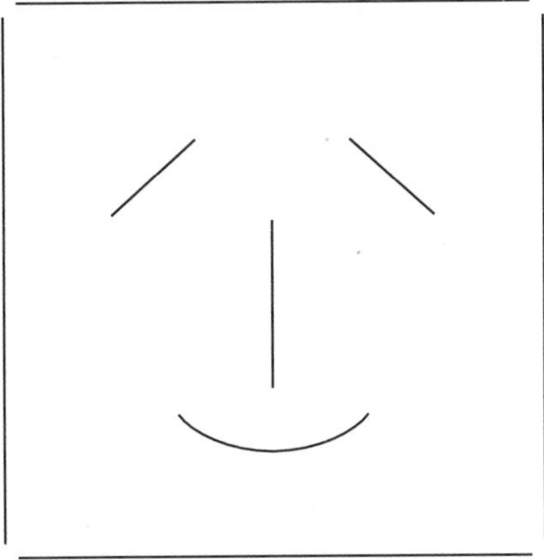

Figure 1

If we actually saw someone on the street who looked like that, we would be inclined to call an ambulance. The disposition of the brain to structure degenerate stimuli into certain structured forms is so powerful that we will naturally tend to see this as a human face. Furthermore, not only do we have our conscious experiences in certain structures, but we tend also to have them as figures against backgrounds. Again, this is most obvious in the case of vision. Thus, when I look at the figure, I see it against the background of the page. I see the page against the background of the table. I see the table against the background of the floor, and I see the floor against the background of the room, until we eventually reach the horizon of my visual consciousness.

The Aspect of Familiarity

It is a characteristic feature of non-pathological states of consciousness that they come to us with what I will call the 'aspect of familiarity'. In order for me to see the objects in front of me as, for example, houses, chairs, people, tables, I have to have a prior possession of the categories of houses, chairs, people, tables. But that means that I will assimilate my experiences into a set of categories which are more or less familiar to me. When I am in an extremely strange environment, in a jungle village, for example, and the houses, people and foliage look very exotic to me, I still perceive that as a house, that as a person, that as clothing, that as a tree or a bush. The aspect of familiarity is thus a scalar phenomenon. There can be greater or lesser degrees of familiarity. But it is important to see that non-pathological forms of consciousness come to us under the aspect of familiarity. Again, one way to consider this is to look at the pathological cases. In Capgras's syndrome, the patients are unable to acknowledge familiar people in their environment as the people they actually are. They think the spouse is not really their spouse but is an impostor, etc. This is a case of a breakdown in one aspect of familiarity. In non-pathological cases it is extremely difficult to break with the aspect of familiarity. Surrealist painters try to do it. But even in the surrealist painting, the threeheaded woman is still a woman, and the drooping watch is still a watch.

Mood

Part of every normal conscious experience is the mood that pervades the experience. It need not be a mood that has a particular name to it, like depression or elation; but there is always what one might call a flavour or tone to any normal set of conscious states. So, for example, at present I am not especially depressed and I am not especially ecstatic, nor, indeed, am I what one would call simply 'blah'. Nonetheless, there is a certain mood to my present experiences. Mood is probably more easily explainable in biochemical terms than several of the features I have mentioned. We may be able to control, for example, pathological forms of depression by mood-altering drugs.

Boundary Conditions

All of my non-pathological states of consciousness come to me with a certain sense of what one might call their 'situatedness'. Though I am not thinking about it, and though it is not part of the field of my consciousness, I nonetheless know what year it is, what place I am in, what time of day it is, the season of the year it is, and usually even what month it is. All of these are the boundary conditions or the situatedness of non-pathological conscious states. Again, one can become aware of the pervasiveness of this phenomenon when it is absent. So, for example, as one gets older there is a certain feeling of vertigo that comes over one when one loses a sense of what time of year it is or what month it is. The point I am making now is that conscious states are situated, and they are experienced as situated, even though the details of the situation need not be part of the content of the conscious states.

IV. Some Common Mistakes About Consciousness

I would like to think that everything I have said so far is just a form of common sense. However, I have to report, from the battlefronts as it were, that the approach I am advocating to the study of consciousness is by no means universally accepted in cognitive science nor even neurobiology. Indeed, until quite recently many workers in cognitive science and neurobiology regarded the study of consciousness as somehow out of bounds for their disciplines. They thought that it was beyond the reach of science to explain why warm things feel warm to us or why red things look red to us. I think, on the contrary, that it is precisely the task of neurobiology to explain these and other questions about consciousness. Why would anyone think otherwise? Well, there are complex historical reasons, going back at least to the seventeenth century, why people thought that consciousness was not part of the material world. A kind of residual dualism prevented people from treating consciousness as a biological phenomenon like any other. However, I am not now going to attempt to trace this history. Instead I am going to point out some common mistakes that occur when people refuse to address consciousness on its own terms.

The characteristic mistake in the study of consciousness is to ignore its essential subjectivity and to try to treat it as if it were an objective third person phenomenon. Instead of recognizing that consciousness is essentially a subjective, qualitative phenomenon, many people mistakenly suppose that its essence is that of a control mechanism or a certain kind of set of dispositions to behavior or a computer program. The two most common mistakes about consciousness are to suppose that it can be analysed behavioristically or computationally. The Turing test disposes us to make precisely these two mistakes, the mistake of behaviorism and the mistake of computationalism.

It leads us to suppose that for a system to be conscious, it is both necessary and sufficient that it has the right computer program or set of programs with the right inputs and outputs. I think you have only to state this position clearly to enable you to see that it must be mistaken. A traditional objection to behaviorism was that behaviorism could not be right because a system could behave as if it were conscious without actually being conscious. There is no logical connection, no necessary connection between inner, subjective, qualitative mental states and external, publicly observable behavior. Of course, in actual fact, conscious states characteristically cause behavior. But the behavior that they cause has to be distinguished from the states themselves. The same mistake is repeated by computational accounts of consciousness. Just as behavior by itself is not sufficient for consciousness, so computational models of consciousness are not sufficient by themselves for consciousness. The computational model of consciousness stands to consciousness in the same way the computational model of anything stands to the domain being modelled. Nobody supposes that the computational model of rainstorms in London will leave us all wet. But they make the mistake of supposing that the computational model of consciousness is somehow conscious. It is the same mistake in both cases.

There is a simple demonstration that the computational model of consciousness is not sufficient for consciousness. I have given it many times before so I will not dwell on it here. Its point is simply this. *Computation is defined syntactically.* It is defined in terms of the manipulation of symbols. But the syntax by itself can never be sufficient for the sort of contents that characteristically go with conscious thoughts. Just having zeros and ones by themselves is insufficient to guarantee mental content, conscious or unconscious. This argument is sometimes called 'the Chinese room argument' because I originally illustrated the point with the example of the person who goes through the computational steps for answering questions in Chinese but does not thereby acquire any understanding of Chinese (Searle, 1980). The point of the parable is clear but it is usually neglected. *Syntax by itself is not sufficient for semantic content.* In all of the attacks on the Chinese room argument, I have never seen anyone come out baldly and say they think that syntax is sufficient for semantic content.

However, I now have to say that I was conceding too much in my earlier statements of this argument. I was conceding that the computational theory of the mind was at least false. But it now seems to me that it does not reach the level of falsity because it does not have a clear sense. Here is why.

The natural sciences describe features of reality that are intrinsic to the world as it exists independently of any observers. Thus, gravitational attraction, photosynthesis, and electromagnetism are all subjects of the natural sciences because they describe intrinsic features of reality. But such features as being a bathtub, being a nice day for a picnic, being a five dollar bill or being a chair are not subjects of the natural sciences because they are not intrinsic features of reality. All the phenomena I named – bathtubs, etc. – are physical objects and as physical objects have features that are intrinsic to reality. But the feature of being a bathtub or a five dollar bill exists only relative to observers and users.

Absolutely essential, then, to understanding the nature of the natural sciences is the distinction between those features of reality that are intrinsic and those that are observer-relative. Gravitational attraction is intrinsic. Being a five dollar bill is observer-relative. Now, the really deep objection to computational theories of the mind can be stated quite clearly. Computation does not name an intrinsic feature of reality but is observer-relative, and this is because computation is defined in terms of symbol manipulation, but the notion of a 'symbol' is not a notion of physics or chemistry. Something is a symbol only if it is used, treated or regarded as a symbol. The Chinese room argument showed that semantics is not intrinsic to syntax. But what this argument shows is that syntax is not intrinsic to physics. There are no purely physical properties that zeros and ones or symbols in general have that determine that they are symbols. Something is a symbol only relative to some observer, user or agent who assigns a symbolic interpretation to it. So the question, 'Is consciousness a computer program?', lacks a clear sense. If it asks, 'Can you assign a computational interpretation to those brain processes which are characteristic of consciousness?' the answer is: you can assign a computational interpretation to anything. But if the question asks, 'Is consciousness intrinsically computational?' the answer is: nothing is intrinsically computational. Computation exists only relative to some agent or observer who imposes a computational interpretation on some phenomenon. This is an obvious point. I should have seen it ten years ago but I did not.

References

Searle, J. R. (1980), 'Minds, Brains, and Programs', *Behavioral and Brain Sciences* 3, 417–57.

Searle, J. R. (1992), *The Rediscovery of the Mind* (Cambridge, Mass.: MIT Press, 1992).

2

HOW TO STUDY CONSCIOUSNESS SCIENTIFICALLY

1. Introduction

The neurosciences have now advanced to the point that we can address – and perhaps, in the long run, even solve – the problem of consciousness as a scientific problem like any other. However there are a number of philosophical obstacles to this project. The aim of this article is to address and try to overcome some of those obstacles. Because the problem of giving an adequate account of consciousness is a modern descendant of the traditional 'mind-body problem', I will begin with a brief discussion of the traditional problem.

The mind-body problem can be divided into two problems; the first is easy to solve, the second is much more difficult. The first is this: what is the general character of the relations between consciousness and other mental phenomena on the one hand and the brain on the other? The solution to the easy problem can be given with two principles: first, consciousness and indeed all mental phenomena are *caused by lower level neurobiological processes in the brain*; and, second, consciousness and other mental phenomena are *higher level features of the brain.* I have expounded this solution to the mind-body problem in a number of writings, so I will not say more about it here (but see Searle 1984, 1992).

The second, and more difficult problem, is to explain in detail how consciousness actually works in the brain. Indeed, I believe that a solution to the second problem would be the most important scientific discovery of the present era. When, and if, it is made, it will be an answer to the question

Reprinted by permission of The Royal Society from *Philosophical Transactions of the Royal Society*, ser. B, 353, no. 1377 (29 November 1998): 1935–1942.

'how exactly do neurobiological processes in the brain cause consciousness?' Given our present models of brain functioning, it would be an answer to the question 'how' exactly do the lower level neuronal firings at synapses cause all of the enormous variety of our conscious (subjective, sentient, aware) experiences?' Perhaps we are wrong to think that neurons and synapses are the right anatomical units to account for consciousness, but we do know that some elements of brain anatomy must be the right level of description for answering our question. We know this because we know that brains do cause consciousness in a way that elbows, livers, television sets, cars and commercial computers do not, and therefore, we know that the special features of brains, features that they do not have in common with elbows, livers, and so forth, must be essential to the causal explanation of consciousness.

The explanation of consciousness is essential for explaining most of the features of our mental life because in one way or another they involve consciousness. How exactly do we have visual perception and other sorts of perceptions? What exactly is the neurobiological basis of memory, and of learning? What are the mechanisms by which nervous systems produce sensations of pain? What, neurobiologically speaking, are dreams and why do we have them? Even: why does alcohol make us drunk and why does bad news make us feel depressed? In fact, I do not believe we can have an adequate understanding of *unconscious* mental states until we know more about the neurobiology of consciousness.

As I said at the beginning, our ability to get an explanation of consciousness – a precise neurobiology of consciousness – is in part impeded by a series of philosophical confusions. This is one of those areas of science (and they are actually more common than one might suppose) where scientific progress is blocked by philosophical error. Since many scientists and philosophers make these errors, I am going to devote this article to trying to remove what I believe are some of the most serious philosophical obstacles to understanding the relation of consciousness to the brain.

Since it will seem presumptuous for a philosopher to try to advise scientists in an area outside his special competence, I want to begin by making a few remarks about the relation of philosophy to science and about the nature of the problem we are discussing. 'Philosophy' and 'science' do not name distinct subject matters in the way that 'molecular biology', 'geology', and 'the history of Renaissance painting' do; rather, at the abstract level at which I am now considering these issues, there is no distinction of subject matter because, in principle at least, both are universal in subject matter. Of the various parts of this universal subject matter, each aims for knowledge.

When knowledge becomes systematic we are more inclined to call it scientific knowledge, but knowledge as such contains no restriction on subject matter. 'Philosophy' is in large part the name for all those questions which we do not know how to answer in the systematic way that is characteristic of science. These questions include, but are not confined to, the large family of conceptual questions that have traditionally occupied philosophers: what is truth, justice, knowledge, meaning, and so forth. For the purposes of this discussion the only important distinction between philosophy and science is this: science is systematic knowledge; philosophy is in part an attempt to reach the point where we can have systematic knowledge. This is why science is always 'right' and philosophy is always 'wrong': as soon as we think we really know something we stop calling it philosophy and start calling it science. Beginning in the seventeenth century, the area of systematic knowledge, that is, scientific knowledge, increased with the growth of systematic methods for acquiring knowledge. Unfortunately, most of the questions that most bother us have not yet been amenable to the methods of scientific investigation. But we do not know how far we can go with those methods and we should be reluctant to say *a priori* that certain questions are beyond the reach of science. I will have more to say about this issue later, because many scientists and philosophers think that the whole subject of consciousness is somehow beyond the reach of science.

A consequence of these points is that there are no 'experts' in philosophy in the way that there are in the sciences. There are experts on the history of philosophy and experts in certain specialized corners of philosophy such as mathematical logic, but on most of the central philosophical questions there is no such thing as an established core of expert opinion. I remark on this because I frequently encounter scientists who want to know what philosophers think about a particular issue. They ask these questions in a way that suggests that they think there is a body of expert opinion that they hope to consult. But in the way that there is an answer to the question 'what do neurobiologists currently think about LTP (long term potentiation)?', there is no comparable answer to the question 'what do philosophers currently think about consciousness?'. Another consequence of these points is that you have to judge for yourself whether what I have to say in this article is true. I cannot appeal to a body of expert opinion to back me up. If I am right, what I say should seem obviously true, once I have said it and once you have thought about it.

The method I will use in my attempt to clear the ground of various philosophical obstacles to the examination of the question 'how exactly do brain processes cause consciousness?' is to present a series of views that I think are false or confused and then, one by one, try to correct them by explaining why I think they are false or confused. In each case, I will discuss views I have found to be widespread among practising scientists and philosophers.

2. Thesis 1

Consciousness is not a suitable subject for scientific investigation because the very notion is ill-defined. We do not have anything like a scientifically acceptable definition of consciousness and it is not easy to see how we could get one, since consciousness is unobservable. The whole notion of consciousness is at best confused and at worst it is mystical.

Answer to Thesis 1

We need to distinguish analytic definitions, which attempt to tell us the essence of a concept, from commonsense definitions, which just clarify what we are talking about. An example of an analytic definition is 'water = df. H_2O'. A common-sense definition of the same word is, for example, 'water is a clear, colourless, tasteless liquid, it falls from the sky in the form of rain, and it is the liquid which is found in lakes, rivers and seas'. Notice that analytic definitions typically come at the *end*, not at the beginning, of a scientific investigation. What we need at this point in our work is a common-sense definition of consciousness and such a definition is not hard to give: 'consciousness' refers to those states of *sentience* or *awareness* that typically begin when we wake from a dreamless sleep and continue through the day until we fall asleep again, die, go into a coma or otherwise become 'unconscious'. Dreams are also a form of consciousness, though in many respects they are quite unlike normal waking states.

Such a definition, the job of which is to identify the target of scientific investigation and not to provide an analysis, is adequate and indeed is exactly what we need to begin our study. Because it is important to be clear about the target, I want to note several consequences of the definition: first, consciousness, so defined, is an inner, qualitative, subjective state typically present in humans and the higher mammals. We do not at present know how far down the phylogenetic scale it goes, and until we obtain an adequate scientific account of consciousness it is not useful to worry about whether, for example, snails are conscious. Second, consciousness, so defined, should not be confused with attention, because in this sense of consciousness there are many things that I am conscious of that I am not paying attention to, such as the feeling of the shirt on my back. Third, consciousness, so defined, should not be confused with self-consciousness. 'Consciousness', as I am using the word, refers to any state of sentience or awareness, but self-consciousness, in which the subject is aware of himself or herself, is a very special form of consciousness, perhaps peculiar to humans and the higher animals. Forms of consciousness such as feeling pain do not necessarily involve a consciousness of the self as a self. Fourth, I experience my own conscious states, but I can neither experience nor observe those of another human or animal, nor can they experience or observe mine. But the fact that the consciousness of others is 'unobservable' does not by itself prevent us from obtaining a scientific account of consciousness. Electrons, black holes and the 'Big Bang' are not observable by anybody, but that does not prevent their scientific investigation.

3. Thesis 2

Science is, by definition, *objective*, but on the definition of consciousness you have provided, you admit it is *subjective*. So, it follows from your definition that there cannot be a science of consciousness.

Answer to Thesis 2

I believe that this statement reflects several centuries of confusion about the distinction between objectivity and subjectivity. It would be a fascinating exercise in intellectual history to trace the vicissitudes of the objective-subjective distinction. In Descartes's writings in the seventeenth century, 'objective' had something close to the opposite of its current meaning (Descartes [1984]: *Meditations on the First Philosophy*, especially the *Third Meditation*, 'but in order for a given idea to contain such and such objective reality, it must surely derive it from some cause which contains at least as much formal reality as there is objective reality in the idea'). Sometime – I don't know when – between the seventeenth century and the present, the objective-subjective distinction rolled over in bed.

However, for present purposes, we need to distinguish between the epistemic sense of the objective-subjective distinction and the ontological sense. In the epistemic sense, objective claims are objectively verifiable or objectively knowable, in the sense that they can be known to be true or false in a way that does not depend on the preferences, attitudes or prejudices of particular human subjects. So, if I say, for example, 'Rembrandt was born in 1606', the truth or falsity of that statement does not depend on the particular attitudes, feelings or preferences of human subjects. It is, as they say, a matter of objectively ascertainable fact. This statement is epistemically objective. It is an objective fact that Rembrandt was born in 1606.

This statement differs from subjective claims whose truth cannot be known in this way. So, for example, if I say 'Rembrandt was a better painter than Rubens', that claim is epistemically subjective, because, as we would say, it's a matter of subjective opinion. There is no objective test, nothing independent of the opinions, attitudes and feelings of particular human subjects, which would be sufficient to establish that Rembrandt was a better painter than Rubens.

I hope that the distinction between objectivity and subjectivity in the epistemic sense is intuitively clear. There is another distinction which is related to the *epistemic* objective-subjective distinction but which should not be confused with it, and that is the distinction between *ontological* objectivity and subjectivity. Some entities have a subjective mode of existence. Some have an objective mode of existence. So, for example, my present feeling of pain in my lower back is ontologically subjective in the sense that it only exists as experienced by me. In this sense, all conscious states are ontologically subjective, because they have to be experienced by a human or an animal subject in order to exist. In this respect, conscious states differ from, for example, mountains, waterfalls or hydrogen atoms. Such entities have an objective mode of existence, because they do not have to be experienced by a human or animal subject in order to exist.

Given this distinction between the *ontological* sense of the objective-subjective distinction and the *epistemic* sense of the distinction, we can see the ambiguity of the claim made in thesis 2. Science is indeed objective in the epistemic sense. We seek truths that are independent of the feelings and attitudes of particular investigators. It does not matter how you feel about hydrogen, whether you like it or don't like it, hydrogen atoms have one electron. It is not a matter of opinion. That is why the claim that Rembrandt was a better painter than Rubens is not a scientific claim. But now, the fact that science seeks objectivity in the epistemic sense should not blind us to the fact that there are ontologically subjective entities that are as much a matter of scientific investigation as any other biological phenomena. We can have epistemically objective knowledge of domains that are ontologically subjective. So, for example, in the epistemic sense, it is an objective matter of fact – not a matter of anybody's opinion – that I have pains in my lower back. But the existence of the pains themselves is ontologically subjective.

The answer, then, to thesis 2, is that the requirement that science be objective does not prevent us from getting an epistemically objective science of a domain that is ontologically subjective.

4. Thesis 3

There is no way that we could ever give an intelligible causal account of how anything subjective and qualitative could be caused by anything objective and quantitative, such as neurobiological phenomena. There is no way to make an intelligible connection between objective third-person phenomena, such as neuron firings, and qualitative, subjective states of sentience and awareness.

Answer to Thesis 3

Of all the theses we are considering, this seems to me the most challenging. In the hands of some authors, for example, Thomas Nagel (1974), it is presented as a serious obstacle to obtaining a scientific account of consciousness using anything like our existing scientific apparatus. The problem, according to Nagel, is that we have no idea how objective phenomena, such as neuron firings, could necessitate, could make it unavoidable, that there be subjective states of awareness. Our standard scientific explanations have a kind of necessity, and this seems to be absent from any imaginable account of subjectivity in terms of neuron firings. What fact about neuron firings in the thalamus could make it necessary that anybody who has those firings in that area of the brain must feel a pain, for example?

However, though I think this is a serious problem for philosophical analysis, for the purpose of the present discussion, there is a rather swift answer to it: we know in fact that it happens. That is, we know as a matter of fact that brain processes cause consciousness. The fact that we do not have a theory that explains how it is possible that brain processes could cause consciousness, is a challenge for philosophers and scientists. But it is by no means a challenge to the fact that brain processes do in fact cause consciousness, because we know independently of any philosophical or scientific argument that they do. The mere fact that it happens is enough to tell us that we should be investigating the form of its happening and not challenging the possibility of its happening.

I accept the unstated assumption behind thesis 3: given our present scientific paradigms, it is not clear how consciousness could be caused by brain processes. But I see this as analogous to the following: within the explanatory apparatus of Newtonian mechanics, it was not clear how there could exist a phenomenon such as electromagnetism; within the explanatory apparatus of nineteenth-century chemistry, it was not clear how there could be a non-vitalistic, chemical explanation of life. That is, I see the problem as analogous to earlier apparently unsolvable problems in the history of science. The challenge is to forget about how we think the world ought to work, and instead figure out how it works in fact.

My own guess – and at this stage in the history of knowledge it is only a speculation – is that when we have a general theory of how brain processes cause consciousness, our sense that it is somehow arbitrary or mysterious will disappear. In the case of the heart, for example, it is clear how the heart pumps the blood. Our understanding of the heart is such that we see the necessity. Given the contractions, it causes blood to flow through the arteries. What we so far lack for the brain is an analogous account of how the brain causes consciousness. But if we had such an account – a general causal account – then it seems to me that our sense of mystery and arbitrariness would disappear.

It is worth pointing out that our sense of mystery has already changed since the seventeenth century. To Descartes and the Cartesians, it seemed mysterious that a physical impact on our bodies should cause a sensation in our souls. But we have no trouble in sensing the necessity of pain given certain sorts of impacts on our bodies. We do not think it at all mysterious that the man whose foot is caught in the punch press is suffering terrible pain. We have moved the sense of mystery inside. It now seems mysterious to us that neuron firings in the thalamus should cause sensations of pain. And I am suggesting that a thorough neurobiological account of exactly how and why it happens would remove this sense of mystery.

5. Thesis 4

All the same, within the problem of consciousness we need to separate out the qualitative, subjective features of consciousness from the measurable objective aspect which can be properly studied scientifically. These subjective features, sometimes called 'qualia', can be safely left on one side. That is, the problem of qualia needs to be separated from the problem of consciousness. Consciousness can be defined in objective third-person terms and the qualia can then be ignored. And, in fact, this is what the best neurobiologists are doing. They separate the general problem of consciousness from the special problem of qualia.

Answer to Thesis 4

I would not have thought that this thesis – that consciousness could be treated separately from qualia – was commonly held until I discovered it in several recent books on consciousness (Crick 1994; Edelman 1989). The basic idea is that the problem of qualia can be carved off from consciousness and treated separately, or, better still, simply brushed aside. This seems to me profoundly mistaken. There are not two separate problems, the problem of consciousness and then a subsidiary problem, the problem of qualia. *The problem of consciousness is identical with the problem of qualia, because conscious states are qualitative states right down to the ground.* Take away the qualia and there is nothing there. This is why I seldom use the word 'qualia', except in sneer quotes, because it suggests that there is something else to consciousness besides qualia, and there is not. Conscious states by definition are inner, qualitative, subjective states of awareness or sentience.

Of course, it is open to anybody to define these terms as they like and use the word 'consciousness' for something else. But then we would still have the problem of what I am calling 'consciousness', which is the problem of accounting for the existence of our ontologically subjective states of awareness. The point for the present discussion is that the problem of consciousness and the problem of so called qualia is the same problem; and you cannot evade the identity by treating consciousness as some sort of third-person, ontologically objective phenomenon and by setting qualia on one side, because to do so is simply to change the subject.

6. Thesis 5

Even if consciousness did exist, as you say it does, in the form of subjective states of awareness or sentience, all the same it could not make a real difference to the real physical world. It would just be a surface phenomenon that did not matter causally to the behaviour of the organism in the world. In the current philosophical jargon, consciousness would be epiphenomenal. It would be like surface reflections on the water of the lake or the froth on the wave coming to the beach. Science can offer an explanation why there are surface reflections or why the waves have a froth, but in our basic account of how the world works, these surface reflections and bits of froth are themselves caused, but are causally insignificant in producing further effects. Think of it this way: if we were doing computer models of cognition, we might have one computer that performed cognitive tasks, and another one, just like the first, except that the second computer was lit up with a purple glow. That is what consciousness amounts to: a scientifically irrelevant, luminous purple glow. And the proof of this point is that for any apparent explanation in terms of consciousness a more fundamental explanation can be given in terms of neurobiology. For every explanation of the form, for example, my conscious decision to raise my arm caused my arm to go up, there is a more fundamental explanation in terms of motor neurons, acetylcholene, and so forth.

Answer to Thesis 5

It might turn out that in our final scientific account of the biology of conscious organisms, the consciousness of these organisms plays only a small or negligible role in their life and survival. This is logically possible in the sense, for example, that it might turn out that DNA is irrelevant to the inheritance of biological traits. It might turn out that way but it is most unlikely, given what we already know. Nothing in thesis 5 is a valid argument in favour of the causal irrelevance of consciousness.

There are indeed different levels of causal explanation in any complex system. When I consciously raise my arm, there is a macro level of explanation in terms of conscious decisions, and a micro level of explanation in terms of synapses and neurotransmitters. But, as a perfectly general point about complex systems, the fact that the macro-level features are themselves caused by the behaviour of the micro-elements and realized in the system composed of the micro-elements does not show that the macro-level features are epiphenomenal. Consider, for example, the solidity of the pistons in my car engine. The solidity of a piston is entirely explainable in terms of the behaviour of the molecules of the metal alloy of which the piston is composed; and for any macro-level explanation of the workings of my car engine given in terms of pistons, the crank shaft, spark plugs, etcetera, there will be micro levels of explanation given in terms of molecules of metal alloys, the oxidization of hydrocarbon molecules, and so forth. But this does not show that the solidity of the piston is epiphenomenal. On the contrary, such an explanation only explains why you can make effective pistons out of steel and not out of butter or 'papier mâché'. Far from showing the macro level to be epiphenomenal, the micro level of explanation shows, among other things, why the macro levels are causally efficacious. That is, in such cases the bottom up causal explanations of macro-level phenomena show why the macrophenomena are not epiphenomenal. An adequate science of consciousness should analogously show how my conscious decision to raise my arm causes my arm to go up by showing how the consciousness, as a biological feature of the brain, is grounded in the micro-level neurobiological features.

The point that I am making here is quite familiar: it is basic to our world view that higher-level or macrofeatures of the world are grounded, or implemented, in microstructures. The grounding of the macro in the micro does not by itself show that the macrophenomena are epiphenomenal. Why then do we find it difficult to accept this point where consciousness and the brain are concerned? I believe the difficulty is that we are still in the grip of a residual dualism. The claim that mental states must be epiphenomenal is supported by the assumption that because consciousness is non-physical, it could not have physical effects. The whole thrust of my argument has been to reject this dualism. Consciousness is an ordinary biological, and therefore physical, feature of the organism, as much as digestion or photosynthesis. The fact that it is a physical biological feature does not prevent it from being an ontologically subjective mental feature. The fact that it is both a higher level and a mental feature is no argument at all that it is epiphenomenal, any more than any other higher level biological feature is epiphenomenal. To repeat, it might turn out to be epiphenomenal, but no valid *a priori* philosophical argument has been given which shows that it must turn out that way.

7. Thesis 6

Your last claims fail to answer the crucial question about the causal role of consciousness. That question is: what is the evolutionary function of consciousness? No satisfactory answer has ever been proposed to that question, and it is not easy to see how one will be forthcoming since it is easy to imagine beings which behave just like us who lack these 'inner, qualitative states' you have been describing.

Answer to Thesis 6

I find this point very commonly made, but if you think about it I hope you will agree that it is a very strange claim to make. Suppose someone asked, what is the evolutionary function of wings on birds? The obvious answer is that for most species of birds the wings enable them to fly and flying increases their genetic fitness. The matter is a little more complicated because not all winged birds are able to fly (consider penguins, for example), and more interestingly, according to some accounts, the earliest wings were really stubs sticking out of the body that functioned to help the organism keep warm. But there is no question that relative to their environments, seagulls, for example, are immensely aided by having wings with which they can fly. Now suppose somebody objected by saying that we could imagine the birds flying just as well without wings. What are we supposed to imagine? That the birds are born with rocket engines? That is, the evolutionary question only makes sense given certain background assumptions about how nature works. Given the way that nature works, the primary function of the wings of most species of birds is to enable them to fly. And the fact that we can imagine a science fiction world in which birds fly just as well without wings is really irrelevant to the evolutionary question. Now similarly with consciousness. The way that human and animal intelligence works is through consciousness. We can easily imagine a science fiction world in which unconscious zombies behave exactly as we do. Indeed, I have actually constructed such a thought experiment, to illustrate certain philosophical points about the separability of consciousness and behaviour (Searle 1992, Chapter 3). But that is irrelevant to the actual causal role of consciousness in the real world.

When we are forming a thought experiment to test the evolutionary advantage of some phenotype, what are the rules of the game? In examining the evolutionary functions of wings, no one would think it allowable to argue that wings are useless because we can imagine birds flying just as well without wings. Why is it supposed to be allowable to argue that consciousness is useless because we can imagine humans and animals behaving just as they do now but without consciousness? As a science fiction thought experiment, that is possible, but it is not an attempt to describe the actual world in which we live. In our world, the question 'what is the evolutionary function of consciousness?' is like the question 'what is the evolutionary function of being alive?' After all, we can imagine beings who outwardly behave much as we do but which are all made of cast iron and reproduce by smelting and who are all quite dead. I believe that the standard way in which the question is asked reveals fundamental confusions. In the case of consciousness the question 'what is the evolutionary advantage of consciousness?' is asked in a tone which reveals that we are making the Cartesian mistake. We think of consciousness not as part of the ordinary physical world of wings and water, but as some mysterious non-physical phenomenon that stands outside the world of ordinary biological reality. If we think of consciousness biologically, and if we then try to take the question seriously, the question 'what is the evolutionary function of consciousness?' boils down to, for example, 'what is the evolutionary function of being able to walk, run, sit, eat, think, see, hear, speak a language, reproduce, raise young, organize social groups, find food, avoid danger, raise crops, and build shelters?', *because for humans all of these activities, as well as countless others essential for our survival, are conscious activities.* That is, 'consciousness' does not name a separate phenomenon, isolatable from all other aspects of life, but rather 'consciousness' names the mode in which humans and the higher animals conduct the major activities of their lives.

This is not to deny that there are interesting biological questions about the specific forms of our consciousness. For example, what evolutionary advantages, if any, do we derive from the fact that our colour discriminations are conscious and our digestive discriminations in the digestive tract are typically not conscious? But as a general challenge to the reality and efficacy of consciousness, the sceptical claim that consciousness serves no evolutionary function is without force.

8. Thesis 7

Causation is a relation between discrete events ordered in time. If it were really the case that brain processes cause conscious states, then conscious states would have to be separate events from brain processes and that result would be a form of dualism, a dualism of brain and consciousness. Any attempt to postulate a causal explanation of consciousness in terms of brain processes is necessarily dualistic and therefore incoherent. The correct scientific view is to see that consciousness is *nothing but* patterns of neuron firings.

Answer to Thesis 7

This thesis expresses a common mistake about the nature of causation. Certainly there are many causal relations that fit this paradigm. So, for example, in the statement 'the shooting caused the death of the man' we describe a sequence of events where first the man was shot and then he died. But there are lots of causal relations that are not discrete events but are permanent causal forces operating through time. Think of gravitational attraction. It is not the case that there is first gravitational attraction, and then, later on, the chairs and tables exert pressure against the floor. Rather, gravitational attraction is a constant operating force and, at least in these cases, the cause is co-temporal with the effect.

More importantly for the present discussion, there are many forms of causal explanation that rely on *bottom-up* forms of 'causings'. Two of my favourite examples are solidity and liquidity. This table is capable of resisting pressure and is not interpenetrated by solid objects. But of course, the table, like other solid objects, consists entirely of clouds of molecules. Now, how is it possible that these clouds of molecules exhibit the causal properties of solidity? We have a theory: solidity is caused by the behaviour of molecules. Specifically, when the molecules move in vibratory movements within lattice structures, the object is solid. Now, somebody might say 'well, but then solidity consists in nothing but the behaviour of the molecules', and in a sense that has to be right. However, solidity and liquidity are causal properties in addition to the summation of the molecule movements. Some philosophers find it useful to use the notion of an 'emergent property'. I do not find this a very clear notion, because it is so confused in the literature. But if we are careful, we can give a clear sense to the idea that consciousness, like solidity and liquidity, is an emergent property of the behaviour of the micro-elements of a system that is composed of those micro-elements. An emergent property, so defined, is a property that is explained by the behaviour of the micro-elements but cannot be deduced simply from the composition and the movements of the micro-elements. In my writings, I use the notion of a 'causally emergent' property (Searle 1992, Chapter 5, pp. 111 ff.), and in that sense, liquidity, solidity and consciousness are all causally emergent properties. They are emergent properties caused by the micro-elements of the system of which they are themselves features.

The point that I am eager to insist on now is simply this: the fact that there is a causal relation between brain processes and conscious states does not imply a dualism of brain and consciousness any more than the fact that the causal relation between molecule movements and solidity implies a dualism of molecules and solidity. I believe that the correct way to see the problem is to see that consciousness is a higher-level feature of the system, the behaviour of whose lower-level elements cause it to have that feature.

But this claim leads to the next problem – that of reductionism.

9. Thesis 8

Science is by its very nature *reductionistic*. A scientific account of consciousness must show that it is but an illusion in the same sense in which heat is an illusion. There is nothing to heat (of a gas), except the kinetic energy of the molecule movements. There is nothing else there. Now, similarly, a scientific account of consciousness will be reductionistic. It will show that there is nothing to consciousness except the behaviour of the neurons. There is nothing else there. And this is really the death blow to the idea that there will be a causal relation between the behaviour of the micro-elements, in this case neurons, and the conscious states of the system.

Answer to Thesis 8

The concept of reductionism is one of the most confused notions in science and philosophy. In the literature on the philosophy of science, I found at least half a dozen different concepts of reductionism. It seems to me that the notion has probably outlived its usefulness. What we want from science are general laws and causal explanations. Now, typically when we get a causal explanation, say, of a disease, we can redefine the phenomenon in terms of the cause and so reduce the phenomenon to its cause. For example, instead of defining measles in terms of its symptoms, we redefine it in terms of the virus that causes the symptoms. So, measles is reduced to the presence of a certain kind of virus. There is no factual difference between saying 'the virus causes the symptoms which constitute the disease' and 'the presence of the virus is just the presence of the disease, and the disease causes the symptoms'. The facts are the same in both cases. The reduction is just a matter of different terminology. This is the point: what we want to know is what are the facts?

In the case of reduction and causal explanations of the sort that I just gave, it seems to me that there are two sorts of reductions: those that eliminate the phenomenon being reduced, by showing that there is really nothing there in addition to the features of the reducing phenomena, and those that do not eliminate the phenomenon but simply give a causal explanation of it. I do not suppose that this is a very precise distinction but some examples of it will make it intuitively clear. In the case of heat, we need to distinguish between the movement of the molecules with a certain kinetic energy on the one hand and the subjective sensations of heat on the other. There is nothing there except the molecules moving with a certain kinetic energy and this then causes in us the sensations that we call sensations of heat. The reductionist account of heat carves off the subjective sensations and defines heat as the kinetic energy of the molecule movements. We have an eliminative reduction of heat because there is no objective phenomenon there except the kinetic energy of the molecule movements. Analogous remarks can be made about colour. There is nothing there but the differential scattering of light and these cause in us the experiences that we call colour experiences. But there is not any colour phenomenon there beyond the causes in the form of light reflectances and their subjective effects on us. In such cases, we can do an eliminative reduction of heat and colour. We can say there is nothing there but the physical causes and these cause the subjective experiences. Such reductions are eliminative reductions in the sense that they get rid of the phenomenon that is being reduced. But in this respect they differ from the reductions of solidity to the vibratory movement of molecules in lattice structures. Solidity is a causal property of the system which cannot be eliminated by the reduction of solidity to the vibratory movements of molecules in lattice type structures.

But now why can we not do an eliminative reduction of consciousness in the way that we did for heat and colour? The pattern of the facts is parallel: for heat and colour we have physical causes and subjective experiences. For consciousness we have physical causes in the form of brain processes and the subjective experience of consciousness. So it seems we should reduce consciousness to brain processes. And of course we could if we wanted to, at least in this trivial sense: we could redefine the word 'consciousness' to mean the neurobiological causes of our subjective experiences. But if we did, we would still have the subjective experiences left over, and the whole point of having the concept of consciousness was to have a word to name those subjective experiences. The other reductions were based on carving off the subjective experience of heat, colour, and so forth, and redefining the notion in terms of the causes of those experiences. But where the phenomenon that we are discussing is the subjective experience itself, you cannot carve off the subjective experience and redefine the notion in terms of its causes, without losing the whole point of having the concept in the first place. The asymmetry between heat and colour on the one hand and consciousness on the other has not to do with the facts in the world, but rather with our definitional practices. We need a word to refer to ontologically subjective phenomena of awareness or sentience. And we would lose that feature of the concept of consciousness if we were to redefine the word in terms of the causes of our experiences.

You cannot make the appearance-reality distinction for conscious states themselves, as you can for heat and colour, because for conscious states, the existence of the appearance is the reality in question. If it seems to me that I am conscious, then I am conscious. And that is not an epistemic point. It does not imply that we have certain knowledge of the nature of our conscious states. On the contrary, we are frequently mistaken about our own conscious states, for example, in the case of phantom limb pains. It is a point about the ontology of conscious states.

When we study consciousness scientifically, I believe we should forget about our old obsession with reductionism and seek causal explanations.

What we want is a causal explanation of how brain processes cause our conscious experiences. The obsession with reductionism is a hangover from an earlier phase in the development of scientific knowledge.

10. Thesis 9

Any genuinely scientific account of consciousness must be an information processing account. That is, we must see consciousness as consisting of a series of information processes, and the standard apparatus that we have for accounting for information processing in terms of symbol manipulation by a computing device must form the basis of any scientific account of consciousness.

Answer to Thesis 9

I have actually, in a number of works, answered this mistake in detail (Searle 1980; see also, Searle 1984, 1992). But for present purposes, the essential thing to remember is this: consciousness is an intrinsic feature of certain human and animal nervous systems. The problem with the concept of 'information processing' is that information processing is typically in the mind of an observer. For example, we treat a computer as a bearer and processor of information, but intrinsically, the computer is simply an electronic circuit. We design, build and use such circuits because we can interpret their inputs, outputs, and intermediate processes as information bearing, but in such a case the information in the computer is in the eye of the beholder, it is not intrinsic to the computational system. What goes for the concept of information goes *a fortiori* for the concept of 'symbol manipulation'. The electrical state transitions of a computer are symbol manipulations only relative to the attachment of a symbolic interpretation by some designer, programmer or user. The reason we cannot analyse consciousness in terms of information processing and symbol manipulation is that consciousness is intrinsic to the biology of nervous systems, but information processing and symbol manipulation are observer-relative.

For this reason, any system at all can be interpreted as an information processing system. The stomach processes information about digestion; the falling body processes information about time, distance, and gravity. And so on.

The exceptions to the claim that information processing is observer-relative are precisely cases where some conscious agent is thinking. If I as a conscious agent think, consciously or unconsciously, '2 + 2 = 4', then the information processing and symbol manipulation are intrinsic to my mental processes, because they are the processes of a conscious agent. But in that respect my mental processes differ from my pocket calculator adding 2 + 2 and getting 4. The addition in the calculator is not intrinsic to the circuit, the addition in me is intrinsic to my mental life.

The result of these observations is that in order to make the distinction between the cases which are intrinsically information bearing and symbol manipulating from those which are observer-relative we need the notion of consciousness. Therefore, we cannot explain the notion of consciousness in terms of information processing and symbol manipulations.

11. Conclusion

There are other mistakes I could have discussed, but I hope the removal of those I have listed will actually help us make progress in the study of consciousness. My main message is that we need to take consciousness seriously as a biological phenomenon. Conscious states are caused by neuronal processes, they are realized in neuronal systems and they are intrinsically inner, subjective states of awareness or sentience.

We want to know how they are caused by, and realized in, the brain. Perhaps they can also be caused by some sort of chemistry different from brains altogether, but until we know how brains do it we are not likely to be able to produce it artificially in other chemical systems. The mistakes to avoid are those of changing the subject – thinking that consciousness is a matter of information processing or behaviour, for example – or not taking consciousness seriously on its own terms. Perhaps above all, we need to forget about the history of science and get on with producing what may turn out to be a new phase in that history.

References

Crick, F. 1994. *The astonishing hypothesis: the scientific search for the soul.* New York: Simon & Schuster.

Descartes, R. 1984. *The philosophical writings of Descartes*, vol. II (translated by J. Cottingham, R. Stoothoff & D. Murdoch). Cambridge University Press.

Edelman, G. 1989. *The remembered present: a biological theory of consciousness.* New York: Basic Books.

Nagel, T. 1974. What is it like to be a bat? *Philosoph. Rev.* **83**, 435–450.

Searle, J. R. 1980. Minds, brains and programs. *Behav. Brain Sci.* **3**, 417–457.

Searle, J. R. 1984. *Minds, brains and science.* Cambridge, MA: Harvard University Press.

Searle, J. R. 1992. *The rediscovery of the mind.* Cambridge, MA: MIT Press.

3

CONSCIOUSNESS

Resistance to the Problem

As recently as two decades ago there was little interest among neuroscientists, philosophers, psychologists, and cognitive scientists generally in the problem of consciousness. Reasons for the resistance to the problem varied from discipline to discipline. Philosophers had turned to the analysis of language, psychologists had become convinced that a scientific psychology must be a science of behavior, and cognitive scientists took their research program to be the discovery of the computer programs in the brain that, they thought, would explain cognition. It seemed especially puzzling that neuroscientists should be reluctant to deal with the problem of consciousness, because one of the chief functions of the brain is to cause and sustain conscious states. Studying the brain without studying consciousness would be like studying the stomach without studying digestion, or studying genetics without studying the inheritance of traits. When I first got interested in this problem seriously and tried to discuss it with brain scientists, I found that most of them were not interested in the question.

The reasons for this resistance were various but they mostly boiled down to two. First, many neuroscientists felt – and some still do – that consciousness is not a suitable subject for neuroscientific investigation. A legitimate

Reprinted, with permission, from the *Annual Review of Neuroscience*, Volume 23, © 2000, by Annual Reviews.

I am indebted to many people for discussion of these issues. None of them is responsible for any of my mistakes. I especially wish to thank Samuel Barondes, Dale Berger, Francis Crick, Gerald Edelman, Susan Greenfield, Jennifer Hudin, John Kihlstrom, Jessica Samuels, Dagmar Searle, Wolf Singer, Barry Smith, and Gunther Stent.

brain science can study the microanatomy of the Purkinje cell, or attempt to discover new neurotransmitters, but consciousness seems too airy-fairy and touchy-feely to be a real scientific subject. Others did not exclude consciousness from scientific investigation, but they had a second reason: "We are not ready" to tackle the problem of consciousness. They may be right about that, but my guess is that a lot of people in the early 1950s thought we were not ready to tackle the problem of the molecular basis of life and heredity. They were wrong; and I suggest for the current question, the best way to get ready to deal with a research problem may be to try to solve it.

There were, of course, famous earlier twentieth-century exceptions to the general reluctance to deal with consciousness, and their work has been valuable. I am thinking in particular of the work of Sir Arthur Sherrington, Roger Sperry, and Sir John Eccles.

Whatever was the case 20 years ago, today many serious researchers are attempting to tackle the problem. Among neuroscientists who have written recent books about consciousness are Cotterill (1998), Crick (1994), Damasio (1999), Edelman (1989, 1992), Freeman (1995), Gazzaniga (1988), Greenfield (1995), Hobson (1999), Libet (1993), and Weiskrantz (1997). As far as I can tell, the race to solve the problem of consciousness is already on. My aim here is not to try to survey this literature but to characterize some of the neurobiological problems of consciousness from a philosophical point of view.

Consciousness as a Biological Problem

What exactly is the neurobiological problem of consciousness? The problem, in its crudest terms, is this: How exactly do brain processes cause conscious states and how exactly are those states realized in brain structures? So stated, this problem naturally breaks down into a number of smaller but still large problems: What exactly are the neurobiological correlates of conscious states (NCC), and which of those correlates are actually causally responsible for the production of consciousness? What are the principles according to which biological phenomena such as neuron firings can bring about subjective states of sentience or awareness? How do those principles relate to the already well understood principles of biology? Can we explain consciousness with the existing theoretical apparatus or do we need some revolutionary new theoretical concepts to explain it? Is consciousness localized in certain regions of the brain or is it a global phenomenon? If it is confined to certain regions, which ones? Is it correlated with specific anatomical features, such as specific types of neurons, or is it to be explained functionally with a variety of anatomical correlates? What is the right level for explaining consciousness? Is it the level of neurons and synapses, as most researchers seem to think, or do we have to go to higher functional levels such as neuronal maps (Edelman 1989, 1992), or whole clouds of neurons (Freeman 1995); or are all of these levels much too high so that we have to go below the level of neurons and synapses to the level of the microtubules (Penrose 1994; Hameroff 1998a, b)? Or do we have to think much more globally in terms of Fourier transforms and holography (Pribram 1976, 1991, 1999)?

As stated, this cluster of problems sounds similar to any other such set of problems in biology or in the sciences in general. It sounds like the problem concerning microorganisms: How, exactly, do they cause disease symptoms and how are those symptoms manifested in patients? Or the problem in genetics: By what mechanisms exactly does the genetic structure of the zygote produce the phenotypical traits of the mature organism? In the end I think that is the right way to think of the problem of consciousness – it is a biological problem like any other, because consciousness is a biological phenomenon in exactly the same sense as digestion, growth, or photosynthesis. But unlike other problems in biology, there is a persistent series of philosophical problems that surround the problem of consciousness and before addressing some current research I would like to address some of these problems.

Identifying the Target: The Definition of Consciousness

One often hears it said that "consciousness" is frightfully hard to define. But if we are talking about a definition in common-sense terms, sufficient to identify the target of the investigation, as opposed to a precise scientific definition of the sort that typically comes at the end of a scientific investigation, then the word does not seem to me hard to define. Here is the definition: Consciousness consists of inner, qualitative, subjective states and processes of sentience or awareness. Consciousness, so defined, begins when we wake in the morning from a dreamless sleep and continues until we fall asleep again, die, go into a coma, or otherwise become "unconscious." It includes all of the enormous variety of the awareness that we think of as characteristic of our waking life. It includes everything from feeling a pain, to perceiving objects visually, to states of anxiety and depression, to working out crossword puzzles, playing chess, trying to remember your aunt's phone number, arguing about politics, or to just wishing you were somewhere else. Dreams on this definition are a form of consciousness, though of course they are in many respects quite different from waking consciousness.

This definition is not universally accepted and the word consciousness is used in a variety of other ways. Some authors use the word to refer only to states of self-consciousness, that is, the consciousness that humans and some primates have of themselves as agents. Some use it to refer to the second-order mental states about other mental states; so according to this definition, a pain would not be a conscious state, but worrying about a pain would be a conscious state. Some use "consciousness" behavioristically to refer to any form of complex intelligent behavior. It is, of course, open to anyone to use any word anyway he likes, and we can always redefine consciousness as a technical term. Nonetheless, there is a genuine phenomenon of consciousness in the ordinary sense, however we choose to name it; and it is that phenomenon that I am trying to identify now, because I believe it is the proper target of the investigation.

Consciousness has distinctive features that we need to explain. Because I believe that some, not all, of the problems of consciousness are going to have a neurobiological solution, what follows is a shopping list of what a neurobiological account of consciousness should explain.

The Essential Feature of Consciousness: The Combination of Qualitativeness, Subjectivity, and Unity

Consciousness has three aspects that make it different from other biological phenomena and, indeed, different from other phenomena in the natural world. These three aspects are qualitativeness, subjectivity, and unity. I used to think that for investigative purposes we could treat them as three distinct features, but because they are logically interrelated, I now think it best to treat them together, as different aspects of the same feature. They are not separate because the first implies the second, and the second implies the third. I discuss them in order.

Qualitativeness

Every conscious state has a certain qualitative feel to it, and you can see this clearly if you consider examples. The experience of tasting beer is very different from hearing Beethoven's Ninth Symphony, and both of those have a different qualitative character from smelling a rose or seeing a sunset. These examples illustrate the different qualitative features of conscious experiences. One way to put this point is to say that for every conscious experience there is something that it feels like, or something that it is like, to have that conscious experience. Nagel (1974) made this point over two decades ago when he pointed out that if bats are conscious, then there is something that "it is like" to be a bat. This distinguishes consciousness from other features of the world, because in this sense, for a nonconscious entity such as a car or a brick there is nothing that "it is like" to be that entity. Some philosophers describe this feature of consciousness with the word "qualia," and they say there is a special problem of qualia. I am reluctant to adopt this usage because it seems to imply that there are two separate problems, the problem of consciousness and the problem of qualia. But as I understand these terms, "qualia" is just a plural name for conscious states. Because "consciousness" and "qualia" are coextensive, there seems no point in introducing a special term. Some people think that qualia are characteristic of only perceptual experiences, such as seeing colors and having sensations such as pains, but that there is no qualitative character to thinking. As I understand these terms, that is wrong. Even conscious thinking has a qualitative feel to it. There is something it is like to think that two plus two equals four. There is no way to describe it except by saying that it is the character of thinking consciously "two plus two equals four." But if you believe there is no qualitative character to thinking that, then try to think the same thought in a language you do not know well. If I think in French, "deux et deux fait quatre," I find that it feels quite different. Or try thinking, more painfully, "two plus two equals one hundred eighty-seven." Once again, I think you will agree that these conscious thoughts have different characters. However, the point must be trivial; that is, whether or not conscious thoughts are qualia must follow from our definition of qualia. As I am using the term, thoughts definitely are qualia.

Subjectivity

Conscious states exist only when they are experienced by some human or animal subject. In that sense, they are essentially subjective. I used to treat subjectivity and qualitativeness as distinct features, but it now seems to me that properly understood, qualitativeness implies subjectivity, because in order for there to be a qualitative feel to some event, there must be some subject that experiences the event. No subjectivity, no experience. Even if more than one subject experiences a similar phenomenon, say, two people listening to the same concert, all the same, the qualitative experience can exist only as experienced by some subject or subjects. And even if the different token experiences are qualitatively identical, that is they all exemplify the same type, nonetheless each token experience can exist only if the subject of that experience has it. Because conscious states are subjective in this sense, they have what I call a first-person ontology, as opposed to the third-person ontology of mountains and molecules, which can exist even if no living creatures exist. Subjective conscious states have a first-person ontology ("ontology" here means mode of existence) because they exist only when they are experienced by some human or animal agent. They are experienced by some "I" that has the experience, and it is in that sense that they have a first-person ontology.

Unity

All conscious experiences at any given point in an agent's life come as part of one unified conscious field. If I am sitting at my desk looking out the window, I do not just see the sky above and the brook below shrouded by the trees, and at the same time feel the pressure of my body against the chair, the shirt against my back, and the aftertaste of coffee in my mouth. Rather I experience all of these as part of a single unified conscious field. This unity of any state of qualitative subjectivity has important consequences for a scientific study of consciousness. I say more about them later on. At present I just want to call attention to the fact that the unity is already implicit in subjectivity and qualitativeness for the following reason: If you try to imagine that my conscious state is broken into 17 parts, what you imagine is not a single conscious subject with 17 different conscious states but rather 17 different centers of consciousness. A conscious state, in short, is by definition unified, and the unity will follow from the subjectivity and the qualitativeness because there is no way you could have subjectivity and qualitativeness except with that particular form of unity.

There are two areas of current research where the aspect of unity is especially important. These are, first, the study of the split-brain patients by Gazzaniga (1998) and others (Gazzaniga et al. 1962, 1963) and, second, the study of the binding problem by a number of contemporary researchers. The interest of the split-brain patients is that both the anatomical and the behavioral evidence suggest that in these patients there are two centers of consciousness that after commissurotomy are communicating with each other only imperfectly. They seem to have, so to speak, two conscious minds inside one skull.

The interest of the binding problem is that it looks like this problem might give us in microcosm a way of studying the nature of consciousness because just as the visual system binds all of the different stimulus inputs into a single unified visual percept, so the entire brain somehow unites all of the variety of our different stimulus inputs into a single unified conscious experience.

Several researchers have explored the role of synchronized neuron firings in the range of 40 Hz to account for the capacity of different perceptual systems to bind the diverse stimuli of anatomically distinct neurons into a single perceptual experience (Llinas 1990; Llinas & Pare 1991; Llinas & Ribary 1992, 1993; Singer 1993, 1995; Singer & Gray 1995). For example, in the case of vision, anatomically separate neurons specialized for such things as line, angle, and color all contribute to a single, unified, conscious visual experience of an object. Crick (1994) extended the proposal for the binding problem to a general hypothesis about the NCC. He put forward a tentative hypothesis that perhaps the NCC consists of synchronized neuron firings in the general range of 40 Hz in various networks in the thalamocortical system, specifically in connections between the thalamus and layers four and six of the cortex.

This kind of instantaneous unity has to be distinguished from the organized unification of conscious sequences that we get from short-term or iconic memory. For nonpathological forms of consciousness at least some memory is essential in order that the conscious sequence across time can come in an organized fashion. For example, when I speak a sentence, I have to be able to remember the beginning of the sentence at the time I get to the end if I am to produce coherent speech. Whereas instantaneous unity is essential to, and is part of, the definition of consciousness, organized unity across time is essential to the healthy functioning of the conscious organism, but it is not necessary for the very existence of conscious subjectivity.

This combined feature of qualitative, unified subjectivity is the essence of consciousness and it, more than anything else, is what makes consciousness different from other phenomena studied by the natural sciences. The problem is to explain how brain processes, which are objective third-person biological, chemical, and electrical processes, produce subjective states of feeling and thinking. How does the brain get us over the hump, so to speak, from events in the synaptic cleft and the ion channels to conscious thoughts and feelings? If you take seriously this combined feature as the target of explanation, I believe you get a different sort of research project from what is currently the most influential. Most neurobiologists take what I call the building block approach: Find the NCC for specific elements in the conscious field, such as the experience of color, and then construct the whole field out of such building blocks. Another approach, which I call the unified field approach, takes the research problem to be one of explaining how the brain produces a unified field of subjectivity to start with. On the unified field approach, there are no building blocks; rather there are just modifications of the already existing field of qualitative subjectivity. I say more about this later.

Some philosophers and neuroscientists think we can never have an explanation of subjectivity: We can never explain why warm things feel warm and red things look red. To these skeptics there is a simple answer: We know it happens. We know that brain processes cause all of our inner qualitative, subjective thoughts and feelings. Because we know that it happens, we ought to try to figure out how it happens. Perhaps in the end we will fail but we cannot assume the impossibility of success before we try.

Many philosophers and scientists also think that the subjectivity of conscious states makes it impossible to have a strict science of consciousness. For, they argue, if science is by definition objective, and consciousness is by definition subjective, it follows that there cannot be a science of consciousness. This argument is fallacious. It commits the fallacy of ambiguity over the terms objective and subjective. Here is the ambiguity: We need to distinguish two different senses of the objective-subjective distinction. In one sense, the epistemic sense ("epistemic" here means having to do with knowledge), science is indeed objective. Scientists seek truths that are equally accessible to any competent observer and that are independent of the feelings and attitudes of the experimenters in question. An example of an epistemically objective claim would be "Bill Clinton weighs 210 pounds." An example of an epistemically subjective claim would be "Bill Clinton is a good president." The first is objective because its truth or falsity is settleable in a way that is independent of the feelings and attitudes of the investigators. The second is subjective because it is not so settleable. But there is another sense of the objective-subjective distinction, and that is the ontological sense ("ontological" here means having to do with existence). Some entities, such as pains, tickles, and itches, have a subjective mode of existence, in the sense that they exist only as experienced by a conscious subject. Others, such as mountains, molecules, and tectonic plates, have an objective mode of existence, in the sense that their existence does not depend on any consciousness. The point of making this distinction is to call attention to the fact that the scientific requirement of epistemic objectivity does not preclude ontological subjectivity as a domain of investigation. There is no reason whatever why we cannot have an objective science of pain, even though pains only exist when they are felt by conscious agents. The ontological subjectivity of the feeling of pain does not preclude an epistemically objective science of pain. Though many philosophers and neuroscientists are reluctant to think of subjectivity as a proper domain of scientific investigation, in actual practice we work on it all the time. Any neurology textbook will contain extensive discussions of the etiology and treatment of such ontologically subjective states as pains and anxieties.

Some Other Features

To keep this list short, I mention some other features of consciousness only briefly.

Feature 2: Intentionality

Most important, conscious states typically have "intentionality," that property of mental states by which they are directed at or about objects and states of affairs in the world. Philosophers use the word intentionality not just for "intending" in the ordinary sense but for any mental phenomena at all that have referential content. According to this usage, beliefs, hopes, intentions, fears, desires, and perceptions all are intentional. So if I have a belief, I must have a belief about something. If I have a normal visual experience, it must seem to me that I am actually seeing something, and so forth. Not all conscious states are intentional and not all intentionality is conscious; for example, undirected anxiety lacks intentionality, and the beliefs a man has even when he is asleep lack consciousness then and there. But I think it is obvious that many of the important evolutionary functions of consciousness are intentional: For example, an animal has conscious feelings of hunger and thirst, engages in conscious perceptual discriminations, embarks on conscious intentional actions, and consciously recognizes both friend and foe. All of these are conscious intentional phenomena and all are essential for biological survival. A general neurobiological account of consciousness will explain the intentionality of conscious states. For example, an account of color vision will naturally explain the capacity of agents to make color discriminations.

Feature 3: The Distinction Between the Center and the Periphery of Attention

It is a remarkable fact that within my conscious field at any given time I can shift my attention at will from one aspect to another. So, for example, right now I am not paying any attention to the pressure of the shoes on my feet or the feeling of the shirt on my neck. But I can shift my attention to them any time I want. There is already a fair amount of useful work done on attention.

Feature 4: All Human Conscious Experiences Are in Some Mood or Other

There is always a certain flavor to one's conscious states, always an answer to the question "How are you feeling?" The moods do not necessarily have names. Right now I am not especially elated or annoyed, not ecstatic or depressed, not even just blah. But all the same I will become acutely aware of my mood if there is a dramatic change, if I receive some extremely good or bad news, for example. Moods are not the same as emotions, though the mood we are in will predispose us to having certain emotions.

We are, by the way, closer to having pharmacological control of moods with such drugs as Prozac than we are to having control of other internal features of consciousness.

Feature 5: All Conscious States Come to Us in the Pleasure/Unpleasure Dimension

For any total conscious experience there is always an answer to the question of whether it was pleasant, painful, unpleasant, neutral, and so forth. The pleasure/unpleasure feature is not the same as mood, though of course some moods are more pleasant than others.

Feature 6: Gestalt Structure

The brain has a remarkable capacity to organize very degenerate perceptual stimuli into coherent conscious perceptual forms. I can, for example, recognize a face, or a car, on the basis of very limited stimuli. The best known examples of Gestalt structures come from the researches of the Gestalt psychologists.

Feature 7: Familiarity

There is in varying degrees a sense of familiarity that pervades our conscious experiences. Even if I see a house I have never seen before, I still recognize it as a house; it is of a form and structure that is familiar to me. Surrealist painters try to break this sense of the familiarity and ordinariness of our experiences, but even in surrealist paintings the drooping watch still looks like a watch, and the three-headed dog still looks like a dog.

One could continue this list, and I have done so in other writings (Searle 1992). The point now is to get a minimal shopping list of the features that we want a neurobiology of consciousness to explain. In order to look for a causal explanation, we need to know what the effects are that need explanation. Before examining some current research projects, we need to clear more of the ground.

The Traditional Mind-Body Problem and How to Avoid It

The confusion about objectivity and subjectivity I mentioned earlier is just the tip of the iceberg of the traditional mind-body problem. Though ideally I think scientists would be better off if they ignored this problem, the fact is that they are as much victims of the philosophical traditions as anyone else, and many scientists, like many philosophers, are still in the grip of the traditional categories of mind and body, mental and physical, dualism and materialism, etcetera. This is not the place for a detailed discussion of the mind-body problem, but I need to say a few words about it so that, in the discussion that follows, we can avoid the confusions it has engendered.

The simplest form of the mind-body problem is this: What exactly is the relation of consciousness to the brain? There are two parts to this problem, a philosophical part and a scientific part. I have already been assuming a simple solution to the philosophical part. The solution, I believe, is consistent with everything we know about biology and about how the world works. It is this: Consciousness and other sorts of mental phenomena are caused by neurobiological processes in the brain, and they are realized in the structure of the brain. In a word, the conscious mind is caused by brain processes and is itself a higher level feature of the brain.

The philosophical part is relatively easy but the scientific part is much harder. How, exactly, do brain processes cause consciousness and how, exactly, is consciousness realized in the brain? I want to be very clear about the philosophical part because it is not possible to approach the scientific question intelligently if the philosophical issues are unclear. Notice two features of the philosophical solution. First, the relationship of brain mechanisms to consciousness is one of causation. Processes in the brain cause our conscious experiences. Second, this does not force us to any kind of dualism because the form of causation is bottom-up, and the resulting effect is simply a higher-level feature of the brain itself, not a separate substance. Consciousness is not like some fluid squirted out by the brain. A conscious state is rather a state that the brain is in. Just as water can be in a liquid or solid state without liquidity and solidity being separate substances, so consciousness is a state that the brain is in without consciousness being a separate substance.

Notice that I stated the philosophical solution without using any of the traditional categories of "dualism," "monism," "materialism," and all the rest of it. Frankly, I think those categories are obsolete. But if we accept those categories at face value, then we get the following picture: You have a choice between dualism and materialism. According to dualism, consciousness and other mental phenomena exist in a different ontological realm altogether from the ordinary physical world of physics, chemistry, and biology. According to materialism, consciousness as I have described it does not exist. Neither dualism nor materialism, as traditionally construed, allows us to get an answer to our question. Dualism says that there are two kinds of phenomena in the world, the mental and the physical; materialism says that there is only one, the material. Dualism ends up with an impossible bifurcation of reality into two separate categories and thus makes it impossible to explain the relation between the mental and the physical. But materialism ends up denying the existence of any irreducible subjective qualitative states of sentience or awareness. In short, dualism makes the problem insoluble; materialism denies the existence of any phenomenon to study, and hence of any problem.

On the view that I am proposing, we should reject those categories altogether. We know enough about how the world works to know that consciousness is a biological phenomenon caused by brain processes and realized in the structure of the brain. It is irreducible not because it is ineffable or mysterious, but because it has a first-person ontology and therefore cannot be reduced to phenomena with a third-person ontology. The traditional mistake that people have made in both science and philosophy has been to suppose that if we reject dualism, as I believe we must, then we have to embrace materialism. But on the view that I am putting forward, materialism is just as confused as dualism because it denies the existence of ontologically subjective consciousness in the first place. Just to give it a name, the resulting view that denies both dualism and materialism I call biological naturalism.

How Did We Get into This Mess? A Historical Digression

For a long time I thought scientists would be better off if they ignored the history of the mind-body problem, but I now think that unless you understand something about the history, you will always be in the grip of historical categories. I discovered this when I was debating people in artificial intelligence and found that many of them were in the grip of Descartes, a philosopher many of them had not even read.

What we now think of as the natural sciences did not really begin with ancient Greece. The Greeks had almost everything, and in particular they had the wonderful idea of a "theory." The invention of the idea of a theory – a systematic set of logically related propositions that attempt to explain the phenomena of some domain – was perhaps the greatest single achievement of Greek civilization. However, they did not have the institutionalized practice of systematic observation and experiment. That came only after the Renaissance, especially in the seventeenth century. When you combine systematic experiment and testability with the idea of a theory, you get the possibility of science as we think of it today. But there was a feature of the seventeenth century that was a local accident and is still blocking our path. It is that in the seventeenth century, there was a very serious conflict between science and religion, and it seemed that science was a threat to religion. Part of the way that the apparent threat posed by science to orthodox Christianity was deflected was due to Descartes and Galileo. Descartes, in particular, argued that reality divides into two kinds, the mental and the physical, *res cogitans* and *res extensa.* Descartes made a useful division of the territory: Religion had the territory of the soul, and science could have material reality. But this gave people the mistaken concept that science could deal only with objective third-person phenomena, it could not deal with the inner qualitative subjective experiences that make up our conscious life. This was a perfectly harmless move in the seventeenth century because it kept the church authorities off the backs of the scientists. (It was only partly successful. Descartes, after all, had to leave Paris and live in Holland where there was more tolerance, and Galileo had to make his famous recantation to the church authorities of his heliocentric theory of the planetary system.) However, this history has left us with a tradition and a tendency not to think of consciousness as an appropriate subject for the natural sciences, in the way that we think of disease, digestion, or tectonic plates as subjects of the natural sciences. I urge us to overcome this reluctance, and in order to overcome it, we need to overcome the historical tradition that made it seem perfectly natural to avoid the topic of consciousness altogether in scientific investigation.

Summary of the Argument to This Point

I am assuming that we have established the following: Consciousness is a biological phenomenon like any other. It consists of inner qualitative subjective states of perceiving, feeling, and thinking. Its essential feature is unified, qualitative subjectivity. Conscious states are caused by neurobiological processes in the brain, and they are realized in the structure of the brain.

To say this is analogous to saying that digestive processes are caused by chemical processes in the stomach and the rest of the digestive tract, and that these processes are realized in the stomach and the digestive tract. Consciousness differs from other biological phenomena in that it has a subjective or first-person ontology. But ontological subjectivity does not prevent us from having epistemic objectivity. We can still have an objective science of consciousness. We abandon the traditional categories of dualism and materialism, for the same reason we abandon the categories of phlogiston and vital spirits: They have no application to the real world.

The Scientific Study of Consciousness

How, then, should we proceed in a scientific investigation of the phenomena involved?

Seen from the outside it looks deceptively simple. There are three steps. First, one finds the neurobiological events that are correlated with consciousness (the NCC). Second, one tests to see that the correlation is a genuine causal relation. And third, one tries to develop a theory, ideally in the form of a set of laws, that would formalize the causal relationships.

These three steps are typical of the history of science. Think, for example, of the development of the germ theory of disease. First we find correlations between brute empirical phenomena. Then we test the correlations for causality by manipulating one variable and seeing how it affects the others. Then we develop a theory of the mechanisms involved and test the theory by further experiment. For example, Semmelweis in Vienna in the 1840s found that women obstetric patients in hospitals died more often from puerperal fever than did those who stayed at home. So he looked more closely and found that women examined by medical students who had just come from the autopsy room without washing their hands had an exceptionally high rate of puerperal fever. Here was an empirical correlation. When he made these young doctors wash their hands in chlorinated lime, the mortality rate went way down. He did not yet have the germ theory of disease, but he was moving in that direction. In the study of consciousness we appear to be in the early Semmelweis phase.

At the time of this writing we are still looking for the NCC. Suppose, for example, we found, as Crick once put forward as a tentative hypothesis, that the neurobiological correlate of consciousness was a set of neuron firings between the thalamus and the cortex layers four and six, in the range of 40 Hz. That would be step one, and step two would be to manipulate the phenomena in question to see if you could show a causal relation. Ideally, we need to test for whether the NCC in question is both necessary and sufficient for the existence of consciousness. To establish necessity, we find out whether a subject who has the putative NCC removed thereby loses consciousness; to establish sufficiency, we find out whether an otherwise unconscious subject can be brought to consciousness by inducing the putative NCC. Pure cases of causal sufficiency are rare in biology, and we usually have to understand the notion of conditions against a set of background presuppositions, that is, within a specific biological context. Thus, our sufficient conditions for consciousness would presumably operate only in a subject who was alive, had his brain functioning at a certain level of activity, at a certain appropriate temperature, and so forth. But what we are trying to establish ideally is a proof that the element is not just correlated with consciousness, but that it is both causally necessary and sufficient, other things being equal, for the presence of consciousness. Seen from the outsider's point of view, that looks like the ideal way to proceed. Why has it not yet been done? I do not know. It turns out, for example, that it is very hard to find an exact NCC, and the current investigative tools, most notably in the form of positron emission tomography scans, CAT scans, and functional magnetic resonance imaging techniques, have not yet identified the NCC. There are interesting differences between the scans of conscious subjects and sleeping subjects with REM sleep, on the one hand, and slow-wave sleeping subjects on the other. But it is not easy to tell how much of the differences are related to consciousness. Many things are going on in both the conscious and the unconscious subjects' brains that have nothing to do with the production of consciousness. Given that a subject is already conscious, you can get parts of his or her brain to light up by getting him or her to perform various cognitive tasks, such as perception or memory. But that does not give you the difference between being conscious in general and being totally unconscious. So, to establish this first step, we still appear to be in an early state of the technology of brain research. In spite of all of the hype surrounding the development of imaging techniques, we still, as far as I know, have not found a way to image the NCC.

With all this in mind, let us turn to some actual efforts at solving the problem of consciousness.

The Standard Approach to Consciousness: The Building Block Model

Most theorists tacitly adopt the building block theory of consciousness. The idea is that any conscious field is made of its various parts: the visual experience of red, the taste of coffee, the feeling of the wind coming in through the window. It seems that if we could figure out what makes even one building block conscious, we would have the key to the whole structure. If we could, for example, crack visual consciousness, that would give us the key to all the other modalities. This view is explicit in the work of Crick & Koch (1998). Their idea is that if we could find the NCC for vision, then we could explain visual consciousness, and we would then know what to look for to find the NCC for hearing and for the other modalities, and if we put all those together, we would have the whole conscious field.

The strongest and most original statement I know of the building block theory is by Bartels & Zeki (1998) (Zeki & Bartels 1998). They see the binding activity of the brain not as one that generates a conscious experience that is unified, but rather one that brings together a whole lot of already conscious experiences. As they put it (Bartels & Zeki 1998, p. 2327), "[C]onsciousness is not a unitary faculty, but . . . it consists of many microconsciousnesses." Our field of consciousness is thus made up of a lot of building blocks of microconsciousnesses. "Activity at each stage or node of a processing-perceptual system has a conscious correlate. Binding cellular activity at different nodes is therefore not a process preceding or even facilitating conscious experience, but rather bringing different conscious experiences together" (Bartels & Zeki 1998, p. 2330).

There are at least three lines of research that are consistent with, and often used to support, the building block theory.

Blindsight

Blindsight is the name given by the psychologist Weiskrantz to the phenomenon whereby certain patients with damage to V1 can report incidents occurring in their visual field even though they report no visual awareness of the stimulus. For example, in the case of DB, the earliest patient studied, if an X or an O were shown on a screen in that portion of DB's visual field where he was blind, the patient when asked what he saw, would deny that he saw anything. But if asked to guess, he would guess correctly that it was an X or an O. His guesses were right nearly all the time. Furthermore, the subjects in these experiments are usually surprised at their results. When the experimenter asked DB in an interview after one experiment, "Did you know how well you had done?" DB answered, "No, I didn't, because I couldn't see anything. I couldn't see a darn thing" (Weiskrantz 1986, p. 24). This research has subsequently been carried on with a number of other patients, and blindsight is now also experimentally induced in monkeys (Stoerig & Cowey 1997).

Some researchers suppose that we might use blindsight as the key to understanding consciousness. The argument is the following: In the case of blindsight, we have a clear difference between conscious vision and unconscious information processing. It seems that if we could discover the physiological and anatomical difference between regular sight and blindsight, we might have the key to analyzing consciousness because we would have a clear neurological distinction between the conscious and the unconscious cases.

Binocular Rivalry and Gestalt Switching

One exciting proposal for finding the NCC for vision is to study cases where the external stimulus is constant but where the internal subjective experience varies. Two examples of this are the Gestalt switch, where the same figure, such as the Neckar cube, is perceived in two different ways, and binocular rivalry, where different stimuli are presented to each eye but the visual experience at any instant is of one or the other stimulus, not both. In such cases, the experimenter has a chance to isolate a specific NCC for the visual experience independently of the neurological correlates of the retinal stimulus (Logothetis 1998, Logothetis & Schall 1989). The beauty of this research is that it seems to isolate a precise NCC for a precise conscious experience. Because the external stimulus is constant and there are (at least) two different conscious experiences *A* and *B*, it seems there must be some point in the neural pathways where one sequence of neural events causes experience *A* and another point where a second sequence causes experience *B*. Find those two points and you have found the precise NCCs for two different building blocks of the whole conscious field.

The Neural Correlates of Vision

Perhaps the most obvious way to look for the NCC is to track the neurobiological causes of a specific perceptual modality, such as vision. In a recent article, Crick & Koch (1998) assume as a working hypothesis that only some specific types of neurons will manifest the NCC. They do not think that any of the NCCs of vision are in V1 (Crick & Koch 1995). The reason for thinking that V1 does not contain the NCC is that V1 does not connect to the frontal lobes in such a way that would make V1 contribute directly to the essential information-processing aspect of visual perception. Their idea is that the function of visual consciousness is to provide visual information directly to the parts of the brain that organize voluntary motor output including speech. Thus, because the information in V1 is recoded in subsequent visual areas and does not transmit directly to the frontal cortex, they believe that V1 does not correlate directly with visual consciousness.

Doubts About the Building Block Theory

The building block theory may be right but it has some worrisome features. Most important, all the research done to identify the NCCs has been carried out with subjects who are already conscious, independently of the NCC in question. Going through the cases in order, the problem with the blindsight research as a method of discovering the NCC is that the patients in question only exhibit blindsight if they are already conscious. That is, it is only in the case of fully conscious patients that we can elicit the evidence of information processing that we get in the blindsight examples. So we cannot investigate consciousness in general by studying the difference between the blindsight patient and the normally sighted patient because both patients are fully conscious. It might turn out that what we need in our theory of consciousness is an explanation of the conscious field that is essential to both blindsight and normal vision or, for that matter, to any other sensory modality.

Similar remarks apply to the binocular rivalry experiments. All this research is immensely valuable, but it is not clear how it will give us an understanding of the exact differences between the conscious brain and the unconscious brain because for both experiences in binocular rivalry the brain is fully conscious.

Similarly, Crick (1996) and Crick & Koch (1998) investigated only subjects who were already conscious. What one wants to know is, how is it possible for the subject to be conscious at all? Given that a subject is conscious, his consciousness will be modified by having a visual experience, but it does not follow that the consciousness is made up of various building blocks of which the visual experience is just one.

I wish to state my doubts precisely. There are (at least) two possible hypotheses.

1. The building block theory: The conscious field is made up of small components that combine to form the field. To find the causal NCC for any component is to find an element that is causally necessary and sufficient for that conscious experience. Hence, to find even one is, in an important sense, to crack the problem of consciousness.
2. The unified field theory (explained in more detail below): Conscious experiences come in unified fields. In order to have a visual

experience, a subject has to be conscious already and the experience is a modification of the field. Neither blindsight, binocular rivalry, nor normal vision can give us a genuine causal NCC because only already conscious subjects can have these experiences.

It is important to emphasize that both hypotheses are rival empirical hypotheses to be settled by scientific research and not by philosophical argument. Why then do I prefer hypothesis 2 to hypothesis 1? The building block theory predicts that in a totally unconscious patient, if the patient meets certain minimal physiological conditions (he is alive, the brain is functioning normally, he has the right temperature, etc.), and if you could trigger the NCC for, say, the experience of red, then the unconscious subject would suddenly have a conscious experience of red and nothing else. One building block is as good as another. Research may prove me wrong, but on the basis of what little I know about the brain, I do not believe that is possible. Only a brain that is already over the threshold of consciousness, that already has a conscious field, can have a visual experience of red.

Furthermore, on the multistage theory of Bartels & Zeki (1998) (Zeki & Bartels 1998), the microconsciousnesses are all capable of a separate and independent existence. It is not clear to me what this means. I know what it is like for me to experience my current conscious field, but who experiences all the tiny microconsciousnesses? And what would it be like for each of them to exist separately?

Basal Consciousness and a Unified Field Theory

There is another way to look at matters that implies another research approach. Imagine that you wake from a dreamless sleep in a completely dark room. So far you have no coherent stream of thought and almost no perceptual stimulus. Save for the pressure of your body on the bed and the sense of the covers on top of your body, you are receiving no outside sensory stimuli. All the same there must be a difference in your brain between the state of minimal wakefulness you are now in and the state of unconsciousness you were in before. That difference is the NCC I believe we should be looking for. This state of wakefulness is basal or background consciousness.

Now you turn on the light, get up, move about, and so forth. What happens? Do you create new conscious states? Well, in one sense you obviously do because previously you were not consciously aware of visual stimuli and now you are. But do the visual experiences stand to the whole field of consciousness in the part-whole relation? Well, that is what nearly everybody thinks and what I used to think, but here is another way of looking at it. Think of the visual experience of the table not as an object in the conscious field the way the table is an object in the room, but think of the experience as a modification of the conscious field, as a new form that the unified field takes. As Llinas and his colleagues put it, consciousness is "modulated rather than generated by the senses" (Llinas et al. 1998, p. 1841).

I want to avoid the part-whole metaphor but I also want to avoid the proscenium metaphor. We should not think of my new experiences as new actors on the stage of consciousness but as new bumps or forms or features in the unified field of consciousness. What is the difference? The proscenium metaphor gives us a constant background stage with various actors on it. I think that is wrong. There is just the unified conscious field, nothing else, and it takes different forms.

If this is the right way to look at things (and again this is a hypothesis on my part, nothing more), then we get a different sort of research project. There is no such thing as a separate visual consciousness, so looking for the NCC for vision is barking up the wrong tree. Only the already conscious subject can have visual experiences, so the introduction of visual experiences is not an introduction of consciousness but a modification of a preexisting consciousness.

The research program that is implicit in the hypothesis of unified field consciousness is that at some point we need to investigate the general condition of the conscious brain as opposed to the condition of the unconscious brain. We will not explain the general phenomenon of unified qualitative subjectivity by looking for specific local NCCs. The important question is not what the NCC for visual consciousness is, but how does the visual system introduce visual experiences into an already unified conscious field, and how does the brain create that unified conscious field in the first place. The problem becomes more specific. What we are trying to find is which features of a system that is made up of a hundred billion discrete elements, neurons, connected by synapses can produce a conscious field of the sort that I have described. There is a perfectly ordinary sense in which consciousness is unified and holistic, but the brain is not in that way unified and holistic. So what we have to look for is some massive activity of the brain capable of producing a unified holistic conscious experience. For reasons that we now know from lesion studies, we are unlikely to find this as a global property of the brain, and we have very good reason to believe that activity in the thalamocortical system is probably the place to look for unified field consciousness. The working hypothesis would be that consciousness is in large part localized in the thalamocortical system and that the various other systems feed information to the thalamocortical system that produces modifications corresponding to the various sensory modalities. To put it simply, I do not believe we will find visual consciousness in the visual system and auditory consciousness in the auditory system. We will find a single, unified, conscious field containing visual, auditory, and other aspects.

Notice that if this hypothesis is right, it will solve the binding problem for consciousness automatically. The production of any state of consciousness at all by the brain is the production of a unified consciousness.

We are tempted to think of our conscious field as made up of the various components – visual, tactile, auditory, stream of thought, etcetera. The approach whereby we think of big things as being made up of little things has proved so spectacularly successful in the rest of science that it is almost irresistible to us. Atomic theory, the cellular theory in biology, and the germ theory of disease are all examples. The urge to think of consciousness as likewise made of smaller building blocks is overwhelming. But I think it may be wrong for consciousness. Maybe we should think of consciousness holistically, and perhaps for consciousness we can make sense of the claim that "the whole is greater than the sum of the parts." Indeed, maybe it is wrong to think of consciousness as made up of parts at all. I want to suggest that if we think of consciousness holistically, then the aspects I have mentioned so far, especially our original combination of subjectivity, qualitativeness, and unity all in one feature, will seem less mysterious. Instead of thinking of my current state of consciousness as made up of the various bits – the perception of the computer screen, the sound of the brook outside, the shadows cast by the evening sun falling on the wall – we should think of all of these as modifications, forms that the underlying basal conscious field takes after my peripheral nerve endings have been assaulted by the various external stimuli. The research implication of this is that we should look for consciousness as a feature of the brain emerging from the activities of large masses of neurons, and which cannot be explained by the activities of individual neurons. I am, in sum, urging that we take the unified field approach seriously as an alternative to the more common building block approach.

Variations on the Unified Field Theory

The idea that one should investigate consciousness as a unified field is not new – it goes back at least as far as Kant's doctrine of the transcendental unity of apperception (Kant 1787). In neurobiology I have not found any contemporary authors who state a clear distinction between what I have been calling the building block theory and the unified field theory, but at least two lines of contemporary research are consistent with the approach urged here, the work of Llinas and his colleagues (Llinas 1990, Llinas et al. 1998) and that of Tononi, Edelman, and Sporns (Tononi & Edelman 1998; Tononi et al. 1992, 1998).

On the view of Llinas and his colleagues (Llinas et al. 1998), we should not think of consciousness as produced by sensory inputs but rather as a functional state of large portions of the brain, primarily the thalamocortical system, and we should think of sensory inputs serving to modulate a preexisting consciousness rather that creating consciousness anew. On their view, consciousness is an "intrinsic" state of the brain, not a response to sensory stimulus inputs. Dreams are of special interest to them, because in a dream the brain is conscious but unable to perceive the external world through sensory inputs. They believe the NCC is synchronized oscillatory activity in the thalamocortical system (Llinas et al. 1998, p. 1845).

Tononi & Edelman have advanced what they call the dynamic core hypothesis (1998). They are struck by the fact that consciousness has two remarkable properties, the unity mentioned earlier and the extreme differentiation or complexity within any conscious field. This suggests to them that we should not look for consciousness in a specific sort of neuronal type, but rather in the activities of large neuronal populations. They seek the NCC for the unity of consciousness in the rapid integration that is achieved through the reentry mechanisms of the thalamocortical system. The idea they have is that in order to account for the combination of integration and differentiation in any conscious field, they have to identify large clusters of neurons that function together, that fire in a synchronized fashion. Furthermore, this cluster, which they call a functional cluster, should also show a great deal of differentiation within its component elements in order to account for the different elements of consciousness. They think that synchronous firing among cortical regions between the cortex and the thalamus is an indirect indicator of this functional clustering. Then once such a functional cluster has been identified, they wish to investigate whether it contains different activity patterns of neuronal states. The combination of functional clustering together with differentiation they submit as the dynamic core hypothesis of consciousness. They believe a unified neural process of high complexity constitutes a "dynamic core." They also believe the dynamic core is not spread over the brain but is primarily in the thalamocortical regions, especially those involved in perceptual categorization, and contains reentry mechanisms of the sort that Edelman discussed in his earlier books (1989, 1992). In a new study, they and their colleagues (Srinivasan et al. 1999) claim to find direct evidence of the role of reentry mapping in the NCC.

Like the adherents of the building block theory, they seek such NCCs of consciousness as one can find in the studies of binocular rivalry.

As I understand this view, it seems to combine features of both the building block and the unified field approach.

Conclusion

In my view, the most important problem in the biological sciences today is the problem of consciousness. I believe we are now at a point where we can address this problem as a biological problem like any other. For decades research has been impeded by two mistaken views: first, that consciousness is just a special sort of computer program, a special software in the hardware of the brain; and second, that consciousness is just a matter of information processing. The right sort of information processing – or on some views any sort of information processing – would be sufficient to guarantee consciousness. I have criticized these views at length elsewhere (Searle 1980, 1992, 1997) and do not repeat these criticisms here. But it is important to remind ourselves how profoundly antibiological these views are. On these views brains do not really matter. We just happen to be implemented in brains, but any hardware that could carry the program or process the information would do just as well. I believe, on the contrary, that understanding the nature of consciousness crucially requires understanding how brain processes cause and realize consciousness. Perhaps when we understand how brains do that, we can build conscious artifacts using some nonbiological materials that duplicate, and not merely simulate, the causal powers that brains have. But first we need to understand how brains do it.

Literature Cited

Bartels A, Zeki S. 1998. The theory of multistage integration in the visual brain. *Proc. R. Soc. London Ser. B* 265:2327–32

Cotterill R. 1998. *Enchanted Looms: Consciousness Networks in Brains and Computers.* Cambridge, UK: Cambridge Univ. Press

Crick F. 1994. *The Astonishing Hypothesis: The Scientific Search for the Soul.* New York: Scribner

Crick F. 1996. Visual perception: rivalry and consciousness. *Nature* 379:485–86

Crick F, Koch C. 1995. Are we aware of neural activity in primary visual cortex? *Nature* 374:121–23

Crick F, Koch C. 1998. Consciousness and neuroscience. *Cereb. Cortex* 8:97–107

Damasio A. 1999. *The Feeling of What Happens, Body and Emotion in the Making of Consciousness.* New York: Harcourt Brace Jovanovich

Edelman G. 1989. *The Remembered Present: A Biological Theory of Consciousness.* New York: Basic Books

Edelman G. 1992. *Bright Air, Brilliant Fire: On the Matter of the Mind.* New York: Basic Books

Freeman W. 1995. *Societies of Brains, A Study in the Neuroscience of Love and Hate.* Hillsdale, NJ: Erlbaum

Gazzaniga M. 1988. *How Mind and Brain Interact to Create Our Conscious Lives.* Boston: Houghton Mifflin; and Cambridge, MA: in association with MIT Press

Gazzaniga M. 1998. The split brain revisited. *Sci. Am.* 279:35–39

Gazzaniga M, Bogen J, Sperry R. 1962. Some functional effects of sectioning the cerebral commissures in man. *Proc. Natl. Acad. Sci. USA* 48:1765–69

Gazzaniga M, Bogen J, Sperry R. 1963. Laterality effects in somesthesis following cerebral commissurotomy in man. *Neuropsychologia* 1:209–15

Greenfield S. 1995. *Journeys to the Centers of the Mind: Toward a Science of Consciousness.* New York: Freeman

Hameroff S. 1998a. Funda-Mentality: Is the conscious mind subtly linked to a basic level of the universe? *Trends Cogn. Sci.* 2(4):119–27

Hameroff S. 1998b. Quantum computation in brain microtubules? The Penrose-Hameroff "Orch OR" model of consciousness. *Phil. Trans. R. Soc. London Ser. A* 356:1869–96

Hobson J. 1999. *Consciousness.* New York: Sci. Am Lib./Freeman

Kant I. 1787. *The Critique of Pure Reason.* Riga: Hartknock

Libet B. 1993. *Neurophysiology of Consciousness: Selected Papers and New Essays.* Boston: Birkhauser

Llinas R. 1990. Intrinsic electrical properties of mammalian neurons and CNS function. *Fidea Res. Found. Neurosci. Award Lect.* 4:1–10

Llinas R, Pare D. 1991. Of dreaming and wakefulness. *Neuroscience* 44:521–35

Llinas R, Ribary U. 1992. Rostrocaudal scan in human brain: a global characteristic of the 40-Hz response during sensory input. In *Induced Rhythms in the Brain,* ed. Basar, Bullock, pp. 147–54. Boston: Birkhauser

Llinas R, Ribary U. 1993. Coherent 40-Hz oscillation characterizes dream state in humans. *Proc. Natl. Acad. Sci. USA* 90:2078–2081.

Llinas R, Ribary, U, Contreras D, Pedroarena C. 1998. The neuronal basis for consciousness. *Phil. Trans. R. Soc. London Ser. B* 353:1841–49

Logothetis N. 1998. Single units and conscious vision. *Phil. Trans. R. Soc. London Ser. B* 353:1801–18

Logothetis N, Schall J. 1989. Neuronal correlates of subjective visual perception. *Science* 245:761–63

Nagel T. 1974. What is it like to be a bat? *Philos. Rev.* 83:435–50

Penrose R. 1994. *Shadows of the Mind: A Search for the Missing Science of Consciousness.* New York: Oxford Univ. Press

Pribram K. 1976. Problems concerning the structure of consciousness. In *Consciousness and Brain: A Scientific and Philosophical Inquiry,* ed. G Globus, G Maxwell, I Savodnik, pp. 297–313. New York: Plenum

Pribram K. 1991. *Brain and Perception: Holonomy and Structure in Figural Processing.* Hillsdale, NJ: Erlbaum

Pribram K. 1999. Brain and the composition of conscious experience. *J. Conscious. Stud.* 6:5:19–42

Searle JR. 1980. Minds, brains and programs. *Behav. Brain Sci.* 3:417–57

Searle JR. 1992. *The Rediscovery of the Mind.* Cambridge, MA: MIT Press

Searle JR. 1997. *The Mystery of Consciousness.* New York: NY Rev. Book

Singer W. 1993. Synchronization of cortical activity and its putative role in information processing and learning. *Annu. Rev. Physiol.* 55:349–75

Singer W. 1995. Development and plasticity of cortical processing architectures. *Science* 270:758–64

Singer W, Gray C. 1995. Visual feature integration and the temporal correlation hypothesis. *Annu. Rev. Neurosci.* 18:555–86

Srinivasan R, Russell D, Edelman G, Tononi G. 1999. Frequency tagging competing stimuli in binocular rivalry reveals increased synchronization of neuromagnetic responses during conscious perception. *J. Neurosci.*

Stoerig P, Cowey A. 1997. Blindsight in man and monkey. *Brain* 12:535–59

Tononi G, Edelman G. 1998. Consciousness and complexity. *Science* 282:1846–51

Tononi G, Edelman G, Sporns O. 1998. Complexity and coherency: integrating information in the brain. *Trends Cogn. Sci.* 2:12:474–84

Tononi G, Sporns O, Edelman G. 1992. Reentry and the problem of integrating multiple cortical areas: simulation of dynamic integration in the visual system. *Cereb. Cortex* 2:310–35

Tononi G, Srinivasan R, Russell D, Edelman G. 1998. Investigating neural correlates of conscious perception by frequency-tagged neuromagnetic responses. *Proc. Natl. Acad. Sci. USA* 95:3198–203

Weiskrantz L. 1986. *Blindsight: A Case Study and Implications.* New York: Oxford Univ. Press

Weiskrantz L. 1997. *Consciousness Lost and Found.* Oxford, UK: Oxford Univ. Press

Zeki S, Bartels A. 1998. The autonomy of the visual systems and the modularity of conscious vision. *Phil. Trans. R. Soc. London Ser. B* 353:1911–14

4

ANIMAL MINDS

I

Many species of animals have consciousness, intentionality, and thought processes. By "consciousness" I mean those subjective states of sentience and awareness that we have during our waking life (and at a lower level of intensity in our dreams); by "intentionality" I mean that feature of the mind by which it is directed at or about objects and states of affairs in the world; and by "thought processes" I mean those temporal sequences of intentional states that are systematically related to each other, where the relationship is constrained by some rational principles. Examples of conscious states are such things as feeling a pain or hearing a sound. Examples of intentional states are such things as wanting to eat food or believing that someone is approaching. Examples of thought processes are such things as figuring how to get a banana that is out of reach or monitoring the behavior of prey who is on the move and is trying to escape. Though these three phenomena – consciousness, intentionality, and thought processes – overlap, they are not identical. Some conscious states are intentional, some not. Some intentional states are conscious, many are not. For example, my current thought that it is unlikely to rain is conscious, my belief when I am asleep that Bill Clinton is president of the United States is unconscious. All thought processes, as I have defined them, are intentional; but not every intentional state occurs as part of a thought process. For example, a pang of undirected anxiety, though conscious, is not intentional. A sudden desire for a cold beer is both conscious and intentional. An animal who has a sudden

Reprinted by permission from *Midwest Studies in Philosophy*, vol. XIX, 1994: 206–219.

pang of hunger can have that pang without it being part of any thought process.

I have said that many species of animals have consciousness, intentionality, and thought processes. Now why am I so confident about that? Why, for example, am I so confident that my dog, Ludwig Wittgenstein Searle, is conscious? Well, why is he so confident I am conscious? I think part of the correct answer, in the case of both Ludwig and me, is that any other possibility is out of the question. We have, for example, known each other now for quite a while so there is not really any possibility of doubt.

Philosophically speaking the interesting question is why in philosophy and science we have so much trouble seeing that such sorts of answers are the correct ones? I will come back to this point later. Now I want to turn the original question around and ask, why have so many thinkers denied what would appear to be obvious points, that many species of animals other than our own have consciousness, intentionality, and thought processes? Think for a moment how counterintuitive such denials are: I get home from work and Ludwig rushes out to meet me. He jumps up and down and wags his tail. I am certain that (a) he is conscious; (b) he is aware of my presence (intentionality); and (c) that awareness produces in him a state of pleasure (thought process). How could anyone deny either a, b or c? As his namesake might have said, "This is how we play the language game with 'certain'." I now turn to consider some of these denials.

II

In the seventeenth and eighteenth centuries, in response to the Cartesian revolution, it made sense both philosophically and theologically to wonder whether animals had minds. If, as Descartes had taught us, there were two kinds of substances in the universe, mental substance whose essence was thinking or consciousness, and physical substance whose essence was extension, then the question becomes pressing: Which of the animate extended substances had minds? Which of the living substances contained consciousness?

The basic Aristotelian dichotomy between the living and the non-living was transcended by an even more fundamental dichotomy between those things that had minds and those that did not. The question became even more pressing when people reflected on the theological implications of any philosophical answer that they might care to give. The commonsense view that higher animals are conscious in exactly the same sense that human beings are conscious has the result that every such animal possesses an immortal soul. This is because the Cartesian theory of the nature of the mental, and of the distinction between the mental and the physical, has the implication that consciousness is indestructible. Any mental substance is indivisible and so lasts eternally. But if animals have consciousness, then it follows immediately that they have immortal souls, and the afterlife will, to put it mildly, be very much overpopulated. Worse yet, if consciousness extends very far down the phylogenetic scale, then it might turn out that the population of the afterlife includes a very large number of the souls of fleas, snails, ants, and so forth. This is an unwelcome theological consequence of what seemed a plausible philosophical doctrine.

Another problem that arose even for theologians who were not Cartesians is this: If animals are conscious then they can suffer. But if they can suffer then how is their suffering to be justified, given that they do not have original sin and presumably do not have free will? The arguments that were used to reconcile the existence of an omnipotent and beneficent God with a suffering human population do not seem to work for animals.

We now regard these ways of thinking about the problem of animal minds as completely implausible, and the Cartesians gave an equally implausible solution: On their view, animals simply do not have minds. Animals are unconscious automatons and though we feel sympathy for the dog crushed beneath the car wheel, our sympathy is misplaced. It is just as if a computer had been run over.

Ridiculous as this view now seems to us, I believe it is an inevitable consequence of the rest of the Cartesian system. If every mind is an immortal soul, then only beings that can have immortal souls can have minds. The natural way out of this puzzle is to abandon dualism, both property dualism and substance dualism. And if one abandons dualism, if one really abandons it, then one must also abandon materialism, monism, the identity thesis, behaviorism, token-token identity, functionalism, Strong Artificial Intelligence, and all of the other excrescences that dualism has produced in the nineteenth and twentieth centuries. Properly understood, all these absurd views are forms of dualism.[1]

If one thoroughly abandons dualism, what is the result as far as animal minds are concerned? Before answering that, I want to consider some other more recent attempts to show that animals do not have certain sorts of mental phenomena.

[1] See John R. Searle, *The Rediscovery of the Mind* (Cambridge, Mass., 1992) for arguments to substantiate this claim.

III

Very few people today would be willing to argue that animals lack consciousness altogether. But several thinkers, both philosophers and scientists, have argued either that animals lack intentionality in general or at least that animals cannot think, that is, they cannot have thought processes in my sense. I am frankly extremely suspicious *a priori* of any argument of this form because we know in advance that humans do have intentionality and thought processes and we know that humans are biologically continuous with the rest of the animal kingdom. Whatever its surface logical form, any argument against animal intentionality and thinking has to imply the following piece of speculative neurobiology: the difference between human and animal brains is such that the human brain can cause and sustain intentionality and thinking, and animal brains cannot.

Given what we know about the brains of the higher mammals, especially the primates, any such speculation must seem breathtakingly irresponsible. Anatomically the similarities are too great for such a speculation to seem even remotely plausible, and physiologically we know that the mechanisms that produce intentionality and thought in humans have close parallels in other beasts. Humans, dogs, and chimpanzees all take in perceptual stimuli through visual, tactile, auditory, olfactory, and other sensory receptors; they all send the signals produced by these stimuli to the brain where they are processed; and eventually the resultant brain processes cause motor outputs in the forms of intentional actions such as socializing with other conspecific beasts, eating, playing, fighting, reproducing, raising their young, and trying to stay alive. It seems out of the question, given the neurobiological continuity, to suppose that only humans have intentionality and thoughts.

However, let us turn to the actual arguments against the possibility of animal thinking. The form of the arguments is and has to be the same: humans satisfy a necessary condition on thinking which animals do not and cannot satisfy. Given what we know of the similarities and differences between human and animal capacities, the alleged crucial difference between humans and animals, in all of the arguments I know, is the same: the human possession of language makes human thought possible and the absence of language in animals makes animal thought impossible.

The Cartesians also thought that language was the crucial differentiating feature that distinguished humans from animals. But they thought the significance of language was epistemic. The possession of language was a sure sign that humans are conscious and its absence a sure sign that animals are not conscious. This view has always seemed very puzzling to me.

Why should linguistic behavior be epistemically essential for the presence of consciousness? We know in the case of human beings that children are conscious long before they are able to speak a language and we know that many human beings never acquire the ability to speak a language, but we do not for that reason doubt that they are conscious.

More recent thinkers concede that animals are conscious but think of language as somehow playing a constitutive role in thought, such that beings without language could not have thoughts.

The major premise, then, of these arguments is always that humans have language in a sense in which animals do not have a language, and so far that premise seems to me to be correct. Even those of us who would be willing to describe the waggle dance of the bees as a language and the achievements of the chimpanzees Washoe, Lana, and others as genuinely linguistic would still grant that such symbolizing behavior is vastly weaker than any natural human language. So let us grant that, in some important sense of "language," humans have language, and as far as we know, no other species does. What follows about the mind? Well one thing follows immediately: If there are any intentional states whose possession requires a language, animals cannot have those states, and *a fortiori* they cannot have thought processes involving those states. Clearly there are such states. My dog can want me to take him for a walk but he cannot want me to get my income tax returns in on time for the 1993 tax year. He can want to be let out but he cannot want to write a doctoral thesis on the incidence of mononucleosis among American undergraduates. To have these latter sorts of desires he would have to have, at the very least, linguistic abilities that he lacks. Is there a principle? How do we decide which intentional states require language and which do not? I think there are several principles involved, and I will come back to this question later. Right now I want to continue to follow the arguments against the possibility of any intentionality and thought among linguistically deprived beasts. The argument that there are some intentional states that animals cannot have does not show that they can have no intentional states. Here are some arguments for the stronger thesis.

One argument is that in order to attribute beliefs to a system we have to have a way of distinguishing cases where the system genuinely believes that *p* from cases where the system merely supposes that *p*, hypothesizes that *p*, reckons that *p*, has a hunch that *p*, is certain that *p*, or is merely inclined to think that on balance, all things considered, that *p*.[2] But we cannot

[2] This was an argument popular during my student days at Oxford in the 1950s. I first heard it in lectures and seminars by Stuart Hampshire. I do not know if he ever published it.

make these distinctions for a being that cannot make them for itself, and a being can only make them for itself if it has the relevant vocabulary. The vocabulary need not be the same as or translatable exactly into English, but there must be some vocabulary for marking the different types of intentional states within the range or there is no sense to the attribution of the states.

What are we to make of this argument? Even if we grant the premise that such discriminations require a language, it does not follow that we need to be able to make fine-grained distinctions before we can make any attributions of intentional states at all. In fact this premise just seems wrong. Very general psychological verbs like "believe" and "desire" are often used in such a way as to allow for a slack, an indeterminacy, as to which of the subsidiary forms of the general attitude are exemplified by the agent. Thus I may believe that it is going to rain, without it being the case that I myself could say without reflection whether it is a strong or weak belief, a hunch, a conviction, or a supposition. And even if I can answer these questions on reflection, the reflection itself may fix the relevant attitude. Before I thought about it there simply may not have been any fact of the matter about which kind of belief it was, I just believed that it was going to rain. So I conclude that the fact that fine-grained discriminations cannot be made for animal beliefs and desires does not show that animals do not have beliefs and desires.

A related argument has been considered by Davidson (I am not sure if he accepts it).[3] The fine discriminations we make about the propositional content of beliefs and desires cannot be made for the alleged intentional attributions to animals. We say that the dog believes his master is at home, but does it believe that Mister Smith (who is his master) is at home or that the president of the bank (who is that same master) is at home? Without an answer to such questions we cannot attribute beliefs to the dog.

This argument is parallel to one mentioned earlier. According to that argument, unless there is a determinate fact of the matter about *psychological type*, there is no intentional state; according to this argument, unless there is a determinate fact of the matter about *propositional content* there is no intentional state. The argument is subject to the same objection we made to the earlier one. The premise seems to be false. Even if we assume that there is no fact of the matter as to which is the correct translation of the dog's mental representations into our vocabulary; that, by itself does not show that the dog does not have any mental representations, any beliefs and desires, that we are trying to translate.

[3] D. Davidson, "Thought and Talk" in *Truth and Interpretation* (Oxford, 1984), 155–70.

Davidson mentions this argument only in passing. An argument he presents more seriously against animal thoughts goes as follows. In order that an animal have a thought, the thought must occur in a network of beliefs. His example is: in order to think the gun is loaded I must believe that guns are a type of weapon, and that a gun is an enduring physical object. So in order to have a thought there must be beliefs. But, and this is the crucial step, in order to have beliefs a creature must have the concept of belief. Why? Because in order to have a belief one must be able to distinguish true from false beliefs. But this contrast, between the true and the false, "can only emerge in the context of interpretation" (of language).[4] The notion of a true belief or a false belief depends on the notion of true and false utterances, and these notions cannot exist without a shared language. So, only a creature who is the possessor and interpreter of a language can have thoughts. The basic idea in this argument seems to be that since "truth" is a metalinguistic semantic predicate and since the possession of belief requires the ability to make the distinction between true and false beliefs, it seems to follow immediately that the possession of beliefs requires metalinguistic semantic predicates, and that obviously requires a language.

This argument is not as clear as it might be, and one might object to various of its steps. The feature on which I want to concentrate here is what I take to be the central core of the argument: In order to tell the difference between true and false beliefs one must have a linguistically articulated concept of belief.

The claim is that only within a language can one distinguish correct from incorrect beliefs. I agree with the presupposition of this claim: having an intentional state requires the capacity to discriminate conditions which satisfy from those that do not satisfy the intentional state. Indeed, I wish to generalize this point to all intentional states and not just confine it to beliefs. In general, in order to have intentional states one must be able to tell the difference between satisfied and unsatisfied intentional states. But I see no reason at all to suppose that this necessarily requires a language, and even the most casual observation of animals suggests that they typically discriminate the satisfaction from the frustration of their intentional states, and they do this without a language.

How does it work? Well, the first and most important thing to notice is that beliefs and desires are embedded not only in a network of other beliefs and desires but more importantly in a network of perceptions and actions, and these are the biologically primary forms of intentionality. We have all along

[4] Ibid., 170.

in this discussion been talking as if perception and action were not forms of intentionality but of course they are; they are the biologically primary forms. Typically, for animals as well as humans, perception fixes belief, and belief together with desire determines courses of action. Consider real-life examples: Why is my dog barking up that tree? Because he *believes* that the cat is up the tree, and he wants to catch up to the cat. Why does he believe the cat is up the tree? Because he *saw* the cat run up the tree. Why does he now stop barking up the tree and start running toward the neighbor's yard? Because he no longer believes that the cat is up the tree, but in the neighbor's yard. And why did he correct his belief? Because he just saw (and no doubt smelled) the cat run into the neighbor's yard; and *seeing and smelling is believing.* The general point is that animals correct their beliefs all the time on the basis of their perceptions. In order to make these corrections they have to be able to distinguish the state of affairs in which their belief is satisfied from the state of affairs in which it is not satisfied. And what goes for beliefs also goes for desires.

But why do we need to "postulate" beliefs and desires at all? Why not just grant the existence of perceptions and actions in such cases? The answer is that the behavior is unintelligible without the assumption of beliefs and desires; because the animal, for example, barks up the tree even when he can no longer see or smell the cat, thus manifesting a belief that the cat is up the tree even when he cannot see or smell that the cat is up the tree. And similarly he behaves in ways that manifest a desire for food even when he is neither seeing, smelling, nor eating food.

In such cases animals distinguish true from false beliefs, satisfied from unsatisfied desires, without having the concepts of truth, falsity, satisfaction, or even belief and desire. And why should that seem surprising to anyone? After all, in vision some animals distinguish between red-colored and green-colored objects without having the concepts vision, color, red, or green. I think many people suppose there must be something special about "true" and "false," because they suppose them to be *essentially* semantic predicates in a metalanguage. Given our Tarskian upbringing, we tend to think that the use of "true" and "false" to characterize beliefs must somehow be derived from a more fundamental use to characterize linguistic entities, sentences, and statements, for example. And then it seems to us that if a creature could tell true from false beliefs it would first have to have an object language to give any grip to the original metalanguage distinction between truth and falsity, now being applied by extension to something nonlinguistic.

But all of this is a mistake. "True" and "false" are indeed metalinguistic predicates, but more fundamentally they are *metaintentional* predicates.

They are used to assess success and failure of representations to achieve fit in the mind-to-world direction of fit, *of which statements and sentences are a special case.* It is no more mysterious that an animal, at least sometimes, can tell whether its belief is true or false, than that it can tell whether its desire is satisfied or frustrated. For neither beliefs nor desires does the animal require a language; rather what it requires is some device for recognizing whether the world is the way it seemed to be (belief) and whether the world is the way the animal wants it to be (desire). But an animal does not have to have a language in order to tell true from false beliefs, any more than it has to have a language to tell satisfied from unsatisfied desires. Consider the example of the dog chasing the cat, for an illustration.

IV

I conclude that the arguments I have seen which deny mental phenomena to animals, ranging from Descartes to Davidson, are without force. I now turn to a remaining question: How do we distinguish those intentional states that require a language, and hence are impossible for animals, from those that do not? I believe the best way to answer this question is to list some of the categories of intentional states which require a language and explain the reasons why they require a language. I doubt that I have thought of all of these, but here are five for a start.

1. *Intentional states that are about language.* For example, a creature cannot think that "eat" is a transitive verb or wonder how to translate "Je n'aurais pas pu" into English if it does not possess the capacity to speak a language.
2. *Intentional states that are about facts which have language as partly constitutive of the fact.* For example an animal cannot think that the object in front of it is a twenty-dollar bill or that the man it sees is the Chairman of the Philosophy Department at the University of California, because the facts represented, facts involving human institutions such as money and universities, require language as a constitutive element of the facts.
3. *Intentional states that represent facts that are so remote in space and time from the animal's experience as to be unrepresentable without language.* For example, my dog might think that I am now eating good food, but it cannot think that Napolean ate good food.
4. *Intentional states that represent complex facts, where the complexity cannot be represented without language.* This is a very large class. Thus my dog

can fear a falling object, but he cannot believe the law of gravity even though the falling object instantiates the law of gravity. He can probably have some simple conditional thoughts, but he cannot have subjunctive counterfactual thoughts. Perhaps he can think: "If he gives me that bone I will eat it," but not "If only he had given me a bigger bone I would have enjoyed it more!"

5. *Intentional states that represent facts where the mode of presentation of the fact locates it relative to some linguistic system.* For example, my dog can believe that it is warm here now, but he cannot believe that the 30th of April, 1993, is a warm day, because the system of representing days is essentially linguistic.

No doubt this list could be continued. What it shows so far is that the reasons that an intentional state essentially requires a language for its existence fall into two classes. Either the state has conditions of satisfaction that are essentially linguistic or the mode of representing the conditions of satisfaction is essentially linguistic. Or, quite commonly, both. A third type of reason would be that the type of the state requires language for the very possession of a state of that type. I have seen it claimed that there are such types of state – perhaps hope and resentment would be examples – but I have never seen a convincing argument.

V

I now return to the question: How should we think of animals' mental phenomena in a philosophy purged of dualism? The answer is a form of what I have elsewhere called biological naturalism. Consciousness and other forms of mental phenomena are biological processes occurring in human and certain animal brains. They are as much a part of the biological natural history of animals as are lactation, the secretion of bile, mitosis, meiosis, growth, and digestion. Once we remind ourselves of what we know about the brain and we forget our dualist upbringing, the general outline of the solution to the so-called mind-body problem, whether for humans or animals, is quite simple. Mental phenomena are caused by lower-level neuronal processes in human and animal brains and are themselves higher-level or macro features of those brains. Of course, we do not yet know the details of how it works, how the quite specific neurobiology of human and animal nervous systems causes all the enormous variety of our mental lives. But from the fact that we do not yet know *how* it works it does not follow that we do not know *that* it works.

From the fact that human and animal brains cause consciousness it also does not follow that only human and animal brains could do it. Perhaps one could create consciousness of the sort that exists in us and other animals using some artificial device; perhaps one might be able to create it in systems not made of carbon-based molecules at all. And for all we know, consciousness may have evolved among beasts in other galaxies, or other solar systems within our own dear galaxy, that do not have our local obsession with carbon, hydrogen, nitrogen, and oxygen. But one thing we know for certain: any system capable of causing consciousness and other mental phenomena must have causal capacities to do it equivalent to the threshold biological capacities of animal brains, both our own human brains and the brains of other kinds of animals. From the fact that brains do it causally, it is a trivial logical consequence that any other system capable of doing it causally must have threshold causal powers to do it equivalent to brains. If that sounds trivial, it should. It is, however, routinely denied by any amount of confused contemporary philosophy of mind that tries to treat consciousness as some purely formal abstract phenomenon independent of any biological or physical reality at all. Contemporary versions of this view are sometimes called 'Strong Artificial Intelligence'.[5] They are expressions of one of the major tenets of traditional dualism, the view that where the mind is concerned the specific neurobiology of the brain is of little importance.

So far, we have not the faintest idea how to create consciousness artificially in some other medium, because we do not know exactly how it is created in our own brains. Some of our best contemporary theories tell us that it is a matter of variable rates of neuron firings relative to certain specific neuronal architectures. But what is it exactly about the peculiar electrochemistry of neurons, synapses, transmitters, receptors, and so forth, that enables them to cause consciousness? At present, we do not know. So, the prospects of artificial consciousness are extremely remote, even though the existence of consciousness in brains other than human brains is not seriously in doubt.

Well, what about the special problems having to do with animal minds? I have so far been talking as if humans and animals were in the same boat, but what about the special features of animal minds? Problems in this area can be divided roughly into two categories and it is important to keep them separate. First, *ontological* problems which have to do with the nature, character, and causal relations of animal mental phenomena, both what causes them and what they in turn cause. Second, *epistemic* problems which have to

[5] Cf. John R. Searle, "Minds, Brains and Programs," *Behavioral and Brain Sciences* 3 (1980): 417–24.

do with how we find out about animal mental states, how we know that animals have mental states, and how we know which animals have which sorts of mental states. It is a consequence of the views that I have enunciated so far, that there are not very many interesting philosophical questions about the ontology of animal mental life in general and animal consciousness in particular. The most important questions in this are largely questions for animal psychologists, biologists, and especially neurobiologists. Specifically, if we know that our brains cause consciousness, and we know therefore that any other system capable of causing consciousness must have the relevant threshold causal powers equivalent to our own brains, then the question becomes a factual empirical question: which sorts of animal brains are capable of causing and sustaining consciousness?

Often however in this area epistemology and ontology are confused. The Turing Test tempts us to precisely such a confusion, because the behaviorism behind the test leads to arguments like the following: If two systems behave the same way we have the same grounds for attributing mental states to one as we do to the other. For example, both snails and termites are capable of exhibiting what appears to be goal-directed behavior, so what sense could be attached, for example, to the claim that snails had consciousness and termites did not have it? In fact, since the appearance of goal-directed behavior seems to be a feature of all sorts of artifacts, mouse traps and heat-seeking missiles, for example, if we are going to attribute consciousness to snails or termites on the basis of the appearance of goal-directed behavior, why not to any system that appears to be goal directed, such as mouse traps or heat-seeking missiles?

But if, as I am claiming, this approach confuses epistemology and ontology, what is the right way to look at such questions? How, for example, would we test the hypothesis that snails had consciousness and termites did not? Well, here is one possible way. Suppose we had a science of the brain which enabled us to establish conclusively the causal bases of consciousness in humans. Suppose we discovered that certain electrochemical sequences were causally necessary and sufficient for consciousness in humans. Suppose we knew that humans that had those features were conscious and humans that lacked them lacked consciousness. Suppose we knew, for example, in our own case, that if we knocked out these specific features through anaesthetics, we became unconscious. We may suppose that this is an extremely complicated electrochemical phenomenon, and following a long philosophical tradition, I will simply abbreviate its description as XYZ. Suppose that the presence of features XYZ in the otherwise normal human brain is causally both necessary and sufficient for consciousness. Now, if we found XYZ present in snails but absent in termites, that would seem very strong empirical evidence that snails had consciousness and termites did not. If we had a rich enough theory so that we could identify XYZ as causally both necessary and sufficient for consciousness, then we might regard the hypothesis as definitely established, pending, of course, the usual hesitations about the ultimate falsifiability in principle of any scientific hypothesis.

VI

If the ontological questions are mostly for specialists, what about the epistemology? Here we find plenty of opportunities to clear up philosophical confusions. I have said that contrary to Descartes we are absolutely confident that the higher animals are conscious; but what are the grounds for our confidence? After all, we can design machines that can behave in some areas just as intelligently as animals, perhaps more so, and we are not inclined to ascribe consciousness to these machines. What's the difference? What, other than biological chauvinism, would lead us to ascribe consciousness to animals but not, for example, to computers?

The standard answer has been that we know of the existence of other minds in animals in the same way we know it in humans, we infer from the *behavior* of the human or animal that it has consciousness and other mental phenomena. Since the behavior of other humans and animals is relevantly similar to my own, I infer that they have conscious states just like mine. On this view, if we could build a mechanical animal out of tinker toy parts that behaved like real animals, we would have to say that it too had consciousness.

In response I want to say that I think this view is hopelessly confused and that behavior by itself is simply irrelevant. Even if we confine ourselves to verbal behavior, as Descartes did, it is important to point out that my car radio exhibits much more intelligent verbal behavior, not only than any animal but even than any human that I know. It will on demand provide me with predictions of the weather, reports of the latest news, discussions of the Stock Market as well as Western songs and rock and roll music, and it will display a large number of other forms of verbal behavior, even some where the same radio speaks with a whole lot of its different voices at once. But I do not for a moment suppose that my radio is conscious, and I have no doubt that my dog is conscious. The reason for the distinction is that I have a theory. I have a theory about how radios work and I have a theory about how dogs work. By 'theory' I do not mean anything fancy, I just mean a kind of commonsense theory. I know that a radio is a machine designed for the purpose of transmitting the voices and music produced by people a long way away in such a fashion that I can hear them in my living room or my car. I know that my dog has a certain inner causal structure that is relevantly similar to my own. I know that my dog has eyes, ears, skin, etcetera, and that these form part of the causal bases of his mental life, just as similar structures form part of the causal bases of my mental life. In giving this answer, I am not trying to "answer skepticism" or trying to "solve the other minds problem." I do not think there is any such problem and I do not take skepticism seriously. Rather, I am explaining what are in fact, in real life, the grounds for our complete confidence that dogs are conscious and radios are not. It is not a matter of behavior as such. By itself, behavior is irrelevant. Behavior is only interesting to us to the extent that we see it as the expression of a more ontologically fundamental causal structure. The principle by which we "solve the other minds problem for animals" is not that intelligent behavior is proof of consciousness but rather the principle is that if the animal has a causally relevant structure similar to our own, then it is likely to produce similar mental states in response to similar stimuli. The "behavior" is simply evidence that it is so responding. Nothing more.

Contrary to the whole epistemological tradition, I am suggesting that the grounds on which we found our certainty that animals are conscious is not that intelligent behavior which is the same or similar to ours is proof of consciousness, but rather that causal structures which are the same or similar causal structures to ours produce the same or similar effects. Behavior, even linguistic behavior, is only relevant given certain assumptions about structure. That is why we attribute consciousness to humans and animals, with or without language, and we do not attribute it to radios.

But even saying this seems to me to concede too much. It will almost unavoidably give the impression that I think there really is an other minds problem, that there are tests that a system must pass in order to have a mind, and that dogs and baboons are passing the tests and computers as well as chairs and tables are failing. I think that is the wrong way to see these matters and I will now try to explain why.

The worst mistake that we inherited from Cartesianism was dualism, together with all of its idealist, monist, materialist, physicalist progeny. But the second worst mistake was to take epistemology seriously, or rather to take it seriously in the wrong way. Descartes together with the British empiricists and right up through the Positivists and the Behaviorists of the twentieth century have given us the impression that the question: "How do you know?" asks the fundamental question, the answer to which will explain the relation between us as conscious beings and the world. The idea is that somehow or other we are constantly in some epistemic stance toward the world whereby we are making inferences from evidence of various kinds. We are busy inferring that the sun will rise tomorrow, that other people are conscious, that objects are solid, that events in the past really occurred, and so forth. In this case, the idea is that the evidence that we have that other people are conscious is based on their behavior, and since we see relevantly similar behavior in dogs and primates, we may reasonably infer that they, too, are conscious. Against this tradition, I want to say that epistemology is of relatively little interest in philosophy and daily life. It has its own little corner of interest where we are concentrating on such things as how to understand certain traditional skeptical arguments, but our basic relationships to reality are seldom matters of epistemology. I do not infer that my dog is conscious, any more than, when I come into a room, I infer that the people present are conscious. I simply respond to them as is appropriate to respond to conscious beings. I just treat them as conscious beings and that is that. If somebody says, "Yes, but aren't you ignoring the possibility that other people might be unconscious zombies, and the dog might be, as Descartes thought, a cleverly constructed machine, and that the chairs and tables might, for all you know, be conscious? Aren't you simply ignoring these possibilities?" The answer is: Yes. I am simply ignoring all of these possibilities. They are out of the question. I do not take any of them seriously. Epistemology is of very little interest in the philosophy of mind and in the philosophy of language for the simple reason that where mind and language are concerned, very little of our relationship to the phenomena in question is epistemic. The epistemic stance is a very special attitude that we adopt under certain special circumstances. Normally, it plays very little role in our dealings with people or animals. Another way to put this is to say that it does not matter really *how* I know whether my dog is conscious, or even *whether* or not I do "know" that he is conscious. The fact is, he is conscious and epistemology in this area has to *start* with this fact.

There are indeed grounds for my certainty in the cases of dogs, chairs, tables, baboons, and other people, and I tried to state some of those grounds earlier, but the important thing to see is that I am certain. When I state the grounds for my certainty I am not trying to answer philosophical skepticism or "prove" that animals have minds and tables and chairs do not.

However, though the general or philosophically skeptical form of the "other animals' minds problem" seems to me confused, there are quite specific questions about specific mechanisms the answers to which are essential to scientific progress in this area. For example, how are cats' visual experiences similar to and different from those of humans'? We know quite a lot about this question because we have studied the cat's visual system fairly extensively, and we have an extra motivation for wanting to answer it because we need to know how much we can learn about the human visual system from work done on cats. Furthermore, we currently suppose that certain species of birds navigate by detecting the earth's magnetic field. And the question arises, if they do this, do they do it consciously? And if so, what are the mechanisms for conscious detection of magnetism? In the same vein, bats navigate by bouncing sonar off solid objects in the dark. We would like to know not only what it feels like to do this but what the mechanisms are that produce the conscious experience of detecting material objects by reflected sound waves. The most general question of all is this: What exactly are the neurobiological mechanisms by which consciousness is produced and sustained in animals and humans? An answer to this question would give us solid epistemic grounds for settling the issue as to which animals are conscious and which are not.

Such epistemic questions seem to me meaningful, important, and indeed crucial for scientific progress in these areas. But notice how different they are from traditional philosophical skepticism. They are answered by doing specific work on specific mechanisms, using the best tools available. For example, no one could have said in advance, just on the basis of philosophical reflection, that using PET scans and CAT scans would prove crucial in studying human and animal minds. To these genuine epistemic questions the answer is always the same: Use your ingenuity. Use any weapon you can lay your hands on and stick with any weapon that works. With this type of epistemology we have the best chance of understanding both human and animal minds.

5

INTENTIONALITY AND ITS PLACE IN NATURE

1

Intentionality is that feature of certain mental states and events that consists in their (in a special sense of these words) being *directed at*, being *about*, being *of*, or *representing* certain other entities and states of affairs. If, for example, Robert has the belief that Ronald Reagan is president, then his belief is an intentional state because in the appropriate sense his belief is directed at, or about, or of, or represents Ronald Reagan and the state of affairs that Ronald Reagan is president. In such a case Ronald Reagan is the *intentional object* of Robert's belief, and the existence of the state of affairs that Ronald Reagan is president is the *condition of satisfaction* of his belief. If there is not anything that a belief is about, then it does not have an intentional object; and if the state of affairs it represents does not obtain, it is not satisfied.

Ascriptions of intentionality are of differing kinds, and as these differences have been a source of confusion, I will begin by sorting out some of them. Consider the statements made in utterances of the following sentences:

A. Robert believes that Ronald Reagan is president.
B. Bill sees that it is snowing.
C. "Es regnet" means it's raining.
D. My car thermostat perceives changes in the engine temperature.

Each of these statements ascribes intentionality, but the status of the ascriptions is different. A simply ascribes an intentional mental state, a belief, to

Reprinted from *Synthese* (1984), 61/1, pp. 3–16, © 1984 by D. Reidel Publishing Company, with kind permission from Kluwer Academic Publishers.

a person; B does more than that, since to say of someone that he sees that something is the case implies not only that he has a certain form of intentionality but also that the intentionality is satisfied, that is, that the conditions of satisfaction actually obtain. "See", like "know" but unlike "believe", is a success verb: *x sees that p* entails *p*. There is an intentional phenomenon reported by B, since in order to see something one has to have a visual experience, and the visual experience is the vehicle of intentionality. But B does more than report a visual experience; it also reports that it is satisfied. Furthermore, visual experiences differ from beliefs in being conscious mental events rather than states. A man asleep can be literally said to believe that such and such, but not to see that such and such. Both beliefs and visual experiences are *intrinsic* intentional phenomena in the minds/brains of agents. To say that they are intrinsic is just to say that the states and events really exist in the minds/brains of agents; the ascription of these states and events is to be taken literally, not just as a manner of speaking, nor as shorthand for a statement describing some more complex set of events and relations going on outside the agents.

In this last respect the ascription of intentionality in A and B differs from C and D. C literally ascribes intentionality, though the intentionality is *not intrinsic*, but *derived*. It is literally true that the sentence "Es regnet" means it's raining, but the intentionality in question is not intrinsic to the sentence. That very sentence might have meant something else or nothing at all. To ascribe this form of intentionality to it is shorthand for some statement or statements to the effect that speakers of German use the sentence literally to mean one thing rather than another, and the intentionality of the sentence is derived from this more basic form of intrinsic intentionality of speakers of German. In D, on the other hand, there is no literal ascription of intentionality at all because my car thermostat does not literally have any perceptions. D, unlike C, is a metaphorical ascription of intentionality; but, like C, its point depends on some intrinsic intentionality of agents. We use car thermostats to regulate engine temperatures and therefore they must be able to respond to changes in temperature. Hence the metaphor; and hence its harmlessness, provided we don't confuse the analysis of A, B, and C, with that of D.

To summarize: even from this short list of statements there emerge several distinctions, which – in addition to the usual distinction between conscious and unconscious forms of intentionality – we will need to keep in mind.

1. The distinction between ascriptions of intentionality that imply that the intentional phenomenon is satisfied and those that do not, as illustrated by A and B.

2. The distinction between intentional states and intentional events, as also illustrated by A and B. (For brevity, I will sometimes call both "intentional states".)
3. The distinction between intrinsic intentionality and derived intentionality, as illustrated by the distinction between the intentionality ascribed in A and B, on the one hand, and C on the other.
4. The distinction between literal ascriptions of intentionality such as A, B, and C, whose truth depends on the existence of some intentional phenomenon, whether intrinsic or derived; and metaphorical ascriptions, such as D, which do not literally ascribe any intentionality at all, even though the point of the metaphorical ascription may depend on some intrinsic intentionality of human agents.

In the rest of this essay I will deal only with intrinsic intentionality and the question I will discuss, to put it broadly, is as follows: What is the place of intrinsic intentionality in nature?

2

Intentional mental phenomena are part of our natural biological life history. Feeling thirsty, having visual experiences, having desires, fears, and expectations, are all as much a part of a person's biological life history as breathing, digesting, and sleeping. Intentional phenomena, like other biological phenomena, are real intrinsic features of certain biological organisms, in the same way that mitosis, meiosis, and the secretion of bile are real intrinsic features of certain biological organisms.

Intrinsic intentional phenomena are caused by neurophysiological processes going on in the brain, and they occur in and are realized in the structure of the brain. We do not know much about the details of how such things as neuron firings at synapses cause visual experiences and sensations of thirst; but we are not totally ignorant, and in the cases of these two intentional phenomena we even have pretty good evidence about their locations in the brain. That is, for at least some intentional phenomena, we have some idea of the special role of certain brain organs, such as the visual cortex or the hypothalamus, in producing the intentional phenomena. More important for our present discussion, our ignorance of how it all works in the brain is an empirical ignorance of details and not the result of a metaphysical gulf between two incommensurable categories, the "Mind" and the "Body", which would prevent us from ever overcoming our ignorance. Indeed, the general sorts of relations involved between mental phenomena and the brain are quite familiar to us from other parts of nature. It is common in nature to discover that higher level features of a system are caused by the behavior of lower level microentities and realized in the structure of the system of microentities. For example, the solidity of the metal in the typewriter I am currently hammering on is caused by the behavior of the microparticles that compose the metal, and the solidity is realized in the structure of the system of microparticles, the atoms and molecules. The solidity is a feature of the system but not of any individual particle. Analogously, from what we know about the brain, mental states are features of the brain that are caused by the behavior of the elements at the microlevel and realized in the structure of the system of microelements, the neurons. A mental state is a feature of the system of neurons but not of any particular neuron. Furthermore, on this account there is no more reason for counting mental states as epiphenomenal than there would be for counting any other intrinsic, higher level features of the world, such as the solidity of this typewriter, as epiphenomenal.

In sum, certain organisms have intrinsic intentional states, these are caused by processes in the nervous systems of these organisms, and they are realized in the structure of these nervous systems. These claims should be understood in as naturalistic a sense as the claims that certain biological organisms digest food, that digestion is caused by processes in the digestive tract, and that it all goes on in the stomach and the rest of the digestive tract. Part of our difficulty in hearing the former claims naturalistically derives from the fact that the traditional vocabulary for discussing these problems is designed around a seventeenth-century conception of the "mind/body problem". If we insisted on using the traditional jargon we might say: monism is perfectly compatible with dualism, provided it is a property dualism; and property dualism is compatible with complete physicalism, provided that we recognize that mental properties are just one kind of higher level property along with any number of other kinds. The view is not so much dualism as polyism, and it has the consequence that intrinsic mental properties are just one kind of higher level physical property among many others (which is perhaps a good reason for not using the traditional jargon at all).

It is a remarkable fact about contemporary intellectual life that the existence of intrinsic intentional phenomena is frequently denied. It is sometimes said that the mind with its intentional states is something abstract, such as a computer program or a flow chart; or that mental states have no intrinsic *mental* status because they can be entirely defined in terms of their causes and effects; or that there aren't any *intrinsic* mental states, but rather that talk about mental states is just a manner of speaking that enables us to cope with our environment; and it is even sometimes said that mental terms should not be thought of as standing for actual things in the world at all. To catalogue the reasons that people have had for holding these views and denying everything that biology has to tell us about the brain would be to catalogue some of the leading intellectual confusions of the epoch. One, though only one, of the sources of confusion is the deeply held belief that if we grant the existence of intrinsic intentional states we will be confronted with an insoluble "mind/body" or "mind/brain" problem. But, to paraphrase Darwin, it is no more mysterious that the brain should cause mental phenomena than that bodies should have gravity. One might, and indeed one should, have a sense of awe and mystery in the face of both facts, but that sense would no more justify us in the denial of the existence of mental states than it would justify us in the denial of the existence of gravity.

Some philosophers feel that I am unjustified in simply asserting the existence of intrinsic intentional mental states and events in the world. For, they argue, might not the progress of science show them to be an illusion in the way that the appearance of the sun rising and setting over a stationary earth was shown to be an illusion? Isn't it just as prescientific to believe in intrinsic mental states as it is to believe that the earth is flat and in a fixed position in the universe?[1]

But if we confine our attention for the moment to conscious intentional mental events and states – and they are, after all, the primary forms of intentionality – we can see that the analogy between the belief in a flat and fixed earth and the belief in the existence of mental phenomena breaks down. In the case of the earth there is a clear distinction between how things are and how they seem to be, but in the case of the very existence of conscious mental phenomena it is hard to know what a parallel distinction would look like. I know more or less exactly what it means to say that, though the earth seems flat and fixed, it is in fact not flat and fixed but round and mobile; but I haven't the faintest idea what it would mean to say that, though it seems to me that I am now conscious, in fact I am not really conscious but rather I am . . . What?

The reason we are unable to fill in the gap with anything that does not seem preposterous has been familiar since Descartes: If it consciously seems to me that I am conscious then that is enough for me to be conscious. And that is why there cannot be a general "how things seem"/"how they really are" distinction for the very existence of conscious mental states.

[1] Rorty (1982), p. 84.

This is not, of course, to say that we cannot discover all sorts of surprising and counterintuitive things about our mental life, about the nature and mechanisms of both conscious and unconscious mental states. But it is to say that the distinction between how things seem and how they really are cannot apply to the *existence* of our own conscious mental phenomena.

3

Since the resistance to treating consciousness and intentionality naturalistically, as just higher level properties among others, is so pervasive, and since the view of the place of intentionality in nature advanced in this essay is so much out of step with what is currently accepted, I want to probe these issues a little more deeply. If one reads the standard literature on the "mind/body problem" over the past thirty years,[2] since the publication of Ryle's *The Concept of Mind* (1949), one discovers a curious feature of this continuing dispute. Almost all the participants on both sides tacitly assume that the specifically mental features of conscious mental events cannot be ordinary physical features of the world like any other higher level features of the world. This assumption is often masked from us by the way these theses are stated. Thus, when the identity theorist tells us that mental states just *are* brain states, there is a way of hearing that thesis which is perfectly consistent with our common-sense assumption of the intrinsic and irreducible character of consciousness and other forms of intentionality. We can hear the thesis as saying that mental processes are just processes going on in the brain in the way that digestive processes are processes going on in the digestive tract. But in general that is not what identity theorists are claiming. Under close scrutiny of the texts, particularly those parts of the texts where they are replying to dualist adversaries, it turns out that in general identity theorists (materialists, physicalists, functionalists, etc.) end up by denying the existence of intrinsically mental features of the world. J. J. C. Smart, with typical candor, states the position clearly in responding to J. T. Stevenson:

> My reply is that I do not admit that there are any such *P*-properties [i.e., properties of sensations that would prevent us from defining 'sensation' in terms of properties in a physicalist scheme]. (1970, p. 93)

Now why does Smart feel it necessary to deny what seems to Stevenson (and to me) an obvious truth? I believe it can only be because, in common with

[2] I am thinking of the sort of articles to be found in Borst (1970), Rosenthal (1971), and Block (1980).

the tradition since Descartes, he thinks that to grant the reality of conscious mental phenomena is to grant the existence of some mysterious phenomena, some sort of "nomological danglers" beyond the reach of the physical sciences. On the other hand, consider those who challenge the tradition of materialism by asserting such obvious facts as that they are currently having a series of conscious states. They seem to think their claim commits them to some form of dualism, as if in asserting obvious facts about our waking life they are committed to the existence of some ontological category different from that of the ordinary physical world we all live in. One group of philosophers sees itself as defending the progress of science against residual superstitions. The other group sees itself as asserting obvious facts that any moment of introspection will reveal. But both accept the assumption that naive mentalism and naive physicalism must be inconsistent. Both accept the assumption that a purely physical description of the world could not mention any mental entities.

These are false assumptions. Unless one defines "physical" and "mental" in such a way that one is the negation of the other, there is nothing in our ordinary notions of mental phenomena and physical reality that excludes cases of the former from being instances of the latter.

Why then, to continue the investigation a step further, do both sides make this apparently obvious mistake? I think the answer must be that they take very seriously a whole tradition, going back at least to Descartes, with its endless disputes about substance, dualism, interaction, emergence, ontological categories, the freedom of the will, the immortality of the soul, the presuppositions of morality, and the rest of it. And in large measure this tradition revolves around the assumption that "mental" and "physical" name mutually exclusive categories. But suppose for a moment that we could forget all about this entire tradition. Try to imagine that we are simply investigating the place in nature of our own human and animal mental states, intentional and otherwise, given what we know about biology, chemistry, and physics and what we know from our own experiences about our own mental states. I believe if we could forget the tradition, then the question as to the place of such states in nature would have an obvious answer. They are physical states of certain biochemical systems, namely, brains. But there is nothing reductive or eliminative about this view. Mental states with all their glorious or tiresome features – consciousness, intentionality, subjectivity, joy, anguish, and the rest – are exactly as we knew they were all along.

Lest my view be misunderstood, I should like to state it with maximum simplicity. Take the most naive form of mentalism: There really are intrinsic mental states, some conscious, some unconscious; some intentional, some nonintentional. As far as the conscious ones are concerned they pretty much have the mental properties they seem to have, because in general for such properties there is no distinction between how things are and how they seem. Now take the most naive version of physicalism: The world consists entirely of physical particles, including the various sorts of relations between them. As far as real things in the world are concerned there are only physical particles and various arrangements of physical particles. Now, my point is that it is possible to accept both of these views exactly as they stand, without any modification whatever. Indeed the first is simply a special case of the second.

4

Granted that intentional mental states really do exist and are not to be explained away as some kind of illusion or eliminated by some sort of re-definition, what role do they play in a naturalistic or scientific description of nature?

Just as it is a biological fact that certain sorts of organisms have certain sorts of mental states, so it is equally a biological fact that certain mental states function causally in the interactions between the organism and the rest of nature and in the production of the behavior of the organism. It is just a fact of biology that sometimes thirst will cause an organism to drink water, that hunger will cause it to seek and consume food, and that sexual desire will cause it to copulate. In the case of human beings, at a much more sophisticated though equally biological level, the beliefs a person has about what is in his or her economic interest may play a causal role in how he or she votes in political elections, literary preferences may play a causal role in the purchase and reading of books, and the desire to be someplace other than where one is may play a causal role in a person's buying a plane ticket, driving a car, or getting on a bus. Though the fact of causal relations involving intentional mental states is pretty obvious, what is a great deal less obvious is the logical structure of the causal relations involved and the consequent implications that those causal relations have for the logical structure of the explanation of human behavior.

Explanations involving intentionality have certain logical features not common to explanations in the other physical sciences. The first of these is the specific role of intentional causation in the production of certain sorts of animal and human behavior. The essential feature of intentional causation is that the intentional state itself functions causally in the production of its own conditions of satisfaction or its conditions of satisfaction function causally in its production. In the one case the representation, as a representation, produces what it represents; in the other case the object or state of affairs represented functions causally in the production of its representation. This point can be made clear by considering some examples. If I now have a strong desire to drink a cup of coffee and I act on that desire so as to satisfy it, then the desire whose content is

(that I drink a cup of coffee)

causes the very state of affairs, that I drink a cup of coffee. Now, in this simple and paradigmatic case of intentional causation, the desire represents the very state of affairs that it causes. The much discussed "internal connection" between "reasons for action" and the actions that they cause is just a reflection of this underlying feature of intentional causation. Since the cause is a representation of that which it causes, the specification of the cause, as cause, is indirectly already a specification of the effect.

Sometimes, indeed, the intentional state has as part of its conditions of satisfaction, as part of its intentional content, that it must function causally if it is to be satisfied. Thus, for example, intentions can only be satisfied if the actions that they represent are caused by the intentions that represent them. In this respect intentions differ from desires: a desire can be satisfied even if it does not cause the conditions of its satisfaction; whereas an intention can be satisfied only if it causes the rest of its own conditions of satisfaction. For example, if I want to be rich and I become rich, my desire will be satisfied even if that desire played no causal role in my becoming rich; but if I intend to earn a million dollars and I wind up with a million dollars quite by accident, in such a way that my intention to earn the money played no causal role consciously or unconsciously in my getting it, then although the state of affairs represented by my intention came about, the intention itself was not satisfied, that is, the intention was never carried out. Intentions, unlike desires, have intentional causation built into their intentional structure; they are causally self-referential in the sense that they can only be satisfied *if they cause* the very action they represent. Thus, the prior intention to drink a cup of coffee differs in its content from the desire to drink a cup of coffee, as we can see by contrasting the following representation of the conditions of satisfaction of a prior intention with our representation above of the conditions of satisfaction of the corresponding desire:

(that I drink a cup of coffee and that this prior intention causes that I drink a cup of coffee).

Cases of "volition", such as desires and intentions, have what I call the "world-to-mind direction of fit" (the aim of the state is to get the world to change to match the content of the desire or intention) and the "mind-to-world direction of causation" (the mental state causes the state of affairs in the world that it represents). Cases of "cognition", such as perception, memory, and belief, function conversely as far as direction of fit and intentional causation are concerned. Thus, they have the mind-to-world direction of fit (the aim of the mental state is not to create a change in the world, but to match some independently existing reality); and, where intentional causation functions in the production of the intentional state, they have the world-to-mind direction of causation (if I correctly perceive or remember how things are in the world, then their being that way must cause my perceiving them or remembering them as being that way).

5

I believe that a full account of the role of intentionality and its place in nature requires much more study of intentional causation than has yet been done or than I can undertake in this essay. But by way of giving the reader some idea of the importance of intentional causation, I want to mention just three of the implications of this brief sketch of intentional causation for a causal account of human and animal behavior and for ways in which such a causal account differs from certain standard models of what we have as canonical explanations in the usual natural sciences.

1. In any causal explanation, the propositional content of the explanation specifies a cause. But in intentional explanations the cause specified is itself an intentional state with its own propositional content. The canonical specification, therefore, of the cause in an intentional explanation doesn't just *specify* the propositional content of the cause, but it must actually *repeat* in the explanation (at least some of) the propositional content that is functioning causally in the operation of the cause. So, for example, if I buy a plane ticket because I want to go to Rome, then in the explanation:

> I did it because I want to go to Rome.

I repeat the very propositional content functioning in the operation of the desire:

> I want to go to Rome.

Intentional explanations are more or less adequate as they accurately repeat in the explanation the propositional content functioning in the cause itself.

It is a further consequence of this feature that the concepts used in the canonical form of the explanation don't just describe a cause; rather, the very concepts themselves must function in the operation of the cause. So, if I say that a man voted for Reagan because he thought it would increase the probability that he would be rich and happy, such concepts as being rich and being happy can be used in the explanation to specify a cause only if they also function as part of the cause.

These features have no analogue in the standard physical sciences. If I explain the rate of acceleration of a falling body in terms of gravitational attraction together with such other forces as friction operating on the body, the propositional content of my explanation makes reference to features of the event such as gravity and friction, but the features themselves are not propositional contents or parts of propositional contents.

This is a familiar point in the history of discussions of the nature of psychological explanation, but it seems to me that it has not been properly stated or appreciated. I believe it is part of what Dilthey (1962) was driving at when he said that the method of *Verstehen* was essential to the social sciences, and it was part of what Winch (1958) was driving at when he said that concepts used in the explanation of human behavior must also be concepts that are available to the agent whose behavior is being explained. I think an analysis of intentional causation would provide us with a deeper theoretical understanding of the points that Dilthey and Winch were after.

2. Statements of intentional causation do not require the statement of a covering law in order to be validated or in order to be causally explanatory. In a subject like physics we assume that no causal explanation of a phenomenon is fully explanatory unless it can be shown to instantiate some general law or laws. But in the case of intentional causation this is not generally the case. Even if we believe that there are laws, stateable in some terms or other, which any given instance of behavior instantiates, it is not essential to giving a causal explanation of human behavior in terms of intentional causation that we be able to state any such laws or even believe that there are such laws.

3. Teleological forms of explanation are those in which a phenomenon is explained in terms of goals, aims, purposes, intentions, and similar phenomena. If teleological explanation is really a subclass of scientific explanation, it would appear that nature must actually contain teleological phenomena. The account of intentionality and its place in nature that I have been urging has the consequences both that nature contains teleological phenomena and that teleological explanations are the appropriate forms of explanation for certain sorts of events. Indeed, it is an immediate logical consequence

of the claim that goals, aims, purposes, and intentions are intrinsic features of certain biological organisms, that teleology is an intrinsic part of nature, for by definition such phenomena are teleological. And it is an immediate consequence of the characterization I have given of these phenomena that teleological explanations are the appropriate forms for explaining certain sorts of events, since these phenomena cause events by way of the form of intentional causation that is peculiar to teleology.

All the states I have called "teleological" have the world-to-mind direction of fit and the mind-to-world direction of causation. The explanatory role of citing such states in teleological explanations can best be illustrated by example. Consider the case of an animal, say, a lion, moving in an erratic path through tall grass. The behavior of the lion is explicable by saying that it is stalking a wildebeest, its prey. The stalking behavior is caused by a set of intentional states: it is *hungry*, it *wants* to eat the wildebeest, it *intends* to follow the wildebeest with the *aim* of catching, killing, and eating it. Its intentional states represent possible future states of affairs; they are satisfied only if those states of affairs come to pass (world-to-mind direction of fit); and its behavior is an attempt to bring about those states of affairs (mind-to-world direction of causation). The claim that teleology is part of nature amounts to the claim that certain organisms contain future-directed intentional states with the world-to-mind direction of fit, and that these states are capable of functioning causally to bring about their conditions of satisfaction.

It is worth emphasizing the logical features of teleological explanation because on some accounts a teleological explanation explains an event by the occurrence of a future event, as if, for example, the eating of the prey explained the stalking behavior.[3] But on my account this conception has things back to front. All valid teleological explanations are species of explanation in terms of intentional causation, and there is no mysterious backwards operation of intentional causation. The stalking behavior at time t_1 is explained by present and prior intentional states at t_1 and t_0, and these aim at the eating behavior of t_2.

In the great scientific revolution of the seventeenth century the rejection of teleology in physics was a liberating step. Again, in the great Darwinian revolution of the nineteenth century the rejection of a teleological account of the origins of the species was a liberating step. In the twentieth century there was an overwhelming temptation to complete the picture by rejecting teleology in the sciences of man. But ironically the liberating move of the

[3] For a discussion of this conception see Braithwaite (1953), Chapter X.

past has become constraining and counterproductive in the present. Why? Because it is just a plain fact about human beings that they do have desires, goals, intentions, purposes, aims, and plans, and these play a causal role in the production of their behavior. Those human sciences in which these facts are simply taken for granted, such as economics, have made much greater progress than those branches, such as behavioristic psychology, which have been based on an attempted denial of these facts. Just as it was bad science to treat systems that lack intentionality as if they had it, so it is equally bad science to treat systems that have intrinsic intentionality as if they lacked it.

References

Block, N. (ed.): 1980, *Readings in Philosophical Psychology*, Vol. 1, Harvard University Press, Cambridge, Mass.

Borst, C. V. (ed.): 1970, *The Mind-Brain Identity Theory*, Macmillan, London.

Braithwaite, R. B.: 1953, *Scientific Explanation*, Cambridge University Press, Cambridge, England.

Dilthey, W.: 1962, *Meaning in History*, H. P. Rickman (trans. and ed.), New York.

Rorty, R.: 1982, 'Mind as Ineffable', in R. Q. Elvee (ed.), *Mind and Nature*, Harper & Row, San Francisco.

Rosenthal, D. M. (ed.): 1971, *Materialism and the Mind-Body Problem*, Prentice-Hall, Englewood Cliffs, N.J.

Ryle, G.: 1949, *The Concept of Mind*, Hutchinson's University Library, London.

Smart, J. J. C.: 1970, 'Further Remarks on Sensations and Brain Processes', in Borst (1970), pp. 93–94.

Winch, P.: 1958, *The Idea of a Social Science*, Routledge & Kegan Paul, London.

6

COLLECTIVE INTENTIONS AND ACTIONS

This essay begins with an intuition, a notation, and a presupposition. The intuition is: Collective intentional behavior is a primitive phenomenon that cannot be analyzed as just the summation of individual intentional behavior; and collective intentions expressed in the form "we intend to do such-and-such" or "we are doing such-and-such" are also primitive phenomena and cannot be analyzed in terms of individual intentions expressed in the form "I intend to do such-and-such" or "I am doing such-and-such." The notation is: S (p). The "S" stands for the type of psychological state; the "p" stands for the propositional content, the content that determines the conditions of satisfaction. Like all such notations, it isn't neutral; it embodies a theory. The presupposition is: All intentionality, whether collective or individual, requires a preintentional Background of mental capacities that are not themselves representational. In this case that implies that the functioning of the phenomena represented by the notation requires a set of phenomena that cannot be represented by that notation.

The questions this essay addresses are: Is the intuition right? (It is denied by most of the authors I have read on the subject.) And if it is right, can it be made to fit the notation? How, if at all, can we capture the structure of collective intentions within that notation? And what role does the Background play in enabling us to function in social collectives? These questions are not innocent. The larger question they form a part of is: How far can the theory of intentional action in *Intentionality* (Searle, 1983) be extended to become a general theory?

Reprinted by permission from *Intentions in Communication*, ed. P. Cohen, J. Morgan, and M. E. Pollack (Cambridge, Mass.: MIT Press, 1990).

1 The Intuition

Let's start with the intuition. The first half of the intuition could hardly be wrong. It seems obvious that there really is collective intentional behavior as distinct from individual intentional behavior. You can see this by watching a football team execute a pass play or hear it by listening to an orchestra. Better still, you can experience it by actually engaging in some group activity in which your own actions are a part of the group action.

The problem is with the second half of the intuition, the idea that the collective behavior is somehow not analyzable in terms of individual behavior and that the collective intention is somehow not reducible to a conjunction of singular intentions. How, one wants to ask, could there be any group behavior that wasn't just the behavior of the members of the group? After all, there isn't anyone left to behave once all the members of the group have been accounted for. And how could there be any group mental phenomenon except what is in the brains of the members of the group? How could there be a "we intend" that wasn't entirely constituted by a series of "I intend"s? There clearly aren't any bodily movements that are not movements of the members of the group. You can see that if you imagine an orchestra, a corps de ballet, or a football team. So if there is anything special about collective behavior, it must lie in some special feature of the mental component, in the form of the intentionality.

I want to build up to a characterization of the special form of collective intentionality by first trying to justify the first part of the original intuition.

Thesis 1

> There really is such a thing as collective intentional behavior that is not the same as the summation of individual intentional behavior.

I said this seems obvious, but it is important to see how pervasive collective behavior is. It is by no means confined to human beings but rather seems to be a biologically primitive form of animal life. Studies of animal behavior are filled with accounts of cooperative behavior, which it does not take a specialist's knowledge to recognize. Consider two birds building a nest together, or puppies playing on a lawn, or groups of primates foraging for food, or even a man going for a walk with his dog. In humans, collective behavior typically involves language, but even for humans it does not invariably require language or even conventional ways of behaving. For example, I see a man pushing a car in the street in an effort to get it started; and I simply start pushing with him. No words are exchanged and there is no convention according to which I push his car. But it is a case of collective behavior. In such a case *I* am pushing only as part of *our* pushing.

Perhaps the simplest way to see that collective behavior is not the same as the summation of individual behavior is to see that the same type of bodily movements could on one occasion be a set of individual acts and could on another occasion constitute a collective action. Consider the following sort of example: Imagine that a group of people are sitting on the grass in various places in a park. Imagine that it suddenly starts to rain and they all get up and run to a common, centrally located shelter. Each person has the intention expressed by the sentence "I am running to the shelter." But for each person, we may suppose that his or her intention is entirely independent of the intentions and behavior of others. In this case there is no collective behavior; there is just a sequence of individual acts that happen to converge on a common goal. Now imagine a case where a group of people in a park converge on a common point as a piece of collective behavior. Imagine that they are part of an outdoor ballet where the choreography calls for the entire corps de ballet to converge on a common point. We can even imagine that the external bodily movements are indistinguishable in the two cases; the people running for shelter make the same types of bodily movements as the ballet dancers. Externally observed, the two cases are indistinguishable, but they are clearly different internally. What exactly is the difference? Well, part of the difference is that the form of the intentionality in the first case is that each person has an intention that he could express without reference to the others, even in a case where each has mutual knowledge of the intentions of the others. But in the second case the individual "I intend"s are, in a way we will need to explain, derivative from the "we intend"s. That is, in the first case, even if each person knows that the other people intend to run to the shelter and knows that the other people know that he intends to run to the shelter, we still do not have collective behavior. In this case at least, it seems no set of "I intend"s, even supplemented with beliefs about other "I intend"s, is sufficient to get to the "we intend." Intuitively, in the collective case the individual intentionality, expressed by "I am doing act A," is derivative from the collective intentionality "We are doing act A."

Another clue that collective intentions are different from a mere summation of individual intentions is that often the derived form of an individual intention will have a different content from the collective intention from which it is derived. We can see this in the following sort of example. Suppose we are on a football team and we are trying to execute a pass play. That is, the team intention, we suppose, is in part expressed by "We are executing a pass play." But now notice: no individual member of the team has this as the entire content of his intention, for no one can execute a pass play by himself. Each player must make a specific contribution to the overall goal. If I am an offensive lineman, my intention might be expressed by "I am blocking the defensive end." Each member of the team will share in the collective intention but will have an individual assignment that is derived from the collective but has a different content from the collective. Where the collective's is "We are doing A," the individual's will be "I am doing B," "I am doing C," and so on.

But supposing we got the characterization of the "I intend"s just right, couldn't we show how they add up to a "we intend"? I think not, and this leads to our second thesis:

Thesis 2

> We-intentions cannot be analyzed into sets of I-intentions, even I-intentions supplemented with beliefs, including mutual beliefs, about the intentions of other members of a group.

I think most philosophers would agree that collective behavior is a genuine phenomenon; the disagreement comes in how to analyze it. One tradition is willing to talk about group minds, the collective unconscious, and so on. I find this talk at best mysterious and at worst incoherent. Most empirically minded philosophers think that such phenomena must reduce to individual intentionality; specifically, they think that collective intentions can be reduced to sets of individual intentions together with sets of beliefs and especially mutual beliefs. I have never seen any such analysis that wasn't subject to obvious counterexamples, but let us try it out to see why it won't work. To have an actual sample analysis to work with, let us try that of Tuomela and Miller (1988), which is the best I have seen.

Leaving out various technical details, we can summarize their account as follows. An agent A who is a member of a group "we-intends" to do X if

1. A intends to do his part of X.
2. A believes that the preconditions of success obtain; especially, he believes that the other members of the group will (or at least probably will) do their parts of X.
3. A believes that there is a mutual belief among the members of the group to the effect that the preconditions of success mentioned in point 2 obtain.

This account is typical in that it attempts to reduce collective intentions to individual intentions plus beliefs. I, on the contrary, am proposing that no such reduction will work, that "we-intentions" are primitive. And I think it is easy to see what is wrong with the Tuomela-Miller account: a member of a group can satisfy these conditions and still not have a we-intention.

Consider the following situation. Suppose a group of businessmen are all educated at a business school where they learn Adam Smith's theory of the hidden hand. Each comes to believe that he can best help humanity by pursuing his own selfish interest, and they each form a separate intention to this effect; that is, each has an intention he would express as "I intend to do my part toward helping humanity by pursuing my own selfish interest and not cooperating with anybody." Let us also suppose that the members of the group have a mutual belief to the effect that each intends to help humanity by pursuing his own selfish interests and that these intentions will probably be carried out with success. That is, we may suppose that each is so well indoctrinated by the business school that each believes that his selfish efforts will be successful in helping humanity.

Now consider any given member A of the business school graduating class.

1. A intends to pursue his own selfish interests without reference to anybody else, and, thus, he intends to do his part toward helping humanity.
2. A believes that the preconditions of success obtain. In particular, he believes that other members of his graduating class will also pursue their own selfish interests and thus help humanity.
3. Since A knows that his classmates were educated in the same selfish ideology that he was, he believes that there is a mutual belief among the members of his group that each will pursue his own selfish interests and that this will benefit humanity.

Thus, A satisfies the Tuomela-Miller conditions, but all the same, he has no collective intentionality. There is no we-intention. There is even an ideology, which he and the others accept, to the effect that there should not be a we-intention.

This case has to be distinguished from the case where the business school graduates all get together on graduation day and form a pact to the effect that they will all go out together and help humanity by way of each pursuing his own selfish interests. The latter case is a case of collective intentionality; the former case is not. Cooperative collective goals may be pursued by individualistic means, as is also shown by the following example. Suppose one of the members of a softball team loses his wallet at the game. Suppose the members reason that the chances of finding it are best if they each act separately; and each searches for the wallet in his own way, ignoring the others. They then set about in a coordinated and cooperative way to search for the wallet by acting with complete lack of coordination and cooperation. Unlike the original counterexample, these are genuine cases of collective behavior.

Could we avoid such counterexamples by construing the notion of "doing his part" in such a way as to block them? I think not. We are tempted to construe "doing his part" to mean doing his part toward achieving the *collective* goal. But if we adopt that move, then we have included the notion of a collective intention in the notion of "doing his part." We are thus faced with a dilemma: if we include the notion of collective intention in the notion of "doing his part," the analysis fails because of circularity; we would now be defining we-intentions in terms of we-intentions. If we don't so construe "doing his part," then the analysis fails because of inadequacy. Unless the we-intention is built into the notion of "doing his part," we will be able to produce counterexamples of the sort I have outlined above.

The reason that we-intentions cannot be reduced to I-intentions, even I-intentions supplemented with beliefs and beliefs about mutual beliefs, can be stated quite generally. The notion of a we-intention, of collective intentionality, implies the notion of *cooperation*. But the mere presence of I-intentions to achieve a goal that happens to be believed to be the same goal as that of other members of a group does not entail the presence of an intention to cooperate to achieve that goal. One can have a goal in the knowledge that others also have the same goal, and one can have beliefs and even mutual beliefs about the goal that is shared by the members of a group, without there being necessarily any cooperation among the members or any intention to cooperate among the members.

I have not demonstrated that no such analysis could ever succeed. I am not attempting to prove a universal negative. But the fact that the attempts that I have seen to provide a reductive analysis of collective intentionality fail for similar reasons – namely, they do not provide sufficient conditions for cooperation; one can satisfy the conditions in the analysis without having collective intentionality – does suggest that our intuition is right: we-intentions are a primitive phenomenon.

However, my claim that there is a form of collective intentionality that is not the product of some mysterious group mind and at the same time is not reducible to individual intentions has plenty of problems of its own, and we must now set about solving some of them. The most difficult problem we can put in the form: What exactly is the structure of we-intentions? We will not be in a position to answer that question until we answer a prior question about how we can reconcile the existence of collective intentionality with the fact that society consists entirely of individuals and no facts about any individual mental contents guarantee the existence of any other individuals. I believe it is facts such as these that have led people to believe that there must be a reduction of we-intentions to I-intentions.

Anything we say about collective intentionality must meet the following conditions of adequacy:

Constraint 1

It must be consistent with the fact that society consists of nothing but individuals. Since society consists entirely of individuals, there cannot be a group mind or group consciousness. All consciousness is in individual minds, in individual brains.

Constraint 2

It must be consistent with the fact that the structure of any individual's intentionality has to be independent of the fact of whether or not he is getting things right, whether or not he is radically mistaken about what is actually occurring. And this constraint applies as much to collective intentionality as it does to individual intentionality. One way to put this constraint is to say that the account must be consistent with the fact that all intentionality, whether collective or individual, could be had by a brain in a vat or by a set of brains in vats.

These two constraints amount to the requirement that any account we give of collective intentionality, and therefore of collective behavior, must be consistent with our overall ontology and metaphysics of the world, an ontology and metaphysics based on the existence of individual human beings as the repositories of all intentionality, whether individual or collective.[1]

Thesis 3

The thesis that we-intentions are a primitive form of intentionality, not reducible to I-intentions plus mutual beliefs, is consistent with these two constraints.

Actually, I think it is rather simple to satisfy these constraints. We simply have to recognize that there are intentions whose form is: We intend that we perform act A; and such an intention can exist in the mind of each

[1] Readers will recognize that these two constraints are close to "methodological individualism" and "methodological solipsism" as traditionally construed. I am anxious if possible to avoid sinking into the morass of the traditional disputes, so I am trying to present a version of these in which they can be construed as just commonsensical, pretheoretical requirements.

individual agent who is acting as part of the collective. In cases like that of the football team each individual will have further intentional content, which in ordinary English he might express in the form "I am doing act B as part of our doing act A." For example, "I am blocking the defensive end as part of our executing a pass play." We need only note that all the intentionality needed for collective behavior can be possessed by individual agents even though the intentionality in question makes reference to the collective.

In the cases described above, if I am pushing only as part of our pushing, or if I am blocking the defensive end as part of our executing a pass play, the intentionality, both plural and singular, is in my head. Of course, I take it in such cases that my collective intentionality is in fact shared; I take it in such cases that I am not simply acting alone. But I could have all the intentionality I do have even if I am radically mistaken, even if the apparent presence and cooperation of other people is an illusion, even if I am suffering a total hallucination, even if I am a brain in a vat. Collective intentionality in my head can make a purported reference to other members of a collective independently of the question whether or not there actually are such members.

Since this claim is consistent with the brain in the vat fantasy, it is a fortiori consistent with each of our constraints. It is consistent with Constraint 2, because the brain in the vat formulation is just the most extreme form of stating this constraint; it is consistent with Constraint 1, because we are not required to suppose that there is any element in society other than individuals – that is, the supposition is entirely consistent with the fact that society is made up entirely of individuals. It is consistent with the fact that there is no such thing as a group mind or group consciousness, because it only requires us to postulate that mental states can make reference to collectives where the reference to the collective lies outside the bracket that specifies the propositional content of the intentional state. The thought in the agent's mind is simply of the form "We are doing so and so."

Perhaps an uncomfortable feature of the analysis is that it allows for a form of mistake that is not simply a failure to achieve the conditions of satisfaction of an intentional state and is not a simply a breakdown in the Background. It allows for the fact that I may be mistaken in taking it that the "we" in the "we intend" actually refers to a we; that is, it allows for the fact that my presupposition that my intentionality is collective may be mistaken in ways that go beyond the fact that I have a mistaken belief. I do indeed have a mistaken belief if I have a collective intention that is not in fact shared, but on the proposed analysis, something further has gone wrong. Now, this does violate a very deep Cartesian assumption that we feel inclined to make. The assumption is that if I am mistaken, it can only be because one of my beliefs is false. But on my account, it turns out that I can not only be mistaken about how the world is but am even mistaken about what I am in fact doing. If I am having a hallucination in supposing that someone else is helping me push the car, that I am only pushing as part of our pushing, then I am mistaken not only in my belief that there is somebody else there pushing as well but also about what it is that I am doing. I thought I was pushing as part of our pushing, but that is not in fact what I was doing.

2 The Notation

I now turn to the notation. What exactly is the formal structure of collective intentionality? In order to state the structure of collective cases, we need to remind ourselves of the structure of intentionality for singular actions. An action of, say, raising one's arm has two components: a "mental" component and a "physical" component. The mental component both represents and causes the physical component, and because the form of causation is intentional causation, the mental causes the physical by way of representing it. In ordinary English we can say: when I succeed, my trying to do something causes an effect of a certain type, because that is what I was trying to achieve. In the notation that I have found useful and perspicuous we can represent these facts, when the action is one of raising one's arm, as follows:

i.a. (this i.a. causes: my arm goes up) CAUSES: MY ARM GOES UP.

The expressions in lowercase letters represent the mental component. The type of intentional state is specified outside the parentheses; in this case "i.a." stands for intention-in-action; and the expressions inside the parentheses represent the conditions of satisfaction, what must be the case if the state is to be satisfied. Where intentions are concerned, these conditions are causally self-referential; that is, it is part of the conditions of satisfaction that the state itself must cause an event of the type represented in the rest of the conditions of satisfaction. The expressions in capital letters on the right represent actual physical events in the world. If the i.a. is successful, then the action will consist of two components, a "mental" and a "physical" component, and the condition of satisfaction of the mental is that it should cause a physical event of a certain type. Since we are supposing it is successful, the above notation represents the fact that it does cause an event of that type. All of these facts are summarized in the above notation.

I want the notation to seem absolutely clear, so I will write out a paraphrase in ordinary English, treating the whole expression as if it were a sentence instead of a diagram of the structure of an intention:

> There is an intention-in-action that has as its conditions of satisfaction that that very intention-in-action causes it to be the case that my arm goes up; and all of that mental stuff really does cause it to be the case in the physical world that my arm goes up.

Now let us remind ourselves of how it works for a slightly more complex case involving a by-means-of relation. Suppose a man fires a gun by means of pulling the trigger. He has an intention-in-action whose content is that that very intention-in-action should cause the pulling of the trigger, which in turn should cause the firing of the gun. If the intention is satisfied, the whole complex event looks like this:

> i.a. (this i.a. causes: trigger pulls, causes: gun fires) CAUSES: TRIGGER PULLS, CAUSES: GUN FIRES.

Once again, the expressions in lowercase letters represent the contents of the mind, and the expressions in capital letters represent what happens in the real world. Since we are assuming that the contents of the mind are satisfied in subsequent formulations, we can simply leave out the reference to the real world. If satisfied, the contents of the mind can be read off directly onto the world. Previously we introduced the colon, which is read (with appropriate adjustments) as "it to be the case that . . . " and enables us to convert the sentence or other expressions that follow into singular terms. Here we introduce the comma, which is read as "which" and converts the subsequent expressions into a relative clause. Thus, the stuff inside the parentheses in this example is to be read in English as follows:

> This intention-in-action causes it to be the case that the trigger pulls, which causes it to be the case that the gun fires.

Now, let us apply these lessons to the study of collective behavior. To that end, let us look at another case.

Suppose Jones and Smith are engaged in a piece of cooperative behavior. Suppose they are preparing a hollandaise sauce. Jones is stirring while Smith slowly pours in the ingredients. They have to coordinate their efforts because if Jones stops stirring or Smith stops pouring, the sauce will be ruined. Each has a form of collective intentionality that he could express as "We are preparing hollandaise sauce." This is a collective intention-in-action and it has the following form:

i.a. (this i.a. causes: sauce is mixed).

Now the puzzle is, how does this collective intention cause anything? After all, there aren't any agents except individual human beings, and somehow intentional causation has to work through them and only through them. I believe one of the keys to understanding collective intentionality is to see that in general the by and by-means-of relations for achieving the collective goal have to end in individual actions. Thus, we might ask the cooks, "How are you preparing the dinner?" "Well," they might answer, "first by making the sauce; then by cooking the meat." But at some point somebody has to be in a position to say, for example, "I am stirring." In such cases the individual component of the collective actions plays the role of means to ends. Jones's stirring is the means to making the sauce in the same sense that pulling the trigger is the means to firing the gun. Jones has an intentional content that we could express in English as:

We are making the sauce by means of my stirring.

And Smith has the intentional content:

We are making the sauce by means of my pouring.

From the point of view of each agent there are not two actions with two intentions that he is performing. Rather, just as in the gun case, there is only one intention and one action – to fire the gun by means of pulling the trigger – so in the collective case each agent has only one intention that represents his contribution to the single collective action:

Jones: i.a. (this i.a. causes: ingredients are stirred).
Smith: i.a. (this i.a. causes: ingredients are poured).

But we still haven't solved our problem. In the case of the individual action there is a single intention that encompasses the by-means-of relations. I intend to fire the gun by means of pulling the trigger. One intention, one action. The relation of the means-intention to the overall intention is simply part-whole: the whole intention represents both the means and the ends, and it does that by representing the by-means-of relation according to which one achieves the end by means of the means.

But how exactly does it work where the means is individual and the goal is collective? The answer to that question is not at all obvious. Let us try some possibilities. It is tempting to think that such intentions might contain collective intentionality right down to the ground, that there might simply be a special class of collective intentions and that is all that is needed. On this account, from Jones's point of view the intentionality is this:

> collective i.a. (this collective i.a. causes: ingredients are stirred, causes: sauce is mixed).

But this "collectivist" or "socialist" solution can't be right because it leaves out the fact that Jones is making an individual contribution to a collective goal. If I am Jones, this account leaves it as mysterious how the collective intentionality can move my body. Surely, one feels like saying, I personally have to intend to do something if the sauce is ever going to get mixed.

But the opposite view, according to which it is all individual intentionality, a "capitalist" or "individualist" solution, fares no better:

> singular i.a. (this singular i.a. causes: stirred, causes: mixed).

This is unsatisfactory because it is consistent with there being no collective intentionality at all. I might stir in the knowledge that you were doing something that together with my stirring would produce the desired result without any collective intentionality. In short, this formulation is consistent with the claim that there is no such thing as collective intentionality, it is just an accumulation of individual intentionality; and that view we have already rejected.

Well, suppose we try to capture both the collective and individual components in the following way. Suppose we treat the collective intention as causing the singular intention:

> collective i.a. (this collective i.a. causes: singular i.a., causes: stirred, causes: mixed).

The feature of this analysis that makes me think it must be false is the fact that a separate i.a. is in the scope of the collective i.a. This would imply that the collective intention isn't satisfied unless it causes me to have a singular i.a. And that can't be right, because my collective intention isn't an intention to make it be the case that I have a singular intention; it is the intention to achieve some collective goal for which my singular intention stands as means to end. A clue that this must be wrong is provided by the fact that it is quite unlike the case of ordinary singular action where my intention to fire the gun by means of pulling the trigger consists in only one complex intention, not two intentions where one causes the other as part of its conditions of satisfaction. Of course, in the singular cases an intention can cause me to have a subsidiary intention, by practical reasoning. But even in such cases it doesn't necessarily have to cause the subsidiary intention in order to be satisfied. In the singular case there is just one intention in the agent's head: to fire the gun by means of pulling the trigger. Now why should there be two intentions in each agent's head in the collective case?

Well, let's try a new start. Let's ask intuitively what is going on. Intuitively, we are intentionally making the sauce and if I am Jones, my share is that I am intentionally stirring the ingredients. But what exactly is the relation between the collective and the individual intention? It seems to me it is exactly like the relation of the intention to pull the trigger and the intention to fire the gun: just as I fire the gun by means of my pulling the trigger, so We make the sauce by means of My stirring and Your pouring. As far as my part is concerned, We intend to make the sauce by means of My stirring. But don't those have to be two separate intentions, one singular i.a. and one collective i.a.? No, no more than there have to be two separate intentions when I fire the gun by means of pulling the trigger. The real distinction between the singular and the collective case is in the type of intention involved, not in the way that the elements in the conditions of satisfaction relate to each other. The form of the intention in the singular case is to achieve goal B by way of doing means A. That is, it isn't just any old type of i.a., it is an achieve-B-by-means-of-A type of i.a. So we might think of the notation that represents this type of i.a. as containing two free variables, "A" and "B"; and these variables are then bound by clauses inside the parentheses that function as nouns. What we are trying to say is that I have an achieve-B-by-means-of-A sort of intention whose content is that that-the-trigger-pulls-as-A causes it to be the case that-the-gun-fires-as-B. And we can represent this as follows:

> i.a. B by means of A (this i.a. causes: A trigger pulls, causes: B gun fires).

Similarly, in the structure of collective action, there is only one (complex) i.a., and it isn't just any old type of i.a.; it is an achieve-collective-B-by-means-of-singular-A type of i.a. And when it comes to the notation, we bind those free variables in the representation of the type of intention by clauses functioning as singular noun phrases inside the parentheses:

> i.a. collective B by means of singular A (this i.a. causes: A stirred, causes: B mixed).

I am not sure this is the right analysis, but it does seem to be better than the three others we considered. It allows for both the collective and the individual component in the agent's intentions. And it does so in a way that avoids making the paradoxical claim that the collective act causes the individual act. Rather, the individual act is part of the collective act. The intention to stir is part of the intention to mix by means of stirring in the same way that in the gun case the intention to pull is part of the intention to fire by means of pulling.

3 The Presupposition

But now the next question arises, what sort of beings are we that we have the capacity to form such intentions? Ultimately the answer to that has to be biological, but there is a more restricted sense of the question that we can still address: What general Background capacities and phenomena are presupposed by the sketch of collective intentionality I have just given? The manifestation of any particular form of collective intentionality will require particular Background skills, the ability to stir or play football, for example. But are there any features of the Background that are general or pervasive (even if perhaps not universal) for collective behavior? I think there are, but they are not easy to characterize. They are the sorts of things that old-time philosophers were driving at when they said things like "Man is a social animal" or "Man is a political animal." In addition to the biological capacity to recognize other people as importantly like us, in a way that waterfalls, trees, and stones are not like us, it seems to me that the capacity to engage in collective behavior requires something like a preintentional sense of "the other" as an actual or potential agent like oneself in cooperative activities. The football team has the sense of "us against them" and it has that sense against the sense of the larger us of "teams playing the game"; the orchestra has the sense of "us playing in front of them" and it has that sense as part of the larger us of "participants in the concert." "But," one might object, "surely this sense of others as cooperative agents is constituted by the collective intentionality." I don't think so. The collective behavior certainly augments the sense of others as cooperative agents, but that sense can exist without any collective intentionality, and what is more interesting, collective intentionality seems to presuppose some level of sense of community before it can ever function.

It is worth noticing in passing that most forms of competitive and aggressive behavior are forms of higher-level cooperation. Two men engaged in a prizefight are engaged in a form of competition, but it is a form of aggressive competition that exists only within a higher-level form of cooperation. Each prizefighter has the intention to hurt the other, but they have these intentions only within the frame of the higher-order intention to cooperate with each other in engaging in a prizefight. This is the distinction between a prizefight and a case of one man simply assaulting another man in a dark alley. And what goes for the prizefight also goes for football games, business competitions, courtroom trials, and in many cases even armed warfare. For human beings, most social forms of aggressive behavior require higher-level cooperation. For one person even to insult another at a cocktail party requires an extremely sophisticated higher level of cooperation among the participants in the insult.

Not all social groups are engaged in goal-directed behavior all the time. Some of the time they are just, for instance, sitting around in living rooms, hanging out in bars, or riding on the train. Now the form of collectivity that exists in such cases isn't constituted by goal-directed intentionality, because there isn't any. Such groups are, so to speak, ready for action but they are not yet engaged in any actions (they have no collective intentions-in-action) nor are they planning any (they have no collective prior intentions). Nonetheless, they have the type of communal awareness that is the general precondition of collective intentionality.

On the basis of such preliminary reflections I want to advance the following thesis:

Thesis 4

> Collective intentionality presupposes a Background sense of the other as a candidate for cooperative agency; that is, it presupposes a sense of others as more than mere conscious agents, indeed as actual or potential members of a cooperative activity.

Now, what is the argument for this thesis? I don't know of anything like a conclusive argument; nonetheless, the considerations that incline me to this view are something like the following. Ask yourself what you must take for granted in order that you can ever have or act on collective intentions. What you must suppose is that the others are agents like yourself, that they have a similar awareness of you as an agent like themselves, and that these awarenesses coalesce into a sense of *us* as possible or actual collective agents. And these conditions hold even for total strangers. When I go out of my door into the street to help push the stranger's car, part of the Background is that each of us regards the other as an agent and as a candidate to form part of a collective agent. But these are not in the normal case "beliefs." Just as my stance toward the objects around me and the ground underneath me is that of their being solid, without my needing or having a special belief that they are solid; and just as my stance toward others is that of their being conscious agents, without my needing or having a special belief that they are conscious;

so my stance toward others with whom I am engaged in collective behavior is that of their being conscious agents in a cooperative activity, without my needing or having a special belief to that effect.

I believe that if we could fully understand the Background sense of others as possible agents, we would see that certain attempts to understand the character of society must be wrong. It is tempting to think that collective behavior presupposes communication, that speech acts in conversation are the "foundation" of social behavior and hence of society. It is perhaps equally tempting to suppose that conversation presupposes collective behavior, that social behavior is the foundation of conversation and hence of any society in which communication plays an essential role. There is obviously something to be said for each of these views. But I am here suggesting that we cannot explain society in terms of either conversation in particular or collective behavior in general, since each of these presupposes a form of society before they can function at all. The biologically primitive sense of the other person as a candidate for shared intentionality is a necessary condition of all collective behavior and hence of all conversation.

We can now conclude with:

Thesis 5

> The notation, and hence the theory, of *Intentionality* together with a certain conception of the role of the Background can accommodate collective intentions and actions.

References

Searle, John R. (1983). *Intentionality: An essay in the philosophy of mind.* New York: Cambridge University Press.

Tuomela, Raimo, and Kaarlo Miller (1988). We-intentions. *Philosophical Studies* 53, 367–389.

7

THE EXPLANATION OF COGNITION

The Problem

What sorts of systematic explanations should we and can we seek in cognitive science for perception, language comprehension, rational action and other forms of cognition? In broad outline I think the answer is reasonably clear: We are looking for *causal explanations,* and our subject matter is *certain functions* of a biological organ, the human and animal brain.

As with any other natural science there are certain assumptions we have to make and certain conditions that our explanations have to meet. Specifically, we have to suppose that there exists a reality totally independent of our representations of it (in a healthier intellectual era it would not be necessary to say that), and we have to suppose that the elements of that reality that we cite in our explanations genuinely function causally.

Not all functions of the brain are relevant to cognition, so we have to be careful to restrict the range of brain functions we are discussing. Cognitive science is about the *cognitive* functioning of the brain and its relation to the rest of the organism and to the rest of the world in the way that nutrition science is about the digestive functioning of the digestive system and its relation to the rest of the organism and the rest of the world. Like other organs, and indeed like other physical systems, the brain has different levels of description and cognitive science is appropriately concerned with any level of description of the brain that is relevant to the causal explanation of cognition. These can range from conscious processes of decision-making,

Reprinted by permission from John Preston, ed., *Thought and Language* (Cambridge: Cambridge University Press, 1997).

at the top level, to the molecular structure of neurotransmitters, at the bottom.

Typically, the higher levels will be causally emergent properties of the behaviour and organisation of the elements of the brain at the lower levels. Consider an obvious, commonsense example of an explanation at one of these higher levels. If I explain my driving behaviour in Britain by saying I am following the rule 'Drive on the left', I have given a genuine causal explanation by citing a mental process. The operation of the rule is itself caused by lower-level neuronal events in the brain and is realized in the brain at a level higher than that of individual neurons. In what I hope is an unmysterious sense of 'emergent property' the operation of the rule in producing my behaviour is a causally emergent property of the brain system. Another way to put this same point is to say: we can give genuine causal explanations that are not at the bottom level, not at the level of neurons, etcetera, because the higher levels of explanation are also real levels. Talk of them is not just a manner of speaking or a metaphor. In order to be a real level, a putative causal level has to be appropriately related to the more fundamental levels, for example, by being a causally emergent property of those levels. Let us call this constraint, namely, that in explaining cognition we have to cite real features of the real world which function causally, the *causal reality constraint.*

So, just to summarise these constraints, we are seeking *causal explanations* of brain *functioning* at different *levels of description.* We allow ourselves complete freedom in talking about different levels of description, but that freedom is constrained by the requirement that the levels be causally real.

The claim I want to defend here is that some, though of course not all, of the explanatory models in cognitive science fail to meet the causal reality constraint. I will also suggest some revisions that will enable the explanations to meet that constraint.

Marr's Version of the Information-Processing Model

My dog, Ludwig, is very good at catching tennis balls. For example, if you bounce a tennis ball off a wall, he is usually able to leap up and put his mouth at precisely the point the ball reaches as he grasps it in his teeth. He doesn't always succeed, but he is pretty good at it. How does he do it?

According to the current explanatory models in cognitive science, Ludwig performs an information-processing task of enormous complexity. He takes in information in the form of a 2D pattern on his retina, processes it through the visual system until he produces a 3D representation of the external world, and inputs that representation into the motor output system. The computations he is performing, even for the motor output module, are no trivial matter. Here is a candidate for the first formulation of one of the algorithms. Ludwig is unconsciously following the rule: Jump in such a way that the plane of the angle of reflection of the ball is exactly equal to the plane of the angle of incidence of impact, and put your mouth at a point where the ball is in a parabolic arc, the flatness of whose trajectory and whose velocity is a function of impact velocity times the coefficient of elasticity of the tennis ball, minus a certain loss due to air friction. That is, on the standard computational model of cognition, Ludwig unconsciously computes a large number of such functions by unconsciously doing a lot of mathematics.

In form, the explanation of his behaviour is just like that of the person who follows the rule 'drive on the left' except for the fact that there is no way even in principle that he could become consciously aware of the operation of the rule. The rules are not just not present to consciousness in fact, they are not even the sort of rules he could become aware of following. They are what I have called 'deep unconscious' rules (Searle 1992, ch. 7).

I have never been completely satisfied with this mode of explanation. The problem is not just that it attributes an awful lot of unconscious mathematical knowledge to Ludwig's doggy brain, but more importantly, that it leaves out the crucial element that Ludwig is a conscious rational agent trying to do something. The explanatory model seems more appropriate for someone building a machine, a robot canine, that would catch tennis balls. I think in fact that the intuitive appeal of the approach is that it would predict Ludwig's behaviour and it is the sort of information we would put into a robot if we were building a robot to simulate his behaviour.

So let us probe a bit deeper into the assumptions behind this approach.

The classic statement of this version of the cognitive science explanatory paradigm is due to David Marr (Marr 1982), but there are equivalent views in other authors. On this paradigm cognitive science is a special kind of information-processing science. We are interested in how the brain and other functionally equivalent systems, such as certain kinds of computers, process information. There are three levels of explanation. The highest is the computational level, and this Marr defines in terms of the informational constraints available for mapping input information to output information. In Ludwig's case the computational task for his brain is to take in information about a two-dimensional visual array and output representations of muscle contractions that will get his mouth and the tennis ball at the same place at the same time.

Intuitively I think Marr's idea of the computational level is clear. If you were instructing a computer programmer to design a program, the first thing you would tell him is what job you want the program to do. And the statement of that job is a statement of the computational task to be performed at the computational level.

How is it done? Well, that leads to the second level, which Marr calls the algorithmic level. The idea is this. Any computational task can be performed in different ways. The intuitive idea is that the algorithmic level determines how the computational task is performed by a specific algorithm. In a computer we would think of the algorithmic level as the level of the program.

One puzzling feature of cognitive science versions of this level is the doctrine of recursive decomposition. Complex levels decompose into simpler levels until the bottom level is reached and at that level it is all a matter of zeros and ones, or some other binary symbols. That is, there is not really a single intermediate algorithmic level but rather a series of nested levels that bottom out in primitive processors, and these are binary symbols. And the bottom level is the only one that is real. All the others are reducible to it. But even *it* has no physical reality. It is implemented in the physics, as we will see, but *the algorithmic level makes no reference to physical processes.*

I used to think that the computations I gave for Ludwig might be the causally real level on this model, but not so. All Ludwig is really doing is manipulating zeros and ones. All the rest is mere appearance. Any computational claim we make about Ludwig reduces to the claim that he is manipulating zeros and ones.

The bottom level for Marr is the level of implementation, how the algorithm is actually implemented in specific hardware. The same program, the same algorithm, can be implemented in an indefinite range of different hardwares, and it is quite possible, for example, that a program implemented in Ludwig's brain might also be implemented on a commercial computer.

So, on Marr's tripartite model you get the following picture. Cognitive science is essentially the science of information-processing in a very special sense of that notion, and it is primarily concerned with explaining the top level by the algorithmic level. What matters for cognitive science explanation is the intermediate level. Why? Why should we explain brains at the intermediate level and not at the hardware level? The answer is given by my initial characterisation of the brain as a *functional* system. Where other functional systems are concerned, such as cars, thermostats, clocks and carburettors, we are interested in how the function is performed at the level of function, not at the level of microstructure. Thus in explaining a car engine we speak of pistons and cylinders and not of the subatomic particles of which the engine is composed; because, roughly speaking, any old subatomic particles will do as long as they implement the pistons and the cylinders. In Ludwig's case we are interested in the unconscious rule he is actually following and not in the neuronal implementation of that rule-following behaviour. And the rule he is actually following must be statable entirely in terms of zeros and ones, because that is all that is really going on. So on this conception my earlier characterisation of cognitive science as a science of brain function at a certain level or levels of description was misleading. Cognitive science is a science of information-processing, which happens to be implemented in the brain but which could equally well be implemented in an indefinite range of other hardwares. Cognitive science explains the top level in terms of the intermediate level but is not really concerned with the bottom level except in so far as it implements the intermediate level.

One problem with Marr's tripartite analysis of cognitive function is that just about any system will admit of this style of analysis. And the point is not just that clocks, carburettors, and thermostats admit of the three-level analysis (this is welcomed by adherents of the classical model as showing that cognition admits of a functional analysis similar to that of clocks, etc.). The problem is that any system of any complexity at all admits of an information-processing analysis.

Consider a stone falling off the top of a cliff. The 'system', if I may so describe it, has three levels of analysis. The computational task for the stone is to figure out a way to get to the ground in a certain amount of time. It has to compute the function $S = \frac{1}{2}gt^2$. At the intermediate level there is an algorithm that carries out the task. The algorithm instructs the system as to what steps to go through to match time and space in the right way. And there is the familiar hardware implementation in terms of masses of rock, earth and intervening air. So why isn't the falling stone an information-processing system? But if the stone is, then everything is.

This is a crucial question for cognitive science and several authors have answered it. According to them, we need to distinguish between a system being describable by a computation and one actually carrying out the computation. The system just mentioned is *describable* by a computable function, but it does not *carry out* that computation because (a) there are no representations for the computation to operate over and (b) *a fortiori* there is no information encoded in the representations. A genuine science of cognition, an information-processing science, requires computations performed over symbols or other syntactical elements, and these are the representations which encode information which is processed by the algorithm. These conditions are not met by a falling rock, even though the rock is computationally describable.

If we are going to make this reply stick, we will need a satisfactory definition or account of 'information', 'representation', 'symbol' and 'syntax', not to mention 'computation' and 'algorithm'. And these accounts must enable us to explain how information, representation, and so forth, get into the system in such a way as to satisfy the causal reality constraint. The account will have to show how information gets into the system in some intrinsic form in the first place, and then retains its character as information throughout the processing. Furthermore the account would have to show how the real information-processing level is an emergent property of the more fundamental micro-levels. To nail this down to specific cases, it is not going to be enough to say, as Marr did, that there is a two dimensional visual array on the retina as an input to the system, we now have to say what fact about that visual array makes it information, and what exactly the content of the information is.

I have looked at a lot of the literature on this issue, and I cannot find a satisfactory definition of representation or information or the other notions that will solve our problems. To their credit, Palmer and Kimchi (cited in Palmer, 1999) admit that they have not the faintest idea what information, in their sense, might be. I want to explore the notion of information a little more fully. The basic question of this paper is: can we give any empirical sense to the basic concepts of the information-processing model that would make the information-processing version of cognitive science a legitimate empirical discipline?

Following a Rule

If we are going to be clear about the claim that the cognitive agent is following unconscious rules we first have to understand what is involved in rule-following behavior. Consider a case where it seems clear and unproblematic that the agent is following a rule. When I drive in England, I follow the rule: Drive on the left-hand side of the road. And if I stay in England for any length of time, I find that I get used to driving on the left and I don't have to think consciously of the rule. But it seems natural to say that I am still following the rule even when I am not thinking about it. Such an explanation meets the causal reality constraint. When I say that I am following a rule I am saying that there is an intrinsic intentional content in me, the semantic content of the rule, that is functioning causally to produce my behavior. That intentional content is at an emergent level of brain processing. The rule has the world-to-rule direction of fit and the rule-to-world direction of causation.

I want to explore some of the features of this type of explanation to see whether they can be preserved in Marr-style information-processing cognitive science. I will simply list what seem to me some important features of rule-following behaviour:

1. The single most important feature is the one I just mentioned. The intentional content of the rule must function causally in the production of the behaviour in question. To do this it must be at an emergent level of brain functioning. This is how rule explanations in real life meet the causal reality constraint. Any rule-following explanation in cognitive science also has to meet that constraint.

2. Rule-following is normative from the point of view of the agent. The content of the rule determines for the agent what counts as right and wrong, as succeeding or failing.

3. The next feature is a consequence of the first. The rule must have a certain aspectual shape, what Frege called the 'mode of presentation'. This is why extensionally equivalent rules can differ in their explanatory force. I can be following one rule and not another, even though the observable behaviour is the same for both cases. For this reason, that rule explanations must cite specific aspectual shapes, rule explanations are intensional-with-an-s. For example, the rule 'On two-lane roads drive on the left' is extensionally equivalent to the rule 'Drive so that the steering wheel is nearest to the centre line of the road', given the structure of British cars that I drive. But in Britain, I follow the first rule and not the second, even though each would equally well predict my behaviour.

4. In ordinary rule-governed behaviour the rules are either conscious or accessible to consciousness. Even when I am following the rule unthinkingly, still I could think about it. I am not always conscious of the rule, but I can easily become conscious of it. Even if the rule is so ingrained in my unconscious that I cannot think of it, still it must be the sort of thing that *could be* conscious.

5. Accessibility to consciousness implies a fifth requirement. The terms in which the rule is stated must be terms that are in the cognitive repertoire of the agent in question. It is a general characteristic of intentionalistic explanations, of which rule explanations are a special case, that the apparatus appealed to by the rule must be one that the agent is in possession of. If I wish to explain why Hitler invaded Russia, I have to use terms that are part of Hitler's conceptual repertoire. If I postulate some mathematical formula that Hitler never heard of and couldn't have mastered, and couldn't have been aware of, then the explanation cannot be an intentionalistic explanation. It is a peculiarity of cognition, often remarked on by people who

discuss the special features of historical explanation, that explanations that appeal to cognitive states and processes must employ concepts available to the agent.

6. The next feature is seldom remarked on: rule-following is normally a form of voluntary behaviour. It is up to me whether I follow the rule or break it. The rule does indeed function causally but the rule as cause, even the rule together with a desire to follow the rule, does not give causally sufficient conditions.

This is typical of rational explanations of behaviour. It is often said that actions are caused by beliefs and desires, but if we take that to be a claim about causally sufficient conditions, it is false. A test of the rationality of the behaviour is that there is a gap between the intentional contents (beliefs, desires, awareness of rules, etc.) and the actual action. You still have to haul off and do the thing you have decided to do, even in cases where the rule requires you to do it. I am going to call this gap between the rule and other intentional phenomena which are the causes, and the action which is their effect, the 'gap of voluntary action' or simply 'the gap'.

7. A feature, related to the gap, is that rules are always subject to interpretation and to interference by other rational considerations. So, for example, I don't follow the rule 'drive on the left-hand side of the road' blindly. If there is a pothole, or a car parked blocking the road, I will swing around it. Such rules are in this sense *ceteris paribus* rules.

8. The final feature is that the rule must operate in real time. For actual rule-governed behaviour, the rule explanation requires that the time of the application of the rule and the time of the causal functioning are co-extensive.

Just to summarise, then, we have eight features of intentionalistic rule explanations. First, the intentional content of the rule must function causally. Second, the rule sets a normative standard for the agent. Third, rules have aspectual shape and so rule explanations are intensional-with-an-s. Fourth, the rule must be either conscious or accessible to consciousness. Fifth, rules must have semantic contents in the cognitive repertoire of the agent. Sixth, rule-governed behaviour is voluntary, and therefore, because of the gap of voluntary behaviour, the rule explanation does not give causally sufficient conditions. Seventh, rules are subject to interpretation and to interference by other considerations. And finally, eighth, the rule must operate in real time.

Let's compare this with Marr-style cognitivist forms of explanation. In such explanations only features 1 and 3 are unambiguously present. Now one problem with the causal reality constraint on cognitive science explanations is that it is not clear how you can have those two without any of the other six. It is no accident that these features hang together, because rule-following explanations are typical of intentionalistic explanations of rational behavior. How can it be literally the case that Ludwig is following a rule with a specific semantic content, if that rule is not normative for him, is not accessible to his consciousness even in principle, has concepts totally outside his repertoire, is not voluntarily applicable, is not subject to interpretation and appears to operate instantaneously rather than in real time?

Some Preliminary Distinctions

In this section I want to remind you of certain fundamental distinctions. First, we need to recall the familiar distinction between *rule-governed* or *rule-guided* behaviour, on the one hand, and *rule-described behaviour*, on the other. When I follow a rule, such as the rule of the road in England, drive on the left-hand side, the actual semantic content of the rule plays a causal role in my behaviour. The rule does more than predict my behaviour; rather it is part of the cause of my behaviour. In this respect it differs from the laws of nature which describe my behaviour including its causes, but which do not cause the behaviour they describe. The distinction between rule-guided and rule-described can be generalised as a distinction between *intentionality-guided* and *intentionality-described.* All descriptions have intentionality, but the peculiarity of intentionalistic explanations of human cognition is that the intentional content of the explanation functions causally in the production of the explanandum. If I say 'Sally drank because she was thirsty', the thirst functions causally in the production of the behaviour. *It is important to remind ourselves of this distinction because if an information-processing cognitive science is to meet the constraint, the intentionality of the information must not merely describe but must function causally in the production of the cognition that the information-processing explains. Otherwise there is no causal explanation.* To meet the causal reality constraint, the algorithmic level must function causally.

I believe that the standard cognitive science accounts acknowledge this point when they distinguish between being describable by a function and actually computing a function. This a special case of the general distinction between rule-described and rule-guided.

The second important distinction is between observer-relative and observer-independent features of reality. Basic to our whole scientific world-view is the distinction between those features that exist independently of any observer, designer or other intentionalistic agent and those that are dependent on observers, users, etcetera. Often the same object will have both sorts of features. The objects in my pocket have such observer-independent features as a certain mass and a certain chemical composition, but they also have observer-relative features: for example, one is a British £10 note and another is a Swiss Army knife. I want to describe this distinction as that between features of the world that are observer- (or intentionality-) relative, and features that are observer- (or intentionality-) independent. Money, property, marriage, government and correct English pronunciation as well as knives, bathtubs and motor cars are observer-relative; force, mass, and gravitational attraction are observer-independent.

'Observer-relative' does not mean arbitrary or unreal. The fact that something is a knife or a chair or a nice day for a picnic is observer-relative but it is not arbitrary. You can't use just anything as a knife or a chair or a nice day for a picnic. The point about observer-relativity is that observer-relative features, under those descriptions, only exist relative to human observers. The fact that this object in my hand has a certain mass is not observer-relative but observer-independent. That the same object is a knife is relative to the fact that human agents have designed it, sold it, used it, and so forth, as a knife. Same object, different features: some features observer-independent, some observer-relative.

It is characteristic of the natural sciences that they deal with observer-independent features – such as force, mass, the chemical bond, etcetera – and it is characteristic of the social sciences that they deal with observer-relative features, such as money, property, marriage and government. As usual, psychology falls in the middle. Some parts of psychology deal with observer-relative features, but cognitive psychology, the part that is the core of cognitive science, deals with observer-independent features such as perception and memory.

Wherever there is an observer-relative feature, such as being a knife or being money, there must be some agents who use or treat the entities in question as a knife or as money. Now, and this is an important point, though money and knives are observer-relative, the fact that observers treat certain objects as money or knives is not observer-relative, it is observer-independent. It is an intrinsic fact about me that I treat this object as a knife, even though the fact that this object is a knife only exists relative to me and other observers. The attitudes of observers relative to which entities satisfy observer-relative descriptions are not themselves observer-relative.

This is why social science explanations can satisfy the causal reality constraint even though the features appealed to are observer-relative features. So, for example, if I say 'The rise in American interest rates caused a rise in the exchange value of the dollar against the pound', that is a perfectly legitimate *causal* explanation, even though pounds, dollars and interest rates are all observer-relative. The causal mechanisms work in such an explanation even though they work through the attitudes of investors, bankers, money changers, speculators, and so forth. In that respect the rise in the value of the dollar is not like the rise in the pressure of a gas when heated. The rise in pressure of a gas is observer-independent, the rise in the value of the dollar is observer-dependent. But the explanation in both cases can be a causal explanation. The difference comes out in the fact that the explanation of the observer-relative phenomena makes implicit reference to human agents.

The third distinction is an application of the second. It is the distinction between *intrinsic* or original intentionality and *derived* intentionality. If I am currently in a state of thirst or hunger, the intentionality of my state is intrinsic to those states – both involve desires. If I report these states in the utterances of sentences such as 'I am thirsty' or 'I am hungry', the sentences are also intentional because they have truth-conditions. But the intentionality of the sentences is not intrinsic to them as syntactical sequences. Those sentences derive their meaning from the intentionality of English speakers. Mental states such as beliefs, desires, emotions, perceptions, and so forth, have intrinsic intentionality; but sentences, maps, pictures and books have only derived intentionality. In both cases, the intentionality is real and literally ascribed, but the derived intentionality has to be derived from the original or intrinsic intentionality of actual human or animal agents.

I want this distinction to sound obvious, because I believe it is. And I also believe it is a special case of the equally obvious distinction between observer-relativity and observer-independence. Derived intentionality is observer-relative, intrinsic intentionality is observer-independent.

There are, furthermore, intentional ascriptions that do not ascribe either of these kinds of intentionality. These are typically metaphorical or as-if ascriptions. We say such things as 'My lawn is thirsty because we are in a drought', or 'My car is thirsty because it consumes so much gasoline'. I take it that these are harmless metaphorical claims of little philosophical interest. They mean, roughly, my lawn or my car is in a situation similar to and behaves in some ways similar to an organism that is literally thirsty.

Such as-if intentionality should not be confused with derived intentionality. Derived intentionality is genuine intentionality all right but it is derived from the intrinsic intentionality of actual intentional agents such as speakers of a language. Hence, it is observer-relative. But as-if intentionality is not intentionality at all. When I say of a system that it has as-if intentionality, that does not attribute intentionality to it. It merely says that the system behaves as if it had intentionality, even though it does not in fact.

To summarise these distinctions: we need to distinguish between rule-guided and rule-described behaviour. We need to distinguish observer-independent features from observer-relative features. Furthermore, we need to distinguish observer-independent (or intrinsic) intentionality, from both observer-dependent (derived) intentionality and as-if intentionality.

Information and Interpretation

I now want to apply these distinctions to the information-processing model of cognitive explanation. I will argue that if the Marr-style model is to have explanatory force, the behaviour to be explanined by the information-processing rules must be rule-guided and not just rule-described. It can only meet that condition if the information is intrinsic or observer-independent. To make the distinction between Ludwig and the falling rock, we have to show that Ludwig is actually following a rule and that can only be because he has an appropriate intrinsic intentional content. The difficulty with the classical model can now be stated in a preliminary form. Every key notion in the model is observer-relative: *information, representation, syntax, symbol* and *computation,* as typically used in cognitive science, are all observer-relative notions, and this has the consequence that the classical model in its present form cannot meet the causal reality constraint. I will try to state this more precisely in what follows.

Let us go through these notions, starting with 'symbols' and 'syntax'. I take it as obvious that a mark or a shape or a sound is a symbol or a sentence or other syntactical device only relative to some agents who assign a syntactical interpretation to it. And indeed, though it is less obvious, I think it is also true that an entity can only have a syntactical interpretation if it also has a semantic interpretation, because the symbols and marks are syntactical elements only relative to some meaning they have. Symbols have to symbolise something and sentences have to mean something. Symbols and sentences are indeed syntactical entities, but the syntactical interpretation requires a semantics.

When we get to 'representation' the situation is a bit trickier. A representation can be either observer-relative or observer-independent. Thus maps, diagrams, pictures and sentences are all representations and they are all observer-relative. Beliefs and desires are mental representations and they are observer-independent. Furthermore an animal can have such mental representations as beliefs or desires without having any syntactical or symbolic entities at all. When Ludwig wants to eat or wants to drink, for example, he need not use any symbols or sentences at all to have his canine desires. He just feels hungry or thirsty. The tricky part comes from the fact that sometimes observer-independent beliefs and desires make use of sentences, etcetera, which are observer-relative.

Indeed some philosophers have said that all beliefs and desires are 'propositional attitudes' in the sense of being attitudes towards propositions or sentences or some other form of representation. I used to think this was a harmless mistake, but it is not. If I believe that Clinton is president of the United States, I do indeed have an attitude towards Clinton, but not towards a sentence or a proposition. The sentence 'Clinton is president of the United States' is used to express my belief and the proposition that Clinton is president of the United States is the content of my belief. But I have no attitudes towards the sentence or the proposition. Indeed the proposition, construed as believed, just *is* identical with my belief. It is not the object of the belief.

The doctrine of propositional attitudes is a harmful mistake because it leads people to postulate a set of entities in the head, mental representations, and having a belief or desire is supposed to be having an attitude towards one of these symbolic, sentence-like entities. The point for present purposes is that intrinsic mental representations such as beliefs and desires (intentional states, as I prefer to call them) do not require some representing device, some syntactical device, in order to exist. And where there is a syntactical device, the syntactical device, being observer-dependent, inherits its status as syntactical and semantic from the intrinsic intentional content of the mind and not conversely. The crucial point for the present discussion is that all syntactical entities are observer-relative.

This distinction between observer-independent and observer-dependent features of the world applies to information. 'Information' is clearly an intentionalistic notion, because information is always information *about* something and typically the information is: that such and such is the case. Aboutness in this sense is the defining quality of intentionality, and intentional content of this propositional sort is typical of intentionality. So it should not be surprising that the distinctions between the different kinds of intentional ascriptions will apply to information. Thus if I say, 'I know the way to San Jose', I ascribe to myself information which does not depend on any observer. It is intrinsic or observer-independent. If I say 'This book contains information about how to get to San Jose', the book literally contains information, but the interpretation of the inscriptions in the book as information depends on interpreters. The information is observer-dependent.

There are also as-if ascriptions of information. If I say 'These tree rings contain information about the age of the tree', that is not a literal ascription of intentionality. There is no propositional content expressed by the wood. What I am actually saying, stated literally, is that a knowledgeable person can infer the age of the tree from the number of rings, because there is an exact covariance between the number of the tree's rings and its age in years. I think that with the widespread use of the notion of 'information', particularly as a result of information theory, many people would now say that the stump literally contains information. I think they think they are speaking literally when they say that DNA contains information. This is perfectly reasonable, but it is a different meaning of 'information', one that separates information and intentionality. There is no psychological reality to the 'information' in the tree ring or the DNA. They have neither propositional content nor intentionality in the sense in which the thoughts in my head have original intentionality and the sentences in the book have derived intentionality.

Of these three types of intentional ascription only intrinsic information is observer-independent.

Which type of information is appealed to in cognitive science information-processing theories? Well, 'as-if' information won't do. If the explanation is to satisfy the causal reality constraint, some actual informational fact must be appealed to. Why won't derived information satisfy the reality constraint? After all, we can give genuine scientific accounts of the flow of money in the economy; why not scientific accounts of the flow of information in the cognitive system, even though the information, like the money, is an observer-relative phenomenon? The brief answer is that in the case of economics, the agents who treat such and such physical phenomena as money are parts of the subject-matter we are studying. But in cognitive science, if we say we are giving an information-processing explanation of the agent's cognitive processes we cannot accept an explanation in which the agent's information-processing only exists relative to his intentionality, because we then have not explained the intentionality on which all of his cognitive processes depend. We will in short have committed the homunculus fallacy. If, on the other hand, we think of the information as existing relative only to us – the observer – then we have not satisfied the causal reality constraint because we have not identified a fact independent of the theory which explains the data that the theory is supposed to explain. So if cognitive science explanations are going to satisfy the causal reality constraint they are going to have to appeal to information which is intrinsic to the agent, information that is observer-independent.

Computation and Interpretation

Well, why must the requirement be so strong? Why can't we just say that the brain behaves like any other computer? We give causal explanations of ordinary computers, explanations which meet the causal reality constraint but which do not force us to postulate intrinsic intentionality in the computer.

The answer is that the distinction between observer-independent and observer-relative applies to computation as well. When I add 2 plus 2 and get 4, the arithmetical calculation is intrinsic to me. It is observer-independent. When I punch out '2 + 2' and get '4' on my computer, the computation is observer-relative. The electrical state transitions are just that – electrical state transitions – until an interpreter interprets them as a computation. The computation is not intrinsic to the silicon nor to the electric charges. I and others like me are the computer's homunculi. So if we say that the brain is doing computation we need to say whether it is observer-relative or observer-independent. If it is observer-independent then we have to postulate a homunculus inside the brain who is actually manipulating the symbols so as to carry out the computation, just as I am consciously manipulating arabic numerals when I add 2 plus 2 to get 4. If we say it is observer-relative then we are supposing that some outside observer is assigning a computational interpretation to the neuron-firings.

I think this last point is clear if you think about it, but not everyone finds it so and I will therefore explore it a bit further. We are blinded to the observer-relativity of computational ascription because we think that since computation is typically mathematical and we also think that the world satisfies certain mathematical descriptions in an observer-independent fashion, that somehow it must follow that the computation is observer-independent. However, there is a subtle but still important distinction between the observer-independence of certain mathematically described facts and the observer-relativity of computation exploiting those facts. Consider the example I gave earlier of a rock falling off a cliff. The rock satisfies the law $S = \frac{1}{2}gt^2$, and that fact is observer-independent. But notice, we can treat the rock as a computer if we like. Suppose we want to compute the height of the cliff. We know the rule and we know the gravitational constant. All we need is a stopwatch. We can then use the rock as a simple analogue computer to compute the height of the cliff.

So what is the difference between the first case, where the rock is just a rock and is rule-described, and the second case where the rock is a computer carrying out a computation implementing exactly the same rule? The answer is: in the second case we have assigned – that is, there is an observer-relative assignment of – a computational interpretation. But what is true of the rock is true of every computer. What is special about the rock is that the law of nature and the implemented algorithm are the same. In a commercial computer we exploit the laws of nature to assign other algorithms to electronic processes: for addition, subtraction, word-processing, and so forth. But the general principle is this: we cannot appeal to the analogy between the computer and the brain to justify the special character of the tripartite model as applied to the brain, because something is a computer only relative to a computational interpretation.

What I have tried to show with the parable of the falling rock is that one and the same mathematical description can be treated both as a description of an observer-independent process, and as an observer-relative computation. It is just a fact about the stone that it falls in accordance with the laws of physics. There is nothing observer-relative about that. But if we treat that fact computationally, if we think of the stone as carrying out a computation, then that computation only exists relative to us.

I think that you can see this point if I give you a simpler example. If it is a fact that there are three cows in one field and two cows in the next field, both are observer-independent facts. But if I then decide to use these facts in order to perform a mathematical calculation, and I add three plus two to get five by counting the cows, the computational process of addition is not something that is intrinsic to the cows in the field. The process of addition is a process that I perform using the cows as my adding machine.

Now, what is true of the rock and the cows in the field is true of computation generally. If I am consciously doing arithmetic, that computation is intrinsic. If a pocket adding machine is doing arithmetic, that is observer-relative. It is worth pointing out, by the way, that over the years the word 'computer' has changed its meaning. When Turing wrote his famous 1950 article, the world 'computer' meant 'person who computes'. That is why Turing called the article 'Computing Machinery and Intelligence' not 'Computers and Intelligence'. 'Computer' meant: person who computes. Nowadays, the word 'computer' has changed its meaning from an observer-independent to an observer-relative phenomenon. 'Computer' now refers to a class of artefacts. This shift in the meaning of 'computer', like the shift in the meaning of 'information', has tended to blur the distinction between intrinsic intentionality and other sorts of phenomena, and it has tended to foster the confusions I am trying to expose here.

Information-Processing in the Brain

The crucial question for the classical model can now be stated with more precision. What fact exactly corresponds to the claim that there is an algorithmic level of information-processing in the brain? And what fact exactly corresponds to the claim that everything going on at this level reduces to a level of primitive processing which consists entirely in the manipulation of binary symbols? And are these computational information processes observer-independent or observer-relative?

As a first step let's ask how the proponents of the model think of it themselves. The answer to that question is not as clear as it ought to be but I think the answer is something like this. At this level, the brain works like an ordinary commercial computer. Just as there are symbols in the computer and they are information-bearing, so there are sentences in the head and they are information-bearing. Just as the commercial computer is an information-processing device so is the brain.

This answer is unacceptable. As we have already seen, in the commercial computer the symbols, sentences, representation, information and computation are all observer-relative. Intrinsically speaking the commercial computer is just a complicated electronic circuit. For the commercial computer to meet the causal reality constraint we have to appeal to the outside programmers, designers and users who assign an interpretation to the input, to the processes in between, and to the output. For the commercial computer, we are the homunculi who make sense of the whole operation.

This sort of answer can never work for Ludwig because whatever else he is, he is a conscious intentional agent trying to do something, trying to catch a tennis ball; and all of that is intrinsic to him, none of it is observer-relative. We want to know how he works really, intrinsically, not just what sorts of stances we might adopt toward him or what computational interpretations we might impose on him.

Well, why can't Ludwig be computing intrinsically; why can't he be carrying out algorithms unconsciously the way I carry out the algorithm for long division consciously? We can say that he does, but if we do we have abandoned the model, because now the explanatory causal mechanism is not the algorithm, but the mental agent inside who is intentionally going through the steps of the algorithm. This answer, in short, commits the homunculus fallacy. We don't explain Ludwig's intentionally-trying-to-catch-the-ball behaviour by an algorithm if we have to appeal to his intentionally-carrying-out-the-parabolic-trajectory-computation behaviour and then explain that in turn by his intentionally-going-through-millions-of-binary-steps behaviour.

Because now the explanatory mechanism of his system remains his irreducible intentionality. The idea of the model was that the information in the system is carried along by the computational operations over the syntax. The semantics just goes along for the ride. But on this analysis it is the syntax that is going along for the ride. The intrinsic intentionality of the agent is doing all the work. To see this point notice that the psychological explanation of my doing long division is not the algorithm, but my *mastery* of the algorithm and my *intentionally* going through the steps of the algorithm.

The upshot can be stated in the form of a dilemma for the classical model: the crucial notions are taken either in an observer-relative or in an observer-independent sense. If observer-relative then the explanation fails because it fails to meet the causal reality constraint. If observer-independent then it fails because of the homunculus fallacy. The homunculus is doing the work. You get a choice between an outside homunculus (observer-relative) or an inside homunculus (observer-independent). Neither option is acceptable.

Deep Unconscious Rule-Following

I think one way to meet my argument would be to offer a convincing existence proof to the contrary. Are there convincing and unproblematic examples of deep unconscious computational rule-following?

I have argued elsewhere that a specific aspectual shape requires accessibility to consciousness at least in principle. In many cases, blindsight, for example, the content is not accessible to consciousness in fact, but precisely for that reason, we understand such cases as pathological, as due to deficits, repression, and so forth. I won't repeat that argument here but will try to ask a different question: are there any unproblematic examples of deep unconscious rule-following?

If we had some convincing examples, then we would have fewer doubts about the overall principle. If we could agree that there are cases of rule-following in this technical sense, which departs from our ordinary commonsense notion of rule-following, and if we could agree further that these explanations have genuine causal explanatory power, then we would at least have a good beginning of a justification for a general cognitive science strategy of postulating such deep unconscious rule explanations. The two examples that have been presented to me are the operation of modus ponens and other logical rules, and secondly, the operation of the vestibular ocular reflex. (There is a certain irony about the VOR because I presented it as what I thought was an obvious example of a case that superficially seemed to satisfy the causal reality constraint, but where it was obvious that it didn't (Searle 1992, pp. 235–7).)

I will consider each of these in turn. People clearly have a capacity for making logical inferences. They do this, so the account goes, by following rules that they are totally unaware of and that they could not even formulate without professional assistance. So, for example, people are able to make modus ponens inferences, and thus follow the rule of modus ponens, even though they could not formulate the rule of modus ponens and, indeed, do not have the concept of modus ponens.

Well, let's try this out and see how it works. Here is a typical inference using modus ponens. Before the 1996 election I believed that if Clinton could carry the state of California, he would win the election. Having looked over the poll results in California, I came to the conclusion that Clinton would carry California, so I inferred that he would win the election. Now, how did I make that inference?

Well, the cognitive science explanation would go: when you made the inference you were in fact following an unconscious rule. This is the rule of modus ponens, the rule that says if you have premises of the form 'p', and 'if p then q', then you can validly infer 'q'. It seems to me, however, that in cases like this, the rule plays no explanatory role whatsoever. If I believe that Clinton will carry California, and believe that if he carries California he will win the election, that is already enough to enable me to infer that he will win the election. The rule adds nothing to the explanation of my inference. The explanation of the inference is that I can see that the conclusion follows from the premises. But doesn't the conclusion only follow from the premises because it instantiates the rule of modus ponens – doesn't it derive its validity from modus ponens? I believe the answer to these questions is: No. Modus ponens, construed as a syntactical computational rule, is simply a pattern that we use for describing inferences that are *independently* valid. We don't follow the rule of modus ponens in order to make the inference. Rather, we make the valid inference, and the logician can formulate the so-called rule of modus ponens to describe an infinite number of such valid inferences. But the inferences do not derive their validity from modus ponens. Rather, modus ponens derives its validity from the independent validity of the inferences. To think otherwise leads to the Lewis Carroll paradox (Carroll 1895). So, it seems to me, modus ponens plays no explanatory role whatever in an inference of the sort I just described.

But what about purely formal proof-theoretic inferences? Suppose I just have a bunch of symbols and I infer from 'p' and 'p $\rightarrow$ q' to 'q'? Now it seems to me that once we have subtracted the semantic content from the propositions, there actually is a role for the rule of modus ponens. But then precisely because there is such a rule, we are no longer talking about valid inferences as part of human cognitive processes. We are talking about a formal analogue to these valid inferences in some formal proof-theoretic system. That is, if you are given a rule that says whenever you have symbols of the form: 'squiggle blotch squaggle', followed by 'squiggle', you can write down 'squaggle', that is a genuine rule. It tells you what you can do in certain circumstances and it has all of those features that I described as typical of rule-governed behaviour, or rule explanations – every single one. But that is precisely not the operation of the rule of modus ponens in ordinary reasoning. To put this point precisely, if we think of modus ponens as an actual description of the operation of mental contents, then modus ponens plays no explanatory role in valid inferences. If we think of it as a proof-theoretical rule describing operations on meaningless symbols, then it does indeed play a role, but its role is not that of explaining how we actually make inferences in ordinary cognitive processes, but how we can represent the formal or syntactical structure of those inferences in artificially created systems.

I now turn to the vestibular ocular reflex. It looks as if we are unconsciously following the rule: 'Move the eyeball equal and opposite to the movement of the head', when in fact we are not following any such rule. There is a complex reflex mechanism in the brain that produces this behaviour. I thought the point was obvious, but not so. Recently, some of my critics have said that there are even subdoxastic computational states intrinsic to the system that are at a more fine-grained level than the rule I just stated. Martin Davies says,

> Another way to describe the VOR is as a system in which certain information-processing takes place, not just from head-movements of certain velocities to eye-movements of certain velocities, but from representations of head-movement velocities to representations of eye-movement velocities. It is only against the background of this second kind of description that there is any question of crediting the system with tacit knowledge of the rules relating head velocity to eye velocity. (Davies 1995, p. 386)

This assumption of 'semantic content' in the input and output states is a necessary but not a sufficient condition for tacit knowledge of rules. The sufficient condition requires that 'the various input–output transitions that are in conformity with the rule should have the same causal explanation' (ibid.).

The VOR easily satisfies that condition, so it turns out that the VOR is a case of unconscious tacit knowledge of rules and is a case of rule-governed behaviour. To support this, Davies gives various statements of computational descriptions of the VOR from David Robinson, Patricia Churchland and Terry Sejnowski (Churchland and Sejnowski 1993). He thinks mistakenly that I am arguing that the computational ascriptions are trivial. But that is not my point. My point is about the *psychological reality* of the computational ascriptions. I see no reason to treat the computational description of the VOR any differently than the computational description of the stomach or other organs. My question is, is there a causal level distinct from the level of the neurophysiology at which the agent is actually unconsciously carrying out certain computational, information-processing tasks in order to move his eyeball? I see nothing in Davies's account to suppose that the postulation of such a level meets the causal reality constraint. What fact about the vestibular nuclei makes it the case that they are carrying out specifically mental operations at the level of intrinsic intentionality? I do not see an answer to that question. It is not an objection to the usefulness of the computational models of the VOR to point out that they are models of neurophysiology, not examples of actual psychological processes: they are at the level of observer-relative neuronal information-processing not intrinsic intentionality. It is one thing to have a computational description of a process, quite another to actually carry out a mental process of computing.

Conclusion

On the account I am proposing, computational descriptions play exactly the same role in cognitive science that they play in any other branch of biology or in other natural sciences. Except for cases where an agent is actually intentionally carrying out a computation, the computational description does not identify a separate causal level distinct from the level of the physical structure of the organism. When you give a causal explanation, always ask yourself what causal fact corresponds to the claim you are making. In the case of computational descriptions of deep unconscious brain processes, the processes are rule-described and not rule-governed.

And what goes for computation goes *a fortiori* for 'information-processing'. You can give an information-processing description of the brain as you can of the stomach or of an internal combustion engine. But if this 'information-processing' is to be psychologically real, it must be a form of information that is intrinsically intentionalistic. Cognitive science explanations using the deep unconscious typically fail to meet this condition.

I would like to conclude this discussion with a diagnosis of what I think is the mistake. It is very difficult for human beings to accept non-animistic, non-intentionalistic forms of explanation. In our culture we only fully came to accept such explanations in the seventeenth century. Our paradigmatic forms of explanation are intentionalistic: I am eating this food because I am hungry, I am drinking this water because I am thirsty, I am driving on the left because that is the rule of the road. The idea that there are mechanical explanations that cite no intentionality is a very hard idea to grasp. A form of animism still survives in certain research projects in cognitive science. Marr's intermediate level of rule-following at the subdoxastic level in the brain is a form of animism. Now, since these postulated processes are not conscious, are not even accessible to consciousness in principle, we postulate deep unconscious rule-following behaviour. This is the mistake of primitive animism. Now, this is aided by a second mistake: we are misled by the apparent intentionality of computers, thermostats, carburettors and other functional systems that we have designed. It seems apparent to us that these systems have an intentionalistic level of description. Indeed, standard textbooks of cognitive science give Marr's intermediate-level description of the thermostat, as if the algorithmic level explanation obviously satisfied the causal reality constraint. But I think it is clear that it does not. In the case of thermostats we have rigged up physical systems to behave as if they were following computational rules. But the intentional, rule-following computation of the thermostat is entirely observer-relative. It is only because we have designed and used these systems that we can make intentionalistic explanations at all. Now, what goes for the thermostat goes for other functional systems, such as clocks, carburettors and, above all, computers. So, we are making two mistakes. The first is a mistake of preferring animism over naturalistic explanations, and the second is the failure to make the distinction between observer-relativity and observer-independence. In particular, we fail to distinguish the cases where we have genuine intrinsic intentionality as opposed to observer-relative intentionality. The intentionality in thermostats, carburettors, clocks and computers is entirely observer-relative.

The situation we are in is exactly like the following: Suppose cars occurred as natural phenomena and we did not know how they worked. We would be tempted to think that much of what they do is computational information-processing. For example we might try to explain the speedometer system by saying that it computes the speed of the car in miles per hour from the input of information about wheel rotation in revolutions per minute. We might even figure out the algorithm by which it maps rpm onto mph. But such an explanation has no causal reality at all. The actual causal mechanism is that a small electric generator is attached to a wheel in such a way that increases in rpm produce increases in electricity generated. An ammeter with a needle moves higher or lower as the electricity increases or decreases. As far as causation is concerned, that is the entire story. Intrinsically speaking there is no computation and no information. In addition to the straight physics, the computation and the information are all in us. They are observer-relative. There is nothing wrong with observer-relative computation and information. After all, that is what we in fact designed the speedometer system for. The wrong thing is to mistake the observer-relative attribution of computation and information-processing for a causal explanation.

Now, the hard thing to see is that many of the intentionalistic descriptions of brain processes are also observer-relative, and consequently do not give us a causal explanation. What then is the correct model for cognitive science explanation? And, indeed, how do we account for much of the apparent rationality of cognition if we do not postulate rule-governed behaviour at Marr's intermediate level? To answer this, it seems to me we have to remind ourselves of how Darwin solved a similar problem by showing how the apparent goal-directedness in the structure of species could be explained without postulating any intentionality. In a Darwinian style of explanation, we substitute two explanatory levels for one. Instead of saying 'the fish has the shape it has in order to survive in water', we say (1) the fish has the shape it has because of its genetic structure, and (2) fish that have that shape are going to survive better than fish that don't. Notice that survival still functions in the explanation but it is no longer a goal. It is just something that happens. Now, analogously, we should not say 'The eyeball moves because it is following a rule of the vestibular ocular reflex.' We should say that the eyeball moves because of the structure of the visual system – it is just a mechanical process. There is no rule-*following* at all. The rule, however, does *describe* the behaviour of the eyeball, and the eyeball satisfies that description for basically Darwinian reasons. Eyeballs that behave that way are going to produce a more stable retinal image, and organisms that have a stable retinal image are more likely to survive than organisms that don't. Analogously, Ludwig does not follow the parabolic trajectory rule, rather he tries to figure where the ball is going to be and jump to put his mouth at that point. After much practice he gets rather good at it. He has paw–eye co-ordination skills that enable him to be described by the parabolic trajectory rule, but he is not following that rule. Dogs that can develop such skills are more likely to survive than dogs that don't – or at least they are more likely to catch tennis balls.

References

Carroll, L. 1895. 'What the Tortoise Said to Achilles', *Mind* **14**, 278–80

Churchland, P. S. and Sejnowski, T. J. 1993. *The Computational Brain.* Cambridge, MA: MIT Press

Davies, M. 1995. 'Reply: Consciousness and the Varieties of Aboutness', in C. MacDonald and G. MacDonald (eds), *Philosophy of Psychology: Debates on Psychological Explanation.* Oxford: Blackwell

Marr, D. 1982. *Vision.* San Francisco: Freeman and Co.

Palmer, S. E. 1999. *Vision Science: From Photons to Phenomenology.* Cambridge, MA: MIT Press

Searle, J. R. 1992. *The Rediscovery of the Mind.* Cambridge, MA: MIT Press

8

INTENTIONALISTIC EXPLANATIONS IN THE SOCIAL SCIENCES

I

For over a century now there has been a continuing debate about whether the forms of explanation appropriate to the social sciences are essentially the same as or radically different from those used in the natural sciences. On one side is the empiricist philosophical tradition, ranging at least from John Stuart Mill through the logical positivists. According to this view, the covering law model of explanation appropriate for the natural sciences is equally appropriate for subjects such as history, anthropology, linguistics, economics, and other social sciences. On the other side is the interpretivist or hermeneutic tradition which ranges at least from Dilthey in the nineteenth century through the twentieth-century followers of Wittgenstein. According to this tradition, there are special modes of explanation appropriate to human behavior. In the second tradition, for example, Dilthey claims that a special method which he calls *Verstehen* (literally, understanding) is essential to the social sciences. And more recently, Charles Taylor (1985) claimed that human beings are unique in that events are *meaningful* to them in a special way and that any mode of explanation adequate to accounting for human behavior must explain this meaning component.

An unstated but underlying feature of this debate is often the assumption that much larger issues are at stake. There is at least the suggestion that the issue is a version of the dispute between materialism, on one hand, and dualism and idealism, on the other. The positivist tradition insists that

Reprinted from *Philosophy of the Social Sciences* (vol. 21, no. 3), pp. 332–344, the physical world is the only world that there is and that, consequently, the materialist models of explanation that are appropriate to physics and chemistry must be appropriate throughout the rest of science; otherwise there would be no explanation at all. In the interpretivist tradition, on the other hand, there is often the implied claim that not everything can be reduced to physics and chemistry, that some special mental (human, social) facts have a different sort of ontology from the ontology of physics and chemistry. This basic metaphysical dispute between materialism and dualism does not always rise to the surface in these discussions, but I think it is one of the underlying motivations for the persistence of the dispute. On one side are those who think with the positivists that if the material world is the only world there is, then the forms of explanation that have worked well in the material world for the hard sciences must work equally well throughout science. On the other side, in the interpretivist tradition, are those who feel that any such materialistic explanation must be too reductionist, that it must leave out the special features of human beings. It must leave out their mental or spiritual character. According to this view, mechanical forms of explanation are inadequate to capture the special features of human life and behavior; and on the most extreme versions of this view, explanations of human behavior are not even *causal* explanations. In their crudest and most polemical forms, the interpretivists see the empiricists as crass philistines, whereas the empiricists see the interpretivists as muddle-headed sentimentalists.

What are we to make of this dispute? I think we should be very suspicious of the terms in which it is traditionally posed. To begin with, explanations in the natural sciences do not universally employ the covering law form. For example, I recently had an occasion to look at half a dozen standard textbooks on the functioning of the brain. I do not recall a single case of a covering law explanation; indeed, there are almost no references to "laws" of brain functioning. The operation of the brain is explained in these books in the way that one might go about explaining the operation of the internal combustion engine. The brain is a physical system that performs certain functions, and the textbooks describe how the functions are performed. The explanations are indeed causal, but they do not appeal to covering laws.

Furthermore, though it does seem to me that there is a genuine dispute between the empiricist and interpretivist conceptions of the social sciences, I believe that it is a misconception of the nature of this dispute to construe it as essentially about reductionism or the mind-body problem. The question whether the social sciences require a special mode of explanation distinct from that of the natural sciences can be stated in a way which makes it independent of the debate between materialists and dualists. It is possible, for example, to reject dualism completely but still to think that there are certain special logical properties of social science explanations of human behavior. In my own case, for example, though I reject both dualism and materialism as standardly conceived, I still think there is an interesting dispute concerning the distinction between social science explanation and natural science explanation. My own view – just to lay all the cards on the table – is that the world consists entirely of material particles and systems composed of material particles (the materialists are right about that) but that the world also contains subjective mental states that function causally in the production of human and animal behavior (and this is usually – mistakenly – denied by materialists). So, in the discussion that follows, I will be rejecting two commonly accepted assumptions: first, that natural science explanations are invariably covering law explanations and, second, that there is some essential connection between the dispute about the nature of explanation in the social sciences and the materialist-dualist dispute on the mind-body problem.

It seems to me that the interpretivists are right in thinking that the modes of explanation in the social sciences are in certain respects logically distinct from the modes of explanation that we have grown used to in physics and chemistry. My primary aim in this essay is not to *establish* that the mode of explanation is different but simply to describe some of the *actual* differences that we find and explore the consequences of these differences. It is important to keep in mind in this discussion that science progresses not only by the discovery of new facts but by the discovery of new types of explanation. It is not surprising that this should be the case because the discovery of new facts often involves the discovery of new types of causes. Even if we confine our discussion to causal explanations, the discovery of new types of causes will result in the discovery of new types of causal explanation.

II

I do not have a well-worked-out theory of the nature of the explanation of social phenomena, and consequently, it is not my aim here to try to provide one. I have here the much more modest aim of pointing to certain characteristic features of the structure of explanations that we actually use in explaining social phenomena and of calling attention to some features of the ontology of the social phenomena themselves. The basic theses that I wish to argue can be stated as two separate but logically related points. First, characteristically, explanations of human behavior, whether of individual behavior or collective behavior, make reference to intentional causation.

I will give a more precise definition of intentional causation later, but the intuitive idea I can state now is that explanations of human behavior are indeed causal (the empiricists are right about that), but that such explanations, whether of individual behavior or collective behavior, make reference to a special kind of causation – they require a certain form of mental or, as I like to call it, "intentional" causation. Intentional mental states such as desires and intentions represent certain sorts of states of affairs, and intentional causation is that form of causation by which mental states are causally related to the very states of affairs that they represent. Thus, for example, a man whose thirst causes him to drink is engaging in behavior that can only be explained by intentional causation because his desire to drink causes the very behavior that is represented in the content of the desire, namely, his drinking. What is true of this very simple case is true on a much grander scale of the explanation of wars, revolutions, social movements, economic phenomena, and so on.

The second point I want to make is that there is a class of social facts having certain logical features that make them quite unlike the phenomena of physics and chemistry. In the case of phenomena such as marriage, money, divorce, elections, buying and selling, hiring and firing, wars and revolutions, the phenomena are – to speak vaguely at this stage – permeated with mental components; furthermore, the facts in question are self-referential in an odd way because they can only be the facts they are if the people involved think that they are those facts.

I believe the best way to explore the differences between natural science explanation and social science explanation is to list the most striking differences between the basic features of the two types of science. I want to list obvious features, so that at this stage of the argument at least, what I say will seem uncontroversial.

The first and most obvious feature is simply that we have not had the sorts of success in the social sciences that we have had in the physical sciences. We do not have anything in sociology or history to compare with the rich theoretical apparatus that we have developed, for example, in physics. Indeed, there is a sense in which, for the most part, the social sciences have not advanced theoretically beyond a kind of systematized common sense. And the mode of explanation that is appropriate in the social sciences seems to employ categories that we are all familiar with from our ordinary pretheoretical experience. One of the great puzzling features of contemporary intellectual life, as the twenty-first century dawns, is why the methods of the natural sciences have not produced in the social sciences results comparable to those that they have produced in such subjects as physics and chemistry.

It might seem that economics is an exception to this, since it is a formalized mathematical discipline, full of technical terms such as marginal propensity to consume, the multiplier effect, and unstable equilibrium. I believe that economics is not a counterexample at all. Typically what the economic theorist does is to take a lot of commonsense assumptions, such as the fact that consumers are trying to be better off and business people are trying to make money, and then idealize these assumptions (some people would say these assumptions are *over*idealized in economic theory) and work out the systematic implications. Thus the old chestnut in microeconomics that the rational entrepreneur sells where marginal cost equals marginal revenue is, in fact, a strict logical consequence of certain commonsense assumptions about "rational" economic behavior.

A second feature of the social sciences is one mentioned earlier, and it is, I believe, the most important: namely, that of intentional causation as one form of explanation in the social sciences. Intentional causation differs in an important respect from the sorts of causal phenomena that we are familiar with when we discuss such things as gravitation or nuclear forces, for intentional causation is that form of causation involving intentional mental states in virtue of the *actual content* of the mental states. Intentional causation is ascribed in statements such as the following:

> General Robert E. Lee ordered an attack at Gettysburg because he feared that his men would become demoralized if they were told to retreat.

or

> Many Democrats voted for the Republican candidate in the 1988 presidential election because they did not want a rise in taxes and they believed that Dukakis would raise the income tax.

Intentional causation is a reasonably precise notion and can be defined as follows: For any events x and y, x and y are related by intentional causation if and only if either x causes y or y causes x, and either x or y is an intentional state and the term which is not an intentional state is the conditions of satisfaction or part of the conditions of satisfaction of the intentional state (for a detailed discussion of this issue, see Searle 1983, chap. 5).

Intuitively, the idea is that mental states are a type of mental representation, and the special feature of intentional causation is that the intentional content causes the very state of affairs that it represents or is caused by the very state of affairs that it represents. In the case of General Lee, the desire to give an order to attack caused the giving of an order to attack, and ultimately, the desire to attack caused the attack. Furthermore, the desire to attack was itself caused by the desire not to demoralize the troops by ordering a retreat, together with the belief that anything other than an order to attack would cause such demoralization. In the case of the Democrats who voted for the Republicans, their desire to vote against increased taxes caused a desire to vote against the Democratic candidate, and that caused them to vote against the Democratic candidate.

A third distinction between the social and natural sciences is a direct consequence of the nature of intentional causation. The propositional content given by the theorists in the explanation of the behavior must be identical with the propositional content in the actual mind of the agent or agents whose behavior is being explained; otherwise, the behavior is not properly explained. For example, if we explain General Lee's behavior in terms of his fears and we explain the behavior of the Democrats in terms of their desires, in both cases the explanation will be valid only if the actual content that we specify as the content of the fear or the desire is identical with the content in the mind of the agent who had the fear or the desire. Since in the case of intentional causation, the causation works only in virtue of the representational content in the mind of the agent, then any representation of intentional causation will simply be a representation of a representation, and to the extent that it is accurate, there must be an identity between the propositional content given by the theorists and the propositional content in the mind of the person or persons being theorized about. That feature is totally unlike explanations in the natural sciences. In the natural sciences, we simply cite those aspects of events under which they are causally related. So, we cite such phenomena as gravity, pressure, heat, and so on. But since the phenomena in question are not themselves mental, there is no question of there being an identity between the phenomena to be explained and the phenomena occurring in the explanation. I believe that it is this feature of social explanation which accounts for the fact noted by several authors (e.g., Winch 1958) that the terms used in the explanation of human behavior must be available to the agents whose behavior is being explained. We could not, for example, explain Lee's behavior in terms of a fear of communism because as far as we know Lee never heard of communism.

It was a great breakthrough in the development of natural science when the medieval conception of all explanation as essentially intentionalistic was replaced in the seventeenth century by explanations appealing to general nonintentionalistic laws of nature. This was a tremendous advance, but the fact of that advance has blinded us to the fact that there are genuine empirical phenomena to which this covering law model of explanation is simply inadequate. It is inadequate because covering laws of explanation do not have this special feature of intentionalistic explanation. The special feature in question is that the content of the causal explanation and the mental content in the mind of the agent whose behavior is being explained must be identical because if the explanation is really valid, that very content must be functioning causally in the mind of the agent. To put this in brutally simple terms: When we explain human behavior, we are trying to explain people's behavior in terms of what they want and what they do to try to get what they want, given what they believe. But terms like "want," "try to get," and "believe" are intentionalistic notions. We can only specify the particular wants, tryings, and believings in terms of specific propositional contents, but then the propositional content that we specify in the explanation must be identical with the propositional content in the mind of the agent whose behavior is being explained. Otherwise, the explanation will not be adequate.

A fourth feature of social phenomena is also a consequence of intentionality. It is this: For many social phenomena, the phenomenon in question can only exist if people believe it exists. For this reason, the name of the phenomenon is often partly constitutive of the phenomenon so named. These phenomena are completely unlike, for example, such physical phenomena as gravity or kinetic energy and such biological phenomena as diseases or hereditary traits. Whether or not something is a certain disease or whether or not certain relations of gravitational attraction exist between two entities is a fact that is completely independent of how it is represented. The facts exist independently of what anybody thinks about them. But in the case of social facts, the beliefs and the terms that people use are partly constitutive of the facts. Let me give some examples: In general, a certain sort of material is only money if people think that it is money. A certain set of relations constitutes marriage or promise or property or an election only if the people involved think that it is money, marriage, property, or election. Somebody might be mistaken on a particular occasion: I might be married without knowing that I am married, or I might have a counterfeit dollar bill without knowing that it is a counterfeit dollar bill. But for these sorts of facts, it is a logical truth that you cannot fool all the people all the time. If everyone always thinks that it is not money, then it is not money. And what goes for money, goes for elections, private property, wars, voting, promises, marriages, buying and selling, political offices, and so on.

For those of us whose paradigms of reality are scientific phenomena like quarks and protons, these social phenomena ought to seem amazing to us. There is a large class of existing phenomena, a large class of objective facts, where the facts in question essentially involve people's beliefs, where the facts are only the facts they are because people believe that they are the facts they are. The fact that the Oakland Athletics won the 1989 World Series is an objective fact, but that fact is not constituted just by the movements of certain bodies. The movements of those bodies only count as the winning of the World Series by the Oakland team given a very complex network of intentionalistic phenomena, and those phenomena are self-referential in the sense that, for example, people are only playing a game if they believe that they are playing a game. Similarly, it is only a case of winning if people agree that it is the case of winning. Suppose, to take another example, I give a very large party, and at this party a large number of people are killed or injured. Suppose that the casualty rate is comparable to that of the battle of Gettysburg. All the same, as long as people think it is a party and not that it is a battle, then it is a party and not a battle, regardless of the casualty rate. Now, this sounds paradoxical for the following reason: In general, when someone thinks that x is f, if what one thinks is true, then there must be something completely independent of the fact that one thinks that x is f, that makes it the case that x is f. But many social concepts are partly self-referential in this respect; part of what constitutes x's being f is that people think that x is f. This is paradoxical because our notion of truth requires a distinction between the representation of the fact and the fact represented. But in these cases, the representation of the fact is partly constitutive of the fact represented, or at least this is the case for the participants in the fact. But how can our beliefs about social facts be true beliefs if the facts are partly constituted by the fact that we have those beliefs? The paradox dissolves when we see that thinking x is f in the case of social facts is only part of the constitution of the fact that x is f, and the concept expressed by f in all of these cases is simply a way of clustering a whole family of social practices. For social concepts, thinking that x is f involves thinking that whole patterns of behavior and social relationships are appropriate to the phenomenon in question. So, thinking that something is money or property or a party is not just a matter of thinking that certain labels apply but, rather, thinking that a set of attitudes and behavior are appropriate to the situation in its social context. But then, thinking that those attitudes are appropriate is itself partly constitutive of that social situation.

I believe that we will not begin to get a deep analysis of the foundations of the social sciences until we have a more thorough explanation than we now have of social facts. By an explanation of social facts, I mean an explanation of the *ontology* of social facts. The phenomena here that we are trying to analyze are so obvious and pervasive that it is almost impossible for us to see them. It is obvious to me that the piece of paper in my pocket is a dollar bill;

it is also obvious to me that I saw a football game last Sunday. What is not obvious is what facts exactly about this piece of paper make it the case that it is a dollar bill and what facts exactly about the movements that I saw make it the case that some of the organisms involved were playing a game of football. Notice that it is not enough to say that what constitutes the movements being a game of football is that they are in accord with the rules of football because exactly the same physical movements might have been made as part of a dance, outdoor exercise, or religious ceremony. Furthermore, it is not enough to make the obvious point that the fact that this piece of paper is a dollar bill derives from the fact that it was printed as such by the United States Bureau of Engraving and Printing because that only forces the question back a step. What fact makes something the Bureau of Engraving and Printing, and why do we recognize this Bureau as in any way relevant to whether something is a dollar bill? What I intend to do now is briefly discuss the basic elements of the apparatus necessary to give us an analysis of the ontology of social facts.

The first element is *self-referentiality*. Social facts differ from natural facts in that they contain mental representations. But they differ from other sorts of mental facts in that the mental representations have the element of self-referentiality that I was just attempting to adumbrate. The thing is what it is only if people think that that is what it is.

Constitutive rules comprise the second element. In *Speech Acts* (Searle 1969), I made a distinction between constitutive rules and regulative rules. Regulative rules regulate antecedently existing forms of behavior. Constitutive rules not only regulate but create the very possibility of new forms of behavior. The rule that says "Drive on the right side of the road" regulates the activity of driving, but it does not create the very possibility of driving. It is possible to drive on the left-hand side of the road or in the middle of the road as much as it is to drive on the right-hand side. That rule is regulative. But the rules of chess do not in that way regulate the antecedently existing activity of pushing pieces around the chessboard. Rather, acting in accordance with at least a large subset of those rules is part of what constitutes playing chess. The rules do not just regulate but are constitutive of a new form of activity. I believe that similar remarks could be made about the constitutive rules of marriage, money, private property, football, and so on. I am not at all sure that *every* social fact requires systems of constitutive rules, but it seems to me a very large class of social facts only exists within such systems.

The third element is *collective intentionality*. Social facts require social behavior, and social behavior characteristically requires collective intentionality. Collective intentionality is manifested in cooperative forms of behavior, which we characteristically describe by saying it is not just the case that *I* am doing something and *you* are doing something but that *we* are doing something together. It is worth pointing out that most forms of conflict require collective intentionality. In order that two men should engage in a prizefight, for example, there has to be collective intentionality at a higher level. They have to be cooperating in having a fight in order for each of them to try to beat the other up. In this respect, prizefighting differs from simply mugging someone in an alley. The man who creeps up behind another man in an alley and hits him on the head is not engaging in collective behavior. But the man who sticks up a bank by pointing a gun at a teller and demanding money is trying to elicit collective intentionality. Collective intentionality, I believe, is a universal feature of social facts (for a theoretical account of the structure of collective intentionality, see Searle 1990).

Linguistic permeation of the facts is the fourth element. I do not believe that it is possible to have social facts without language. It is possible to have collective behavior without language, and indeed, many forms of animal behavior are precisely collective forms of behavior, expressing collective intentionality. But such forms of behavior do not yet constitute what I am calling social facts. No doubt, there is a continuum between collective behavior in the form of collective animal intentionality and full-blown human social facts, such as electing someone president of the United States. But although there is a continuum, still I believe there is a deep reason why full-blown social facts must be linguistic. This feature derives from the self-referential character of the concepts mentioned earlier here. Money is only money if people think that it is money; a game is only a game if people think that it is a game. But it is impossible for us to have these thoughts without a certain sort of vocabulary. It is not necessary to have the actual word money or some synonym of it, but there has to be a vocabulary appropriate to buying, selling, and exchange generally for us to be able to manifest the collective intentionality which invokes the constitutive rules of private property and the exchange of property in return for money. I do not fully understand this feature, but the hypothesis that I am suggesting might be expressed as follows: There are no social facts without language because it is characteristic of a social fact that in order to be the social fact that it is, it has to be regarded as that fact, but for it to be regarded as that fact there has to be some mechanism for expressing that regard. For human beings, that mechanism is essentially linguistic.

The fifth element comprises *systematic interrelationships among social facts.* Social facts cannot exist in isolation but only in a set of systematic relations to other social facts. Thus, for example, in order that anyone in a society could have money, that society must have a system of exchange, of exchanging goods and services for money, but to have a system of exchange, it must have a system of property and property ownership. Similarly, in order that societies should have marriages, they must have some form of contractual relationships, but to have contractual relationships, they have to understand promising and obligations.

It might seem that games are a counterexample to this general principle because, of course, games are designed precisely with the idea that they should be forms of activity that do not connect with the rest of our lives in a way that social facts characteristically do. Today's baseball game need have no consequences for tomorrow in the way that today's wars, revolutions, buyings, and sellings are intended precisely to have consequences for tomorrow and into the indefinite future. Nonetheless, even in the case of games, there are systematic dependencies on other forms of social facts. The position of the pitcher, the catcher, and the batter, for example, all involve rights and responsibilities, and their positions are unintelligible without an understanding of these rights and responsibilities, but these notions are, in turn, unintelligible without the general notion of rights and responsibilities.

The primacy of acts over objects is the sixth element. It is tempting to think of social objects as independently existing entities on analogy with the objects studied by the natural sciences. It is tempting to think that a government or a dollar bill or a contract is an entity in the sense that a DNA molecule or a tectonic plate or a planet is an entity, an object which admits of study as an object. In the case of social objects, however, the grammar of the noun phrases conceals from us the fact that, in such cases, process is prior to product. Social objects are always created by social acts, and, in a sense, the object is just the continuous possibility of the action. It is a consequence of the account that I have given thus far that social acts are prior to social objects. That is, it is a consequence of the facts that social concepts have the self-referential feature mentioned earlier here and that collective intentionality is essential to the constitution of social facts, that social objects are themselves the product of collective intentionality manifested in the self-referential way that I have tried to characterize. Thus the object in my wallet is indeed a dollar bill and it is indeed an object; however, its status as a dollar bill – as opposed to its status as a piece of paper with ink on it – is constituted by its ability to function in a series of activities: buying, selling, paying bills, and so on. Furthermore, the self-referential concepts that I mentioned earlier serve to focus activities that people engage in in virtue of collective intentionality.

Conclusion

If social explanation has logical features different from explanations in the natural sciences, then it must be because social phenomena have factual features that are logically different from the facts of the natural sciences. I believe that such is indeed the case and I have tried to identify two sorts of facts involved: first, that the form of causation is essentially intentional causation and, second, that social facts have a logical structure different from natural facts.

References

Searle, J. R. 1969. *Speech acts: An essay in the philosophy of language.* New York: Cambridge University Press.

______. 1983. *Intentionality: An essay in the philosophy of mind.* New York: Cambridge University Press.

______. 1990. Collective intentions and actions. In *Intentions in communication,* edited by P. Cohen, J. Morgan, and M. E. Pollack. Cambridge: MIT Press/Bradford Books. Essay 6 of this volume.

Taylor, C. 1985. *Philosophy and the human sciences: Philosophical papers.* Vol. 2. New York: Cambridge University Press.

Winch, P. 1958. *The idea of a social science and its relation to philosophy.* London: Routledge & Kegal Paul.

9

INDIVIDUAL INTENTIONALITY AND SOCIAL PHENOMENA IN THE THEORY OF SPEECH ACTS

Since the early work on speech acts by Austin, Grice, myself and others in the 1950s and '60s, it has been possible to distinguish two apparently inconsistent strands in speech act theory. One strand, most prominently associated with the name of Grice (1957, 1969), treats individual intentionality as the fundamental notion in the theory of speech acts. Meaning is created by individual acts whereby speakers attempt to produce effects on hearers by getting the hearers to recognize their attempt to produce those effects. Meaning is thus the product of individual acts of meaning. On a Gricean analysis, there is no suggestion that conventions, rules, or social practices are in any way essential for the performance of speech acts. A second tradition associated with the name of Austin (1962), as well as with my own early book *Speech Acts* (1969), emphasizes the role of social institutions in the performance of speech acts. On this view, social conventions, rules, and contexts of utterance play a crucial role in the determination of the speech act. Meaning, on this view, is not just a product of individual intentionality, but it is also the result of social practices.

Is there anything to be said for either of these approaches, and in particular, are they, or can they be made to be, consistent with each other? My own view is that if they are stated carefully they can be construed in a way which renders them consistent. I believe they are both trying to say something true. The appearance of inconsistency derives from the fact that we fail to see that they can be construed as non-competing answers to different questions, rather than competing answers to the same question. A primary

Reprinted by permission from *Semiotics and Pragmatics* (Proceedings of the Perpignan Symposium), edited by Gerald Deladalle (Amsterdam: John Benjamins Publishing Co., 1989).

aim of this essay is to offer interpretations of each which would render them consistent.

In order to show the basic consistency of these two views, I want to begin by describing the case to be made for each in as strong terms as I can. To do this, I will present an account of meaning in the subjectivist, or Gricean tradition; I will then present an account of meaning in the objectivist, or social, or Wittgensteinian tradition; and then, I will conclude by showing that they are in fact both accounts of the same phenomenon viewed from two different sides.

1. Meaning as Individual Intentionality

If we approach meaning from the point of view of individual subjectivity, it seems to me essential to make a crucial distinction which Grice does not make. All of Grice's various definitions of meaning, from his earliest 1957 article to his subsequent attempts to improve and refine the original definition, rest on an attempt to define meaning in terms of the intentions that a speaker has to produce effects on heavers. In a word, Grice defines meaning in terms of attempts to communicate. This, I believe, is a mistake. I have argued elsewhere (1983, ch. 6; 1986) that within the theory of speech acts, we need to distinguish between the intention to represent certain states of affairs in certain illocutionary modes and the intention to communicate those representations to a hearer. The first intention, the intention to represent, determines the force and content of the speech act. The second intention, the intention to communicate, is the intention to produce in the hearer the knowledge of the force and content of one's speech act. For example, when I make the assertion to you that it is raining, there is a distinction between my intention to represent assertively the state of affairs that it is raining and my intention to communicate this representation to you. Similarly with promises. If I promise to come and see you on Wednesday, we need to distinguish between my intention to commit myself to come and see you on Wednesday and my intention to communicate this commitment to you. The argument that it is essential to make this distinction can be stated quite simply: in many cases it is possible to have a representing intention without having any intention to communicate the content of that representing intention to the hearer.

It is easy to see why the theory of speech acts leads us to confuse these two forms of intentionality expressed in the performance of the speech act. If a normal speech act is successful, it will involve both the representing intention and the communication intention. When a speaker performs a speech act, he normally intends both to represent a state of affairs in one or more of the possible illocutionary modes, and also to communicate the content of this representation to the hearer. Unless both of these intentions are achieved the speech act is defective. Since illocutionary acts are the basic unit of the speaker's meaning and also the basic unit of communication, it is overwhelmingly tempting to think that meaning is somehow identical with communicating. Nonetheless, within the theory of meaning, we need to distinguish them.

Many of the objections and counterexamples to Grice's definition rest on this distinction. It was always an embarrassment to Grice's account that it did not deal comfortably with cases of soliloquy, or cases in which there was no intended audience, or cases in which the speaker did not intend to produce any effects on his audience. The following example will illustrate the distinction.

I was once detained at the Yugoslav border by some uncooperative customs officials who spoke no English. At one point as I became increasingly cross, I made certain remarks to these officials in colloquial American English. Now I did this in the knowledge that they would not understand a word of what I said. Nonetheless, metaphors apart, I meant everything that I said. This was a defective speech act (fortunately, since if it had not been I would most likely still be at the Yugoslav border), because the hearers never understood what I said, nor were they intended to understand what I said. Nonetheless, I meant what I said, that is to say, I achieved my meaning or representing intention; but I did not intend to communicate – and I did not communicate.

In the analysis of the speech act, we need to distinguish the intention to represent and the intention to communicate. But now which of these is primary in the theory of meaning? It seems to me that the representing intention is prior. It is prior in the sense that one cannot even have the intention to communicate unless one has an illocutionary force and propositional content which one intends to communicate, and these together constitute the content of the representing intention. This is why in the ordinary colloquial use of "meaning", we are prepared to say of someone who has the representing intention that he meant something, even though he may not have intended to communicate it. If one wanted a slogan, one might say, no communication without representation.

In the literature on this subject, there are many counterexamples to the Gricean analysis, some of which have become legendary. On the proposal I am making here, much of the discussion of these counterexamples (much, but not all) can simply be avoided by making the distinction between that part of the speech act which constitutes the meaning intention proper and that part of the speech act which constitutes the intention to communicate that meaning intention to the hearer.

Well, what exactly are these different intentions? If we are to analyze meaning in terms of intentionality, we cannot allow ourselves to talk vaguely about meaning (or representing) intentions and communicating intentions. We have to be able to state precisely what the content of the intentions are. And to do that, we need to say at least a little bit about the nature of intentionality. What follows is a brief summary of some of the features of intentionality described in *Intentionality* (1983).

The key to understanding intentionality is conditions of satisfaction. An intentional state, such as a belief or a desire or a hope or a fear or an intention, with a direction of fit, is a representation of its conditons of satisfaction. Thus, the belief that it is raining represents the state of affairs that it is raining, with the mind-to-world direction of fit. The desire to go to the movies represents oneself as going to the movies, with the world-to-mind direction of fit. If we fully specify the conditions of satisfaction of intentions, however, we find that intending has some special features. Like desires, but unlike beliefs, intentions have the world-to-mind direction of fit. That is to say, it is the aim of the intention not to represent how things are, in the way, for example, that beliefs are supposed to represent how things are, but rather to bring about changes in the world so that the world, specifically one's own behavior, matches the content of the intention. Furthermore, the form in which this satisfaction of the direction of fit is supposed to be achieved by the intention involves the intention itself functioning causally in the bringing about of its own conditions of satisfaction. Thus, if I intend to go to France, but I forget all about my intention, and wind up in France quite by accident on my way to Hong Kong, then my original intention has not been carried out even though the state of affairs that it represented, namely, my going to France, actually occurred. If we are to specify the conditions of satisfaction of an intention fully, not only do we have to specify what it is the agent intends to do, but we have to specify that the intention itself should cause his doing it by way of intentional causation. That is, intentions have causally self-referential conditions of satisfaction. And we see this even in the simplest sort of cases. If I have the intention in action to raise my arm, the conditions of satisfaction are not only that my arm should go up, but that the intention itself should cause my arm to go up.

If the key to understanding intentionality is conditions of satisfaction, it should be possible to give a specification of the sort of intentions that are constitutive of meaning intentions in terms of their conditions of satisfaction.

I think, indeed, that it is fairly easy, but in order to make it explicit we need to back up a second and ask what is peculiar about meaningful entities such as speech acts that we need to explain. For our present discussion, the remarkable thing about speech acts is that in the performance of speech acts ordinary physical events and objects in the world have semantic properties. The remarkable fact is that the noises that come out of my mouth, or the marks that I make on paper, can be said to be true or false, meaningful or meaningless, relevant or irrelevant, and so forth. Now the question we are trying to answer in the theory of meaning might be put very crudely as follows:

How is it possible that mere things in the world can come to have semantic properties? How is it possible that the mind can impose intentionality on entities which construed in one way are just neutral objects and events in the world like any other? And the answer equally can be stated quite simply. If we analyze intentionality in terms of conditions of satisfaction, and if it is of the essence of meaning that entities that are not intrinsically intentional themselves have conditions of satisfaction, then the answer to our questions is: the mind imposes intentionality on objects and events in the world by intentionally imposing conditions of satisfaction on conditions of satisfaction. How does it work? If I say something and mean it, as opposed to just saying it without meaning it, then the conditions of satisfaction of my original intention are not only that that intention itself should cause the production of certain sounds, but that those sounds themselves should have further conditions of satisfaction – truth conditions in the case of assertives, fulfillment conditions in the case of commissives, and obedience conditions in the case of directives. So, for example, if I say in French "Il pleut souvent à Paris" and I intend this not just as the production of a sentence for the sake of practicing my pronunciation, but I intend it as actually making an assertion, that is, I actually mean what I say, then the conditions of satisfaction on my intention are (a) that the intention should cause the production of these sounds, and (b) that these sounds themselves have conditions of satisfaction, with the word-to-world direction of fit, in this case, the truth conditions that it rains often in Paris.

This last point needs to be made more precise. Where I make an assertion, I do not necessarily intend that my assertion be true. It is always possible to lie or otherwise make an insincere assertion. However, it is part of the definition of an assertion that it is a *commitment* to truth. Even if the speaker does not intend to make a true assertion, nonetheless he intends to make an utterance where the category of truth is an applicable standard of criticism. An assertion necessarily commits the speaker to the truth of the proposition, whether or not he in fact believes the proposition to be true. So, the conditions of satisfaction of the intention which the agent has when he makes an utterance are not that that very intention should have as its conditions of satisfaction that it's raining (that would be a case where one was trying to make it rain by saying certain things), but rather the conditions of satisfaction are that the utterance produced by the intention should itself have conditions of satisfaction with a certain direction of fit, in this case, the direction of fit is word-to-world, hence the conditions of satisfaction are truth conditions.

This example will provide us with a model for other examples of how the mind bestows intentionality on entities that are not intrinsically intentional by intentionally imposing conditions of satisfaction on those entities. Let us show how the analysis applies to two additional categories of speech acts – directives and commissives. Most directives and commissives, unlike assertives, have an additional feature of self-referentiality on the conditions of satisfaction of the speech act. This is shown by the fact that the order is not fully carried out, and thus not satisfied, unless the person to whom the order is given acts in the way he does because of the order. That is, to state it more precisely, the conditions of satisfaction of the order are not only that the thing ordered should be done, but rather that it should be done because it was so ordered. And that is just another way of saying that the conditions of satisfaction of the order are self-referential to the very order itself – for what the order orders is its own obedience. Exactly analogous considerations apply to promises. If I make a promise to come to your house on Wednesday night, and I forget all about the promise, but on Wednesday I decide to go over to your house to borrow some money from you, then there is a sense in which in arriving at your house I still haven't kept the promise; because the promise did not function as a reason for my doing what I did. Of course, I didn't break the promise, but then, I didn't exactly keep it either. Why not? Because what the promise promises is not only that a certain action will occur, but that it will occur by way of keeping the promise. To put this in the jargon of conditions of satisfaction, the conditions of satisfaction of the promise are not just that an act should occur, but that it should occur because of the promise. Thus, the conditions of satisfaction of the promise are causally self-referential to the promise itself, for unless the promise functions causally in the production of its own keeping, then it is not fully a case of keeping a promise; the promise is not fully satisfied.

To summarize: the intention that I have when I give an order, such as "Leave the room", involves both (a) that the intention itself should cause the production of the sounds, and (b) that the sounds should have as conditions of satisfaction, this time with the world-to-mind direction of fit, that the agent does the thing ordered and that the utterance itself should function causally in the production of his doing the thing ordered. Analogously with promises: when I promise to come and see you on Wednesday, then the intention behind my utterance is (a) that the intention should produce the utterance, and (b) that the utterance should have as conditions of satisfaction with the world-to-mind direction of fit that I do the thing promised and that the utterance itself should function causally in the production of the behavior that constitutes the doing of the thing promised.

Now notice that so far we have specified all of these meaning intentions without any reference to communication intentions. Of course, in the case of orders especially, and even in the case of some commissives (such as promises, though not for the case of other commissives such as vows), the speech act only takes effect if it is understood by a hearer, only if, to use Austin's jargon, we achieve "illocutionary uptake". In the case of all three types of speech act that we have considered thus far – assertives, directives, and commissives – the communication intention is simply that the hearer should recognize the utterance, and that he should recognize it as having the conditions of satisfaction which the speaker intends it to have. And all of that is just a way of saying that understanding consists in recognizing meaning intentions. Therefore, what has to be added to the meaning intention in order that we should have not only a meaning intention, but also a communicating intention, is the intention that the meaning intention should be recognized. Successful communication consists in the recognition of the speaker's meaning intentions.

Now, these analyses might seem excessively complex, but I think in fact, if anything, they are probably oversimplified. The simplicity, however, enables us to perceive the bare skeleton of the forms of intentionality that are peculiar to meaning. The whole insight behind the theory of speech acts was that the study of language was part of the study of human behavior generally. But if we are to cash in on that insight, if we are to make it fully explicit, then we have to show what is in common between speech acts and other types of acts, and what is different. What is in common is that speech acts, like all acts, involve the intentional production of certain consequences where the intention itself functions causally in the production of those consequences; what is peculiar to speech acts is that in addition to the intention to produce the bodily movements or other physical effects, there is an additional intention that the bodily movement, in this case the utterance act, should itself have further conditions of satisfaction which are not directly causally related to the original intention. In the case of directives and commissives, it is the intention that the utterance function causally in the production of the rest of the conditions of satisfaction, but only by way of further intentionality. That is to say in the case of directives, it isn't that the utterance directly causes something to happen, but rather that, if satisfied, it causes an agent, in this case the person to whom the directive has been issued, to act so as to bring about the rest of the conditions of satisfaction of the utterance by intentional acts. Similarly with promises. In the case of the promise, the agent intends that his utterance should have additional conditions of satisfaction and that, if satisfied, it should function causally by way of his own intentionality in his carrying out of the intentional action that constitutes the rest of the conditions of satisfaction of the utterance.

All of this captures our intuitive insight that what is special about speech acts, what makes them different from other kinds of behavior, is that they have meaning. If I scratch my nose or comb my hair or walk around, my acts don't normally have meaning in the semantic sense. In order for them to have meaning, I must intend them as signals in a certain way, but for me to intend them as signals in that way is precisely for me to impose conditions of satisfaction on them which are additional to the simple conditions of satisfaction of my original intention that the intention itself should produce such and such bodily movements. Another way to get at this very simple insight is this: whatever else speaking and writing a language consists in, it does consist in the production of certain physical events, such as making sounds out of one's mouth or making marks on paper. In that respect, it is just like any other human behavior. What is special is that those sounds and marks acquire semantic properties. They acquire representational properties relating them to the rest of the world. Now the answer to the question "How is such a thing possible?" is that the mind imposes intentionality on these sounds and marks. That is, it imposes intentionality on entities that are not intrinsically intentional to start with.

I said that this analysis would be in the Gricean tradition, but of course it is quite unlike anything that Grice actually ever suggested and I am sure he would find it unappealing. Why? Because I think his main message was that meaning could be analyzed in terms of the intention to communicate. This is the source of many, perhaps most, of the difficulties that his analysis encountered. On the analysis that I am proposing here, we are separating communicating from representing. And the heart of the meaning intention is the intention of representing, as is shown by the fact that one can say something, mean exactly what one says, and still not intend to communicate anything to anybody.

2. Meaning as a Social Phenomenon

So far we have been analyzing meaning and speech acts in terms of individual intentionality. It is as if the solitary subject could solipsistically impose conditions of satisfaction on his utterances and thus bestow meaning on what would otherwise be neutral sounds and marks in the world. But there is something profoundly misleading about this account and something is obviously absent. We can show this by imagining the following sorts of absurd situations. Could I now raise my arm and mean assertively "It is raining in Siberia"? Think what stage setting would be necessary for me to be able to do this. A simple case might be if for some reason we arranged a signalling code in advance, let's say as part of a game or as part of a device of communicating without words. Suppose we agreed in advance that if I raise my left arm, that means it is raining in Siberia; if I raise my right arm, that means the sun is shining in Siberia. Now once we have imagined a prior agreement of this sort, then it is very easy to imagine that I might raise my arm with these meaning intentions. But of course, the prior agreement is precisely the establishment of a convention and the question that that raises is: what is the role of such conventions in setting up the possibility of meaning intentions? Furthermore, the agreement was itself a speech act, or required the performance of speech acts, so it looks like we are in the traditional philosopher's puzzle that in order to explain how speech acts are possible we have to presuppose the performance of speech acts.

So, we now have to turn to the second half of our analysis. Our question is: what exactly is the role of such social phenomena as conventions, rules, practices, etcetera, in the performance of speech acts?

If we were to construct an argument to show that the performance of speech acts, and thus the creation of speaker's meaning, essentially requires human practices, rules, and conventions, the basic form of the argument, I believe, would have to be "transcendental" in the sense that it would assume the existence of speech acts, and then ask what are the conditions of possibility of speech acts. The specific form taken by that transcendental question, I believe, is this: what must be the case in order that on a given occasion by the expression of my intentionality I can, simply by virtue of my intentions, make an assertion or give an order or make a promise?

I will not attempt to develop such a transcendental argument here, but simply point to some of its features and consequences. Assuming that the social phenomena form the conditions of possibility of speech acts, then on this conception, the social-conventional aspects of language do not *replace* individual intentionality, but rather that intentionality is only able to function against the *presupposition* of social rules, conventions, and practices. To paraphrase a question of Wittgenstein's we might ask: would it be possible for one human being to have made a promise to another human being at only one time in the entire history of the universe? And our inclination is to say "No", because something only counts as a promise if it is a part of a general institution or practice of promising. And to deepen this insight, we might ask: what sort of a fact is it that someone made a promise anyhow? And it looks like it could not be just a fact about naked human intentionality and about the perception of that intentionality on the part of hearers. Why not? Well, the sort of intentions that a person has to have in order to make a promise require reference to phenomena which logically require the existence of human institutions, in the same way that the sorts of intentions that one has in buying and selling necessarily make reference to such institutions as those of property and money. So, for example, in order to make a promise a speaker has to have the intention to undertake an obligation. But the notion of an obligation is not, so to speak, a notion of natural history, referring to a natural phenomenon, referring to something that can exist apart from human practices and institutions. And similarly with many of the most interesting kinds of speech acts. For example, if a person makes a statement, his utterance commits him to the truth of the expressed proposition. And if it is to be a genuine statement, it must be intended to commit him to the truth of the proposition. But the notion of a commitment in statements, like the notion of an obligation in promises, is also an institutional notion.

Now when I wrote *Speech Acts,* I made part of this claim by saying: First, that the performance of the speech act, and thus the creation of meaning, was not a matter of brute fact, but for at least a large class of types of speech acts, it essentially involved institutional facts; second, that institutional facts were made possible by systems of constitutive rules; and third, that the same system of constitutive rules could be invoked in different languages by the differing conventions of those languages. The picture that I had at that time was the following: Different languages have different conventions for achieving the same speech act. For example, what I can achieve in English by saying "I promise . . . ", I achieve in French by saying "*Je promets . . .* ", or in German by saying "*Ich verspreche . . .* ". But these three different conventional realizations are all realizations of the same underlying constitutive rule, namely, the rule that says the making of a promise counts as the undertaking of an obligation to do something, normally for the benefit of the hearer. And that rule is not itself a convention of English or French or German, but is a constitutive rule of the institution of promising.

Since I wrote *Speech Acts* I have come to the conclusion that in addition to the constitutive rules of various institutions and the conventional realization of those rules in different languages, a thorough analysis also requires a recognition of the existence of background abilities and practices which enable human beings to communicate at all, or to have intentional states at all. In addition, then, to the apparatus of institutional facts, constitutive rules, and different conventional realizations of constitutive rules in the literal meaning of expressions, it now seems to me we require also what I call the *background*. I will now consider several of these elements in turn and discuss the question of how they relate to the conditions of possibility of the creation of speaker's meaning in the performance of speech acts.

Conventions

The existence of conventions of particular languages is not a necessary condition for the performance of speech acts in general. Such conventions are not conditions of the possibility of there being speech acts at all. This is shown, for example, by the fact that one can perform speech acts to people with whom one shares no common language. However, for the expression of any reasonably complex speech act, such as explaining the operation of an internal combustion engine, or describing the history of the Roman Empire, some system of representation of a conventional kind is necessary, some system other than the sorts of gestures and iconic devices that one is able to use to indicate that one is, for example, thirsty or sleepy.

Rules

Certain types of speech acts require constitutive rules, and certain other types do not. Assertions and promises require constitutive rules. All of those speech acts that require extra-linguistic institutions, such as pronouncing somebody man and wife, declaring war, adjourning a meeting, and so forth, require constitutive rules. But some speech acts, usually of a rather simple kind, such as greetings and simple requests, do not in this way require systems of constitutive rules. Why not? Because in each case the content of the intention which is communicated to the hearer does not make reference to anything that requires the existence of constitutive rules. So for example, if I make a simple request to someone, then I need to represent the state of affairs that I wish brought about and I need to communicate to the hearer the representation of this state of affairs and that my speech act will be satisfied only if the hearer brings about that state of affairs in virtue of the fact that

I have performed the speech act. But I don't in addition need to make reference to any institutional notions, such as commitment or obligation.

The test for whether or not a particular type of speech act requires constitutive rules can now be stated generally: Does the content of the meaning intention or of the communicating intention make reference to entities that require the existence of constitutive rules? Implicit in this test itself is an important negative theoretical claim – namely, the concepts of representation and communication are not themselves institutional in this sense. The concept of imposing conditions of satisfaction on entities that are not intrinsically intentional to start with and the concept of attempting to get hearers to recognize one's intention to do that do not, as such, require the existence of constitutive rules, even though in particular forms, these intentions will require constitutive rules. On my present view, the notions of meaning and communicating are not themselves institutional notions.

Shared Human Background Abilities

All intentional phenomena – whether beliefs, desires, hopes, fears, or whatnot – require non-intentional background capacities in order to function. By that I mean that the intentional states only determine their conditions of satisfaction, and thus only function as intentional states, given a set of capacities for applying the intentional states. Intentionality is not, so to speak, self-interpreting, or self-applying. The easiest way to see this point is to see that one and the same sentence or expression with the same literal meaning will have different applications, will, for example, determine different sets of truth conditions, given different background practices. I have argued for this at some length elsewhere (1983, ch. 5; 1980) using the examples of ordinary, common English verbs like "cut" and "open". For these cases I argue that one and the same literal meaning determines different conditions of satisfaction given different background practices. Thus, "cut" in "Cut the grass" has a different interpretation from "cut" in "Cut the cake", not because of a difference in semantic content, but because of different practices that we have regarding grass and cakes. "Open the door" and "Open your eyes", analogously, have the same semantic content in the verb but are interpreted quite differently given our different abilities as manifested in our practices. The important thing about these background abilities for the present purposes is that they are not themselves representational. They do not consist in a set of rules or beliefs or representations of other sorts. In these cases, knowing how cannot be reduced to knowing that. The argument for this point is first that if you try to specify the background practices as sets of rules or propositions, you get a regress – you never know when to stop because each of the propositions itself requires further background abilities for its interpretation, so you never get finished spelling out the background. But, second, in a sense you never get started either, because the set of propositions you can write down are never quite enough to fix the correct interpretation of the intentional content. The correct inference, I believe, from these, admittedly sketchy, arguments is that the set of capacities that enables us to apply intentional contents do not themselves consist in intentional contents and could not consist in intentional contents.

One of the implications of these points for the present discussion is that the capacity to symbolize itself, the capacity to represent, to use objects and states of affairs as representations of other objects and states of affairs, seems to be precisely one such background capacity. It is presumably innate in human beings, since all normal human beings have it, and (as far as we know) it is developed in humans in a way that is vastly superior to any other animal. If this hypothesis is correct, then the systems of rules and conventions that constitute our actual devices for performing speech acts rest on a background of human mental capacities that are not themselves rules and conventions, but pre-intentional abilities of a non-representational sort.

A second thesis that is suggested by this hypothesis is that in the case of communication it is a precondition of our attempting to communicate that we take other organisms like ourselves as sharing the same background capacities. I do not just exercise my capacities to represent as a solipsistic manoeuvre, but rather, I do it as part of our sharing these capacities and our communicating with each other.

There is in fact a great deal of vague talk in the Wittgensteinian tradition about the role of social practices in language and meaning. Since I believe a fair amount of this involves a confused view that there is an opposition between the role of individual subjectivity and the role of social practices, let me try to state now the relationship between these two as clearly as I can. The social capacities that we are talking about exist only in the minds of individual agents, individual speakers in the society. In addition to what is internalized in the minds/brains of the speakers there isn't some social practice that is, so to speak, out there independent of them. Social capacities are realized entirely in the individual brains of the members of any given society. The feature that makes them *social* practices is that they essentially refer to other agents in the society besides simply the speaker himself. They are social in the sense that their functioning requires contact between different agents in the society. But this in no way prevents them from being entirely realized in the individual brains.

3. Conclusion

This essay has a very limited aim. I am trying to show how two apparently inconsistent approaches to the philosophy of language and meaning can be reconciled. I am arguing that the approaches which emphasize individual subjectivity on the one hand, and social practices on the other hand, are not really in conflict as accounts of meaning and speech acts. My capacities to perform speech acts are realized entirely in my mind and my actual performances of speech acts are expressions of my intentionality. But just as the expressions of my intentionality are often directed at other members of the society, indeed *normally* directed at other members of the society, so the capacities themselves make reference to other members of the society precisely because the capacities are social capacities. I have conversations, engage in buying and selling, and write philosophical articles as part of a social enterprise.

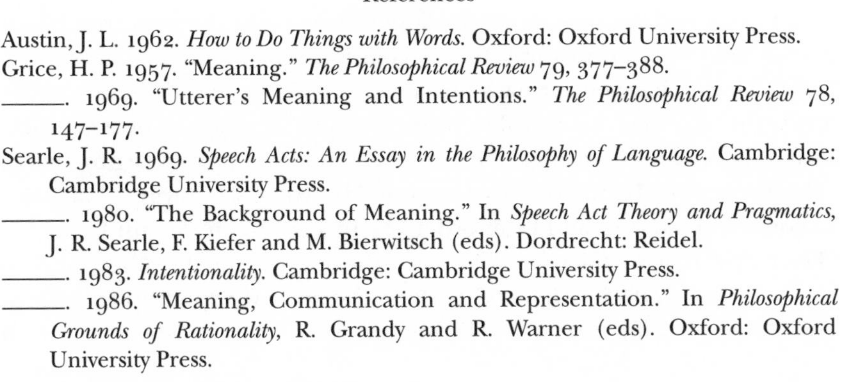

References

Austin, J. L. 1962. *How to Do Things with Words.* Oxford: Oxford University Press.

Grice, H. P. 1957. "Meaning." *The Philosophical Review* 79, 377–388.

_____. 1969. "Utterer's Meaning and Intentions." *The Philosophical Review* 78, 147–177.

Searle, J. R. 1969. *Speech Acts: An Essay in the Philosophy of Language.* Cambridge: Cambridge University Press.

_____. 1980. "The Background of Meaning." In *Speech Act Theory and Pragmatics,* J. R. Searle, F. Kiefer and M. Bierwitsch (eds). Dordrecht: Reidel.

_____. 1983. *Intentionality.* Cambridge: Cambridge University Press.

_____. 1986. "Meaning, Communication and Representation." In *Philosophical Grounds of Rationality,* R. Grandy and R. Warner (eds). Oxford: Oxford University Press.

10

HOW PERFORMATIVES WORK

The notion of a performative is one that philosophers and linguists are so comfortable with that one gets the impression that somebody must have a satisfactory theory. But I have not seen such a theory and in this essay I want to address the question: how exactly do performatives work? I believe that answering that question is not just a fussy exercise in linguistic analysis but can give us insights into the nature of language and the relation between speech acts and actions generally. Some people who have written about performatives[1] seem to think that it is just a semantic fact about certain verbs that they have performative occurrences, but the puzzle is: how could any verbs have such remarkable properties just as a matter of semantics? I can't fix the roof by saying, "I fix the roof" and I can't fry an egg by saying, "I fry an egg," but I can promise to come and see you just by saying, "I promise to come and see you" and I can order you to leave the room just by saying, "I order you to leave the room." Now why the one and not the other? And, to repeat, how exactly does it work? Perhaps the most widely accepted current view is the following: performative utterances are really just statements with

Reprinted from *Linguistics and Philosophy* (1989), 12, pp. 535–558, © 1989 *Kluwer Academic Publishers*, with kind permission from Kluwer Academic Publishers.

An earlier version of this essay was delivered as a forum address to the Linguistics Society of America Summer Institute at Stanford, 1987. I am indebted to several people for helpful comments and criticism, and I especially want to thank J. Boyd, Y. Matsumoto, T. B. Nguyen, D. Searle and E. Sweetser.

There is now a vast literature on the subject of performatives, and I am, of course, indebted to the authors whose works I have read. Specifically, I wish to acknowledge my indebtedness to J. Austin, K. Bach, M. Bierwisch, C. Ginet, R. Harnish, I. Hedenius, J. Lemmon, J. McCawley, F. Récanati, J. Sadock, J. Urmson, and G. Warnock. (See bibliography.)

[1] E.g., McCawley (1979).

truth values like any other statements, and Austin was wrong to contrast performative utterances with some other kind.[2] The only special feature of the performative statement is that the speaker can perform some other speech act indirectly by making the statement. And the task of a theory of performatives is to explain how the speaker can intend and the hearer can understand a second speech act from the making of the first speech act, the statement.

I have not seen an account of performatives that I thought was satisfactory. Therefore, in this essay I will attempt to:

(1) Characterize performatives in a way that will enable us to give a (fairly) precise statement of the problem;
(2) State the conditions of adequacy on any solution;
(3) Show that certain analyses of performatives fail;
(4) Introduce the elements of the apparatus necessary to solve the problem; and
(5) Suggest a solution.

1. What Exactly Is a Performative?

The word 'performative' has had a very confusing history and I need to make clear at the start how I am using it. Austin originally introduced the notion of *performatives* to contrast them with *constatives*; and his idea was that performatives were *actions*, such as making a promise or giving an order; and constatives were *sayings*, such as making a statement or giving a description. Constatives, but not performatives, could be true or false. But that distinction didn't work, because stating and describing are just as much actions as promising and ordering, and some performatives, such as warnings, can be true or false. Furthermore, statements can be made with explicit performative verbs, as in "I hereby state that it is raining." So it looked for a while as if he would have to say that every utterance was a performative, and that would render the notion useless. Another distinction which didn't work is that between explicit and implicit performatives, for example, the distinction between "I promise to come" (explicit) and "I intend to come" (implicit). This distinction doesn't work because in the sense in which the explicit performatives are performatives the implicit cases aren't performative at all. If I say, "I intend to come," I have literally just made a statement

[2] I believe the earliest version of this view is in Lemmon (1962). For another early statement see also Hedenius (1963).

about my intention. (Though, of course, in making such a statement, I might also indirectly be making a promise.)

I believe the correct way to situate the notion of performatives within a general theory of speech acts is as follows: some illocutionary acts can be performed by uttering a sentence containing an expression that names the type of speech act, as in, for example, "I order you to leave the room." These utterances, and only these, are correctly described as performative utterances. On my usage, the only performatives are what Austin called "explicit performatives." Thus, though every utterance is indeed a *performance*, only a very restricted class are *performatives.*

If we adopt this usage, it now becomes essential to distinguish between performative utterances, performative sentences, and performative verbs. As I shall use these expressions, a *performative sentence* is a sentence whose literal utterance in appropriate circumstances constitutes the performance of an illocutionary act named by an expression in that very sentence in virtue of the occurrence of that expression. A *performative utterance* is an utterance of a performative sentence token, such that the utterance constitutes the performance of the act named by the performative expression in the sentence. A *performative verb* is simply a verb that can occur as the main verb in performative sentences. When such a verb occurs in such a sentence in a performative utterance I shall speak of the *performative use* of the sentence and the verb. An utterance of

(1) Leave the room!

can constitute the *performance of* making of an order, but it is not *performative,* whereas an utterance of

(2) I *order* you to leave the room.

would normally be performative.

Furthermore, not every sentence containing a performative verb in the first person present indicative is a performative sentence.

(3) I *promise* to come on Wednesday.

is a performative sentence, but

(4) I *promise* too many things to too many people.

is not a performative sentence. In English most, but not all, performative utterances contain occurrences in the first person present singular indicative of the performative verb. There are also some occurrences in the present continuous, for example,

(5) I am *asking* you to do this for me, Henry, I am *asking* you to do it for me and Cynthia and the children.

and some performative utterances use verbs in the plural, for example,

(6) We *pledge* our lives, our fortunes and our sacred honor.

Furthermore, some performative sentences are in the passive:

(7) Passengers are hereby *advised* that all flights to Phoenix have been cancelled.

Sometimes the performative expression is not a verb and it may be in a separate clause or sentence, as in

(8) I'll come to see you next week, and that's a *promise.*

Not every occurrence of a performative sentence is a performative use. Thus, for example, (3) could be used to report a habitual practice: "Whenever I see you on Tuesday I always do the same thing: I promise to come and see you on Wednesday."[3]

2. What Exactly Is the Problem About Performatives?

Put at its most naive (and in a preliminary formulation we will later have to revise), the puzzle about performatives is simply this: how can there be a class of sentences whose meaning is such that we can perform the action named by the verb just by saying literally we are performing it? How can meaning determine that saying is doing? How does the saying *constitute* the doing? There are other questions related to this: why is the class of verbs restricted in the way that it seems to be? As I mentioned, I can promise by saying "I hereby promise," but I can't fry an egg by saying "I hereby fry an egg." Furthermore, how can one and the same unambiguous sentence have both a literal performative and a literal nonperformative use?

Another crucial question is why is it that in some sense I can't lie or be mistaken or utter a falsehood with the performative part of the performative utterance, in the way that statements normally can be lies, falsehoods or mistakes. This question has to be stated precisely. When I say, "Bill promised to come and see you last week" that utterance can be a lie, a mistake,

[3] Notice that I have restricted the definition of performatives to illocutionary acts. On my definition, utterances of "I am now speaking" or "I am shouting" (said in a loud voice) are not performative utterances.

or some other form of falsehood, just as any statement can. But when I say "I promise to come and see you next week," that utterance could be insincere (if I don't intend to do the act represented by the propositional content) and it can fail to be a promise if certain of the presuppositions fail to obtain (for example, if the person I take myself to be addressing is not a person but a fence post); but I can't be lying or mistaken about its having the *force* of a promise, because, in some sense that we need to explain, my uttering the sentence and meaning literally what I say gives it the force of a promise. Just to have a name I will call this the "self-guaranteeing" character of performative utterances.

Finally, there is a problem about the semantic analysis of performative verbs. Are we to be forced to say that these verbs have two meanings, one performative and one not? Or two senses? Or what?

3. Condition of Adequacy

What are the constraints that we would like to achieve on our analysis of performatives? Well, first we would like the analysis to fit into an overall account of language. Ideally performatives should not just stick out as some oddity or anomaly, but it should seem necessary that these verbs, sentences, and utterances would have these properties given the rest of our account of language. In this connection we would like to preserve the intuition that performative sentences are ordinary sentences in the indicative and that as such they are used to make statements that have truth values, even when uttered performatively. Also, we would like to avoid having to postulate ambiguities, especially since we have independent linguistic evidence that performative verbs are not ambiguous between a performative and a nonperformative sense. For example, we can get something like conjunction reduction in examples of the following sort: the sentence "John promises to come and see you next week, and I promise to come and see you next week" can be paraphrased as "John promises to come and see you next week and so do I." We need further to explain the occurrence of "hereby" in performative sentences. But the hard problem is that we need to meet these constraints in a way that accounts for the special character of performatives, especially the self-guaranteeing feature that I mentioned earlier.

Just so we can see what the problems are, I will simply list the main features that I would like to be able to account for.

(1) Performative utterances are performances of the act named by the main verb (or other performative expression) in the sentence.

(2) Performative utterances are self-guaranteeing in the sense that the speaker cannot be lying, insincere, or mistaken about the type of act being performed (even though he or she can be lying, insincere, or mistaken about the propositional content of the speech act and he or she can fail to perform the act if certain other conditions fail to obtain).

(3) Performative utterances achieve features (1) and (2) in virtue of the literal meaning of the sentence uttered.

(4) They characteristically take "hereby" as in "I hereby promise that I will come and see you."

(5) The verbs in question are not ambiguous between a performative and a nonperformative sense, even though the verbs have both performative and nonperformative literal occurrences.

(6) Performative utterances are not indirect speech acts, in the sense in which an utterance of "Can you pass the salt?" can be an indirect speech act of requesting the hearer to pass the salt.

(7) Performative utterances in virtue of their literal meaning are statements with truth values.

(8) Performative sentences typically use an unusual tense in English, the so-called "dramatic present."

4. Previous Analyses

I am not sure that all these conditions can be met, and perhaps some of them are incorrect, but in any case none of the discussions I have read and heard of performatives meets all of them. Let me review my own earlier writings on this subject. In *Speech Acts* (Searle, 1969) and other writings I pointed out that, in general, illocutionary acts have the structure F(*p*), where the "F" stands for the illocutionary force, and the "(*p*)" stands for the propositional content. If communication is to be successful, the hearer has to be able to figure out from hearing the sentence what is the illocutionary force and what is the propositional content. So there will in general be in the syntax of sentences an illocutionary force indicating device and a representation of the propositional content. In the sentence, "It's raining," the propositional content expressed is: that it is raining, and the illocutionary force of a statement is indicated by such things as word order, intonation contour, mood of the verb and punctuation.

Now on this account, I argued in *Speech Acts* that the performative prefix is just an indicator of illocutionary force like any other. In "I state that it is raining" and "I order you to leave the room" the performative prefixes

"I state" and "I order" function to make explicit the illocutionary force of the utterance of the sentence. As far as it goes, I think that account is right but incomplete in that it doesn't explain how performatives work. In particular, it doesn't so far explain how the same syntactical sequence can occur in some cases as an indicator of illocutionary force and in others as part of propositional content. So the present task can be described in part as an attempt to complete the account I began in *Speech Acts.*

In the *Foundations of Illocutionary Logic* (Searle and Vanderveken, 1985), Daniel Vanderveken and I argued that performative utterances were all cases of declarations. Declarations, just to remind you, are speech acts such as, for example, "The meeting is adjourned" or "War is hereby declared" where the illocutionary point of the speech act is to change the world in such a way that the propositional content matches the world, because the world has been changed to match the propositional content. In a declaration of the form F(*p*) the successful performance of the speech act changes the world to make it the case that *p*. Declarations thus have simultaneously both the word-to-world and the world-to-word directions of fit.[4] Now on this account of performative utterances, just as I can declare the meeting to be adjourned, so I can declare a promise to be made or an order to be issued; and I use a performative prefix to do these things. If we just read off the structure of the speech act from the surface structure of the sentence that account seems obviously right. The propositional content, for example, that I order you to leave the room, is made true by the utterance of the sentence "I order you to leave the room," and such an utterance differs from an utterance of the sentence "Leave the room" because though an utterance of "Leave the room" also makes it the case that I ordered you to leave the room, it does not do so by declaration. It does not do so by representing it as being the case, and thus it differs from a performative.

This analysis of performatives as declarations has the consequence that the illocutionary structure of "I order you to leave the room" is:

Declare (that I order (that you leave the room)).

The propositional content of the declaration is: that I order that you leave the room, even though the propositional content of the order is: that you leave the room.

I think it is correct to say that all performatives are declarations, but that does not really answer our original question, "How do performatives

[4] For an explanation of all these notions, see Searle (1979), Chapter 1.

work"; it only extends it into "How do declarations work?" Also it has consequences of the sort that make philosophers nervous, for example, what about the use of "I declare" as a performative prefix for a declaration?[5] Is that used to make a declaration of a declaration? And if so how far can such a regress go?

Most recent attempts at analyzing performatives have treated them as statements[6] from which some other speech act can be derived; and many, though not all, of these accounts treat them as a type of indirect speech act. I said earlier that intuitively performatives did not seem to be indirect speech acts; but there is something very appealing about any approach that treats them as statements, because it takes seriously the fact that a performative sentence is grammatically an ordinary sentence in the indicative mood. Typical attempts to try to make this approach work treat performative utterances as indirect speech acts on analogy with such cases as "Can you pass the salt?" used to request somebody to pass the salt, or "It's hot in here," used to request somebody to open the window. The idea is that the literal speech act is a statement and then by some mechanism of Gricean implicature the hearer is supposed to infer the intent to perform some other speech act. I do not think these accounts are adequate; but just to consider the best I have seen, I will briefly review the account given by Bach and Harnish.

According to Bach and Harnish, "in the case of performative utterances, even those without the use of 'hereby,' normally the hearer could reason, and could be intended to reason, as follows:

(1) He is saying "I order you to leave."
(2) He is stating that he is ordering me to leave.
(3) If his statement is true, then he must be ordering me to leave.
(4) If he is ordering me to leave, it must be his utterance that constitutes the order. (What else could it be?)
(5) Presusmably, he is speaking the truth.
(6) Therefore, in stating that he is ordering me to leave he is ordering me to leave.[7]

I believe this account is unsatisfactory, because it fails to meet even the most uncontroversial of our conditions of adequacy. Specifically, it fails to explain the performative character and the self-guaranteeing character of

5 "Declare" in English also functions as an assertive prefix, as in "I declare that the contents of this document are true and complete."

6 E.g., Lewis (1972), Bach (1975), Ginet (1979), and Bach and Harnish (1979).

7 Bach and Harnish (1979), p. 208.

performative utterances. It fails to meet conditions (1) and (2). The phenomenon that we are trying to explain is how a statement *could* constitute an order, and on this account, it is just blandly asserted in (4) that it does constitute an order. The fact we were trying to explain is left unexplained by the Bach-Harnish account. Furthermore, we were trying to explain the self-guaranteeing character which performatives have, but other statements do not have. Now, if we are right in thinking that performatives are self-guaranteeing, then it is redundant to suppose that we need an extra presumption that the speaker is telling the truth (their step (5)), because as far as the illocutionary force is concerned, there is no way he could fail to speak the truth.

Their account takes it as given that the utterance can constitute an order, but if we are allowed to assume that utterances can constitute states of affairs described by the utterance, then we do not have an account that explains the differences between sentences which work as performatives and sentences which do not, such as, for example, "I am the King of Spain." They offer no explanation of why their analysis works for ordering but wouldn't work for the following:

(1) He is saying "I am the King of Spain."
(2) He is stating that he is the King of Spain.
(3) If his statement is true, then he must be the King of Spain.
(4) If he is the King of Spain, it must be his utterance that constitutes his being the King of Spain. (What else could it be?)
(5) Presumably, he is speaking the truth.
(6) Therefore, in stating that he is the King of Spain, he is being the King of Spain.

I think it is obvious that "I order you to leave" can be used performatively and "I am the King of Spain" cannot, but there is nothing in the Bach-Harnish account that explains the difference. Why does the one work and not the other? Another way to state the same objection is to point out that they are relying on our understanding of how the sentence "I order you to leave" can be used performatively and not explaining how it can be so used.

Still, there is something very appealing about the idea that performative utterances are statements from which the performative is somehow derived. We have only to look at the syntax of these sentences to feel the appeal. So let's try to make the strongest case for it that we can. What we are trying to explain in the first instance is how the literal meaning of the indicative sentence is such that its serious and literal utterance is (or can be) the performance of the very act named by the main verb.

5. Performatives As Assertives

Notice first that the "hereby" marks a self reference. Whether the "hereby" occurs explicitly or not, the performative utterance is about itself. In "I order you to leave" or "I hereby order you to leave," the speaker in some sense says that that very utterance is an order. Such utterances are no more and no less self-referential than, for example, "This statement is being made in English."[8]

Now, if we were going to take seriously the idea that performatives work by way of being statements to the effect that one performs a certain speech act, we would have to show how the characteristics of such self-referential statements were sufficient to be constitutive of the performance of the speech act named by the performative verb. In the formal mode we could say that we need to show how (assuming certain contextual conditions are satisfied) the statement "John made a self-referential statement to the effect that his utterance was a promise that *p*" entails, as a matter of logic, "John made a promise that *p*." Well, what are the characteristics of such statements, and what are the characteristics of performatives, and what are the relations between them? The characteristics in question are these:

(1) A statement is an intentionally undertaken commitment to the truth of the expressed propositional content.

(2) Performative statements are self-referential.

(3) An essential constitutive feature of any illocutionary act is the intention to perform that act. It is a constitutive feature of a promise, for example, that the utterance should be intended as a promise.

Now our question is a little more precise. Can we show how the first two characteristics combine to guarantee the presence of the third? Can we show how the fact that one made a self-referential statement to the effect that one was making a promise that *p* is sufficient to guarantee that one had the intention to make a promise that *p*? I used to think this was possible, and in fact when I completed an earlier version of this paper I thought I had a pretty good demonstration of how it worked. I now think that it can't be made to work, but I believe its failure is instructive, so let's go through the steps. I will try to set out in some detail an argument designed to show that a self-referential statement to the effect that the utterance is a promise that

[8] Many authors have remarked on this self-referential feature. Perhaps the first was Åqvist (1972).

p necessarily has the force of a promise; and then I will try to show why the argument doesn't work.

Step 1. Suppose someone makes a statement literally uttering the sentence "I promise to come and see you next week." Well, as such it is a statement; and a statement is a commitment to the truth of the proposition, so the speaker is committed to the truth of the proposition that he promises to come to see the hearer next week.

But in general, the making of a statement does not guarantee that it is true or even that the speaker intends that it be true. For even though the statement commits him to its truth, he might lie or he might be mistaken. So from the mere fact that the utterance is a statement that he promises, we cannot derive that it is a promise.

Step 2. The statement is self-referential. It isn't just *about* a promise but it says of itself that it is a promise. It might be paraphrased as "This very utterance is the making of a promise to come and see you next week."

But the addition of self-referentiality by itself is still not enough to guarantee that it is a promise or even that it is intended as a promise. If I say "This very utterance is being made in French," there is nothing in the fact that a self-referential statement has been made that guarantees that it is true or even that it is intended to be true.

Step 3. In the utterance of the sentence, the speaker has made a self-referential truth claim to the effect that his utterance is a promise. But what would make it true, in what would its truth consist? Well obviously, its truth would consist in its being a promise. But in what does its being a promise consist? Given that the preparatory and other conditions are satisfied, *its being a promise consists in its being intended as a promise.* Given that everything else is all right with the speech act, if it is intended as a promise, then it is a promise. So now our question narrows down to this: How do the other features guarantee the intention to make a promise?

Step 4. The main feature of its being a promise is that it is intended as a promise. But now, and this is the crucial point, if the utterance is self-referential and if the intended truth conditions are that it be a promise and if the main component in those truth conditions actually being satisfied is the intention that it be a promise, then the intention to make the self-referential statement that the utterance is a promise is sufficient to guarantee the presence of the intention that it be a promise and therefore sufficient to guarantee that it is a promise. Why?

Step 5. The intention to label the utterance as a promise is sufficient for the intention to be a promise, because the intention to label it as a promise carries a commitment. The commitment in assertives is that the proposition is true. But now, the commitment to its truth, intentionally undertaken, already carries a commitment to the intention that it be a promise. But that intention, in the appropriate circumstances, is sufficient for its being a promise.

So on this account, though statements in general do not guarantee their own truth, performative statements are exceptions for two reasons, first, they are self-referential and, second, the self-reference is to the other speech act being performed in that very utterance. Notice that the self-referentiality is crucial here. If I assert that I will promise or that I have promised, such assertions do not carry the commitments of the actual promise in a way that the assertion "This very speech act is a promise" does carry the commitments both of the assertion and thereby of the promise.

This, I believe, is the best argument to show that performatives are primarily statements. What is wrong with it? For a long time it seemed right to me, but it now seems to me that it contains a mistake. And any mistake, once you see it, is an obvious mistake. The mistake is that the argument confuses *being committed to having an intention* with actually *having the intention.* If I characterize my utterance as a promise, I am committed to that utterance's having been made with the intention that it be a promise, but this is not enough to guarantee that it was actually made with that intention. I thought this objection could be evaded by the self-referentiality, but it can't be. Just self-referentially describing one of my own utterances as a promise is not enough to guarantee that it is made with the intention that it be a promise, even though it is enough to commit me to having made it with that intention.

The point is a fairly subtle one, but I have reluctantly come to the conclusion that it is decisive. So, I will repeat it: The intention to assert self-referentially of an utterance that it is an illocutionary act of a certain type, say, a promise, is simply not sufficient to guarantee the existence of an intention in that utterance to make a promise. Such an assertion does indeed *commit* the speaker to the existence of the intention, but the commitment to having the intention doesn't guarantee the *actual presence* of the intention. And that was what we needed to show. We needed to show that the assertion somehow guaranteed the presence of the performative intention, when the assertion was a self-referential assertion to the effect that it was an illocutionary act named by the performative verb.

It now turns out that the effort to show that performatives are a species of assertion fails. The performative character of an utterance cannot be derived from its literal features as an assertion. I have come to the unfortunate conclusion that any attempt to derive performatives from assertives is doomed to failure because assertives fail to produce the self-guaranteeing feature of performatives, and in failing to account for the self-guaranteeing feature, the analysis fails to account for performativity. The failure to satisfy condition (2) automatically produces a failure to satisfy condition (1). In order to derive the performative from the assertive, we would have to show that given the statement S of certain conditions on the speech act, the conjunction of S and the proposition '*x* made the self-referential assertion that he promised that *p*' entails '*x* promised that *p*'; and this cannot be done because the assertive intention by itself does not guarantee the presence of the performative intention.

6. Performatives as Declarations

Now we have to go back to the drawing board. We were trying to derive the declarational character of performatives from their assertive character and it didn't work. So let's reconsider what is implied by the view that performatives are declarations. We saw earlier that, trivially, performatives are declarations because they satisfy the definition of a declaration. The definition is that an utterance is a declaration if the successful performance of the speech act is sufficient to bring about the fit between words and world, to make the propositional content true. Declarations thus have the double direction of fit ↕ whereas assertives have the word-to-world direction of fit↓.[9] One way to characterize our failure so far is to say that my effort to derive the double direction of fit from the assertive direction of fit was a failure. I thought I could do it with self-referentiality plus the lexical meaning of some peculiar verbs, but it turned out that the apparatus was too weak.

So let us now ask "How do declarations work in general?" and we can then use the answer to that question to locate the special features of performatives.

[9] See Searle (1979), Chapter 1, for further discussion of the notion of direction of fit.

In order intentionally to produce changes in the world through our actions, normally our bodily movements have to set off a chain of ordinary physical causation. If, for example, I am trying to hammer a nail into a board or start the car, my bodily movements – for example, swinging my arm while holding the hammer, turning my wrist while holding the key in the ignition – will cause certain desired effects.

But there is an important class of actions where intention, bodily movement and desired effect are not related by physical causation in this way. If somebody says, "The meeting is adjourned," "I pronounce you husband and wife," "War is declared," or "You're fired," he may succeed in changing the world in the ways specified in these utterances just by performing the relevant speech acts. How is that possible? Well, notice that the literal utterance of the appropriate sentences is not enough. For two reasons: first, for many of these utterances someone might utter the same sentence speaking literally and just be making a report. If the chairman says, "The meeting is adjourned" as a way of adjourning the meeting, I might report to my neighbor at the meeting, "The meeting is adjourned," and my speaker meaning includes the same literal sentence meaning as did the speaker meaning of the chairman; but he and not I performed a declaration. Second, even if I say "The meeting is adjourned" intending thereby to adjourn the meeting, I will not succeed because I lack the authority. How is it that the chairman succeeds and I do not? In general, these sorts of declarations require the following four features:

(1) An extra-linguistic institution.
(2) A special position by the speaker, and sometimes by the hearer, within the institution.
(3) A special convention that certain literal sentences of natural languages count as the performances of certain declarations within the institution.
(4) The intention by the speaker in the utterance of those sentences that his utterance has a declarational status, that it creates a fact corresponding to the propositional content.

As a general point, the difference between pounding a nail and adjourning a meeting is that in the case of adjourning the meeting the intention to perform the action, as manifested in the appropriate bodily movement (in this case, the appropriate utterances) performed by a person duly authorized, and recognized by the audience, is constitutive of bringing about the desired change. When I say in such cases that the intention is constitutive of the action, I mean that the manifestation of the intention in the utterance does not require any further causal effects of the sort we have in hammering a nail or starting a car. It simply requires recognition by the audience.

The more formal the occasion, the more condition (3) is required. The speaker must utter the right expressions or the utterance does not count as marrying you, adjourning the meeting, and so forth. But often on informal occasions, there is no special ritual phrase. I can give you my watch just by saying, "It's yours," "You can have it," "I give it to you," etcetera.

The most prominent exceptions to the claim that declarations require an extra-linguistic institution are supernatural declarations. When God says, "Let there be light!", that I take it is a declaration. It is not a promise; it doesn't mean "When I get around to it, I'll make light for you." And it is not an order; it doesn't mean "Sam over there, turn on the lights." It makes it the case by fiat that light exists. Fairy stories, by the way, are full of declarations performed by witches, wizards, magicians, and so forth. We ordinary humans do not have the ability to perform supernatural declarations, but we do have a quasi-magical power nonetheless of bringing about changes in the world through our utterances; and we are given this power by a kind of human agreement. All of these institutions in question are social institutions, and it is only as long as the institution is recognized that it can continue to function to allow for the performance of declarations.

When we turn to performatives such as "I promise to come and see you," "I order you to leave the room," "I state that it is raining," and so forth, we find that these, like our earlier declarations, also create new facts, but in these cases, the facts created are linguistic facts; the fact that a promise has been made, an order given, a statement issued, etcetera. To mark these various distinctions, let's distinguish between *extra-linguistic* declarations – such as adjourning the meeting, pronouncing somebody man and wife, declaring war, and so on – and *linguistic* declarations – such as promising, ordering, and stating by way of declaration. Both linguistic and extra-linguistic declarations are speech acts, and in that sense they are both linguistic. In the examples we have considered, they are all performed by way of performative utterances. Naively the best way to think of the distinction is this: A declaration is a speech act whose point is to create a new fact corresponding to the propositional content. Sometimes those new facts are themselves speech acts such as promises, statements, orders, etcetera. These I am calling linguistic declarations. Sometimes the new facts are not further speech acts, but wars, marriages, adjournments, light, property transfers, and so forth. These I am calling extra-linguistic declarations. When the chairman says, "The meeting is adjourned," he performs a linguistic *act,* but the *fact* he creates, that the meeting is adjourned, is not a *linguistic fact.* On the other hand, when I say, "I order you to leave the room," I create a new fact, the fact that I have ordered you to leave the room, but that fact is a linguistic fact.

Since the facts created by linguistic declarations are linguistic facts, we don't need an extra-linguistic institution to perform them. Language is itself an institution, and it is sufficient to empower speakers to perform such declarations as promising to come and see someone or ordering someone to leave the room. Of course, extra-linguistic facts may also be required for the performance of the linguistic declaration. For example, I have to be in a position of power or authority in order to issue orders to you. And such facts as that I am in a position of power are not facts of language. Nonetheless, they are conditions required by the rules of linguistic acts. No non-linguistic institution is necessary for me to give an order, and the rules of ordering already specify the extra-linguistic features of the world that are necessary in order to perform a successful and non-defective order.[10]

All performative utterances are declarations. Not all declarations are performatives for the trivial reason that not all declarations contain a performative expression, for example, "Let there be light!" does not. But every declaration that is not a performative could have been one: for example, "I hereby decree that there be light!" The important distinction is not between those declarations which are performatives and those which are not, but between those declarations which create a linguistic entity, a speech act such as an order, promise, or statement, and those which create a non-linguistic entity such as a marriage, a war, or an adjournment. The important distinction is between, for example, "I promise to come and see you" and "War is hereby declared."

Traditionally in speech act theory we have regarded the non-linguistic cases as prototypical of declarations, but it is also important to see how much non-linguistic apparatus they require. Consider "divorce." I am told that in certain Moslem countries a man can divorce his wife by uttering three times the performative sentence "I divorce you." This is a remarkable power for a speech act, but it adds nothing to the meaning of "divorce" or its translations. The ability to create divorces through declarational speech acts derives from legal/theological powers and not from semantics.

[10] Suppose somebody rigs up a transducer device sensitive to acoustic signals which is such that if he stands next to his car and says, "I hereby start the car," the car will start. Has he performed a declaration? Well, obviously not. Why not? *Because the semantic properties played no role.* The acoustic properties are irrelevant except insofar as they are an expression or an encoding of the semantics. Another way to put the same point is to say that declarations can be performed in any language, and there is no set of physical properties that any given declaration has in all and only its occurrences. You can't define the declaration physically.

7. Performatives and Literal Meaning

Since ordinary linguistic declarations are encoded in performative sentences such as "I order you to leave the room" or "Leave, and that's an order," they do not require an extra-linguistic institution. The literal meaning of the sentence is enough. But now the question arises: how could it be enough? How can the literal meaning of an ordinary indicative sentence encode the actual performance of an action named by the main verb? And how can the literal meaning both encode the performative and the assertive meaning without being ambiguous? It is not enough to say that in the one case the speaker intends the utterance as a performative and in the other as an assertion. The question is: how could one and the same literal meaning accommodate both intentions?

With these questions we come to the crux of the argument of this essay. I believe it is the failure to see an answer to these questions – or even to see the questions – that has led to the currently fashionable views that performatives are some kind of indirect speech act where the supposedly non-literal performative is somehow derived from the literal assertion by Gricean mechanisms. On my view, the performative utterance is literal. The speaker utters the sentence and means it literally. If the boss says to me, "I hereby order you to leave the room," I don't have to *infer* that he has made an order, nor do I think that he hasn't quite said exactly what he meant. It is not at all like "Would you mind leaving the room?" said as an order to leave.

The apparatus necessary for answering these questions includes at least the following three elements:

> First, we need to recognize that there is a class of actions where the manifestation of the intention to perform the action, in an appropriate context, is sufficient for the performance of the action.
>
> Second, we need to recognize the existence of a class of verbs which contain the notion of intention as part of their meaning. To say that a person performed the act named by the verb implies that he or she did it intentionally, that if it wasn't intentional, then the agent didn't do it under that description. Illocutionary verbs characteristically have this feature. I cannot, for example, promise unintentionally. If I didn't intend it as a promise, then it wasn't a promise.
>
> Third, we need to recognize the existence of a class of literal utterances which are self-referential in a special way, they are not only *about* themselves, but they also operate on themselves. They are both *self-referential* and *executive.*

Now if you put all these three together you can begin to see how performative sentences can be uttered as linguistic declarations. The first step is to see that for any type of action you can perform, the question naturally arises: how do you do it? By what means do you do it? For some actions you can do it solely by manifesting the intention to do it, and, in general, speech acts fall within this class. Typically we perform a type of illocutionary act by uttering a type of sentence that encodes the intention to perform an act of that type, for example, we perform directive speech acts by uttering sentences in the imperative mood. But another way to manifest the intention to perform an illocutionary act is to utter a performative sentence. Such sentences are self-referential and their meaning encodes the intention to perform the act named in the sentence by the utterance of that very sentence. Such a sentence is "I hereby order you to leave." And an utterance of such a sentence functions as a performative and hence as a declaration because (a) the verb "order" is an intentional verb, (b) ordering is something you can do by manifesting the intention to do it, and (c) the utterance is both self-referential and executive, as indicated by the word "hereby" in a way that I will now explain.

Normally it is a bit pompous to stick in "hereby." It is sufficient to say "I order you . . . " or even "That's an order." Such sentences can be used either just to make assertions or as performatives, without being ambiguous. The sentence uttered as an assertion and the sentence uttered as a performative mean exactly the same thing. Nonetheless, when it is uttered as a performative the speaker's intention is different from when it is uttered as an assertive. Performative speaker meaning includes sentence meaning but goes beyond it. In the case of the performative utterance, the intention is that the utterance should constitute the performance of the act named by the verb. The word "hereby" makes this explicit, and with the addition of this word, sentence meaning and performative speaker meaning coincide. The "here" part is the self-referential part. The "by" part is the executive part. To put it crudely, the whole expression means "by-this-here-very-utterance." Thus, if I say, "I hereby order you to leave the room," the whole thing means "By this here very utterance I make it the case that I order you to leave the room." And it is possible to succeed in making it the case just by saying so, because, to repeat, the utterance is a manifestation (and not just a description or expression) of the intention to order you to leave the room, by making that very utterance. The whole thing implies "This very utterance is intended as an order to you to leave the room," where that implication is to be taken not just as the description of an intention but as its manifestation. And the manifestation of that intention, as we have seen, is sufficient for its being an order.

It is perhaps important to emphasize again a point I made earlier, namely, that the self-referential *assertive* intention is not enough to do the job. Just intending to assert that the utterance is an order or even that it is intended as an order doesn't guarantee the intention to issue an order. But intending that the utterance *make it the case* that it is an order is sufficient to guarantee the intention to issue an order. *And that intention can be encoded in the meaning of a sentence when the sentence encodes executive self-referentiality over an intentional verb.*

To show how the analysis works in more detail, let us go through a derivation from the hearer's point of view. We should *en passant* be able to show how the utterance of a performative sentence constitutes both a declaration and, by derivation, an assertion.

(1) S uttered the sentence "I hereby order you to leave" (or he uttered "I order you to leave" meaning "I hereby order you to leave").
(2) The literal meaning of the utterance is such that by that very utterance the speaker *intends* to make it the case that he orders me to leave.
(3) Therefore, in making the utterance *S manifested an intention* to make it the case by that utterance that he ordered me to leave.
(4) Therefore, in making the utterance S manifested an intention to *order* me to leave by that very utterance.
(5) Orders are a class of actions where the manifestation of the intention to perform the action is sufficient for its performance, given that certain other conditions are satisfied.
(6) We assume those other conditions are satisfied.
(7) S ordered me to leave, by that utterance.
(8) S both said that he ordered me to leave and made it the case that he ordered me to leave. Therefore he made a true statement.

This last step explains how the performative utterance can also be a true statement: Declarations, by definition, make their propositional content true. That's what a successful declaration is. It is an utterance that changes the world in such a way as to bring about the truth of its propositional content. If I say, "The meeting is adjourned," and succeed in my declaration, then I make it the case that what I said is true; similarly with "I order you to leave the room." But it is important to emphasize, contrary to the hypothesis that I considered earlier, that the truth of the statement derives from the declarational character of the utterance and not conversely. In the case of performative utterances, the assertion is derived from the declaration and not the declaration from the assertion.

Now this whole analysis has a somewhat surprising result. If we ask what are the special semantic properties of performativity within the class of intentional verbs which enable a subclass of them to function as performative verbs, the answer seems to be, roughly speaking, there are none. If God decides to fry an egg by saying, "I hereby fry an egg," or to fix the roof by saying, "I hereby fix the roof," He is not misusing English. It is just a fact about how the world works, and not part of the semantics of English verbs, that we humans are unable to perform these acts by declaration. But there is nothing in the semantics of such verbs that prevents us from intending them performatively; it is just a fact of nature that it won't work. If I now say, "I hereby end all wars and produce the eternal happiness of mankind," my attempted declaration will fail, but my failure is not due to semantic limitations. It is due to the facts of nature that in real life, performatives are restricted to those verbs which name actions where the manifestation of the intention is constitutive of the action, and (religious and supernatural cases apart) those verbs are confined to linguistic and institutional declarations.

There are a number of semantic features which *block* a performative occurrence. So, for example, famously, "hint," "insinuate," and "boast" cannot be used performatively, because they imply that the act was performed in a way that was not explicit and overt, and performative utterances are completely explicit and overt. But there is no special *semantic* property of performativity which attaches to verbs and thereby *enables* them to be used performatively. As far as the literal meaning of the verb is concerned, unless there is some sort of block, any verb that describes an intentional action could be used performatively. There is nothing linguistically wrong with the utterance "I hereby make it the case that all swans are purple." The limitation, to repeat, is not in the semantics, it is in the world. Similarly with the perlocutionary verbs. What is wrong with "I hereby convince (persuade, annoy, amuse, etc.) you" is not their semantics but their presumption. The limitation on performatives is provided by the fact that only a very tiny number of changes can be brought about in the world solely by saying that one is making those changes by that very utterance. For non-supernaturally endowed humans beings,[11] these fall into two classes: the creation of purely linguistic institutional facts – such as those created by saying "I hereby promise to come and see you," "I order you to leave the room," etcetera – and extra-linguistic institutional facts – such as "The meeting is adjourned," "I pronounce you husband and wife," and so forth. But the special semantic property of performativity

[11] Again, I am ignoring the religious cases such as blessing, cursing, damning, etc.

simply dissolves. There is nothing there. What we find instead are human conventions, rules, and institutions that enable certain utterances to function to create the state of affairs represented in the propositional content of the utterance. These new facts are essentially social, and the act of creating them can succeed only if there is successful communication between speaker and hearer. Thus the connection between the literal meaning of the sentence uttered and the institutional fact created by its utterance. "I promise" creates a promise; "The meeting is adjourned" creates an adjournment.

8. Summary and Conclusion

The analysis I am proposing runs dead counter to most of the current ways of thinking about this issue and counter to the view I myself held until recently, so it is perhaps useful to summarize the argument so far.

Our problem is to explain how the literal utterance of certain ordinary indicative sentences can constitute, and not merely describe, the acts named by the main verb (or some other performative expression) in that very sentence. It turns out under investigation that that question is the same question as how the literal utterance of these sentences can necessarily manifest the intention to perform those acts; since we discovered for such acts, the manifestation of the intention is constitutive of the performance. So our puzzle was: how can the literal utterance of "I hereby order you to leave the room" constitute an order as much as the literal utterance of "Leave the room" constitutes a directive in general, when the first is obviously an ordinary indicative sentence, apparently purporting to describe some behavior on the part of the speaker?

We found that it was impossible to derive the performative from the assertion because the assertion by itself wasn't sufficient to guarantee the presence of the intention in question. The difference between the assertion that you promise and the making of a promise is that in the making of a promise you have to intend your utterance as a promise, and there is no way that an assertion by itself can guarantee the presence of that intention. The solution to the problem came when we saw that the self-guaranteeing character of these actions derives from the fact that not only are these utterances self-referential, but they are self-referential to a verb which contains the notion of an intention as part of its meaning, and the acts in question can be performed by manifesting the intention to perform them. You can perform any of these acts by an utterance because the utterance can be the manifestation (and not just a commitment to the existence) of the relevant intention. But you can, furthermore, perform them by a performative utterance because the performative utterance is self-referential to a verb which contains the notion of the intention which is being manifested in that very utterance. The literal utterance of "I hereby order you to leave" is – in virtue of its literal meaning – a manifestation of the intention to order you to leave. And this in turn explains why as far as illocutionary force is concerned the speaker cannot lie or be mistaken: assuming the other conditions on the speech act are satisfied, if he intends his utterance to have the force of an order, then it has that force, because the manifested intention is constitutive of that force.

I have so far tried to give an account which will satisfy all but one of our conditions of adequacy, that is, to show:

(1) How performative utterances can be performances of the act named by the performative verb.
(2) How they are self-guaranteeing in the sense explained.
(3) How they have features (1) and (2) in virtue of their literal meaning.
(4) Why they characteristically take "hereby."
(5) How they can achieve all of this without being ambiguous between a performative and a non-performative sense.
(6) How they work without being indirect speech acts.
(7) How it is that they can be statements with truth values.

It remains only to answer:

(8) Why do they take that peculiar tense, the dramatic present?

This tense is used to mark events which are, so to speak, to be construed as instantaneous with the utterance. Thus, the chemistry professor says while giving the demonstration

> I pour the sulphuric acid into the test tube. I then add five grams of pure carbon. I heat the resulting mixture over the Bunsen burner.

In these cases, the sentence describes an event that is simultaneous with its utterance, and for that reason Julian Boyd (in conversation) calls this tense "the present present." Similarly, though less obviously, with the written text of a play. We are to think of sentences such as "John sits" or "Sally raises the glass to her lips" not as reporting a previously occurring set of events nor as predicting what will happen on the stage, but as providing an isomorphic model, a kind of linguistic mirror of a sequence of events. Now, because the performative utterance is both self-referential and executive, the present present is ideally suited to it. "I promise to come and see you" marks an event which is right then and there, simultaneous with the utterance, because the event is achieved by way of making the utterance.

Our analysis had two unexpected consequences, or at least consequences that run counter to the current ways of thinking about these matters. First, most contemporary analyses try to derive the performative from the assertion; but on my proposal, the performative, the declaration, is primary; the assertion is derived. Secondly, it turns out that there is no such thing as a semantic property which defines performative verbs. Unless there is some special feature of the verb which implies non-performativity (as with "hint," "insinuate" and "boast") any verb at all which names an intentional action could be uttered performatively. The limitations on the class that determine which will succeed and which will fail derive from facts about how the world works, not from the meanings of the verbs.

If one looks at the literature on this subject, one finds two apparently absolutely inconsistent and firmly held sets of linguistic intuitions. One set, exemplified powerfully by Austin (1962), insists roundly that performatives are not statements but, rather, performances of some other kind. Another set insists, equally roundly, that all performatives are obviously statements. One of my aims has been to show the truth in both of these intuitions. Austin was surely right in thinking that the primary purpose of saying "I promise to come and see you" is not to make a statement or a description, but to make a promise. His critics are surely right in claiming that, all the same, when one says, "I promise to come and see you," one does make a statement. What my argument attempts to show is how the statement is derivative from the promise and not conversely.

References

Åqvist, L.: 1972, 'Performatives and Verifiability by the Use of Language', *Filosofiska Studier* **14**, University of Uppsala.

Austin, J. L.: 1962, *How to Do Things with Words*, Harvard University Press, Cambridge, Mass.

Bach, K.: 1975, 'Performatives Are Statements Too', in *Philosophical Studies* **28**, 229–36.

Bach, K. and R. Harnish: 1979, *Linguistic Communication and Speech Acts*, MIT Press, Cambridge, Mass.

Bierwisch, M.: 1980, 'Semantic Structure and Illocutionary Force', in J. R. Searle, F. Kiefer and M. Bierwisch (eds.), *Speech Act Theory and Pragmatics*, pp. 1–36, D. Reidel Publishing Company, Dordrecht.

Ginet, C.: 1979, 'Performativity', *Linguistics and Philosophy* **3**, 245–265.

Hedenius, I.: 1963, 'Performatives', *Theoria* **29**, 115–136.

Lemmon, J. E.: 1962, 'Sentences Verifiable by Their Use', *Analysis* **12**, 86–89.

Lewis, D.: 1972, 'General Semantics', in D. Davidson and G. Harman (eds.), *Semantics of Natural Language*, pp. 169–218, D. Reidel Publishing Company, Dordrecht.

McCawley, James D.: 1979, 'Remarks on the Lexicography of Performative Verbs', in *Adverbs, Vowels, and Other Objects of Wonder*, pp. 161–173, University of Chicago Press, Chicago and London.

Récanati, F.: 1980, 'Some Remarks on Explicit Performatives, Indirect Speech Acts, Locutionary Meaning and Truth-value', in J. R. Searle, F. Kiefer and M. Bierwisch (eds.), pp. 205–220, D. Reidel Publishing Company, Dordrecht.

Sadock, J.: 1974, *Toward a Linguistic Theory of Speech Acts*, Academic Press, New York.

Searle, J. R.: 1969, *Speech Acts: An Essay in the Philosophy of Language*, Cambridge University Press, Cambridge.

Searle, J. R.: 1979, *Expression and Meaning: Studies in the Theory of Speech Acts*, Cambridge University Press, Cambridge.

Searle, J. R. and D. Vanderveken: 1985, *Foundations of Illocutionary Logic*, Cambridge University Press, Cambridge.

Urmson, J.: 1977, 'Performative Utterances', *Midwest Studies in Philosophy* **2**, 120–127.

Warnock, G. J.: 1973, 'Some Types of Performative Utterance', in I. Berlin *et al.* (eds), *Essays on J. L. Austin*, pp. 69–89, Clarendon Press, Oxford.

11

CONVERSATION

I

Traditionally speech act theory has a very restricted subject matter. The speech act scenario is enacted by its two great heroes, "S" and "H"; and it works as follows: S goes up to H and cuts loose with an acoustic blast; if all goes well, if all the appropriate conditions are satisfied, if S's noise is infused with intentionality, and if all kinds of rules come into play, then the speech act is successful and nondefective. After that, there is silence; nothing else happens. The speech act is concluded and S and H go their separate ways. Traditional speech act theory is thus largely confined to single speech acts. But, as we all know, in real life speech acts are often not like that at all. In real life, speech characteristically consists of longer sequences of speech acts, either on the part of one speaker, in a continuous discourse, or it consists, more interestingly, of sequences of exchange speech acts in a conversation, where alternately S becomes H, and H, S.

Reprinted by permission from (*On*) *Searle on Conversation*, edited by Herman Parret and Jeff Verschueren (Amsterdam: John Benjamins Publishing Co., 1992).

This essay originated in a lecture I gave at the University of Campinas, Brazil, at a conference on Dialogue in 1981. A later version was given at a conference at Michigan State University in 1984. Much of this version is simply a transcript of the Michigan State lecture. Since that lecture was delivered without a text and without notes, it is somewhat more informal than is generally the case with published articles. The original version was published as "Notes on Conversation," in *Contemporary Issues in Language and Discourse Processing*, edited by D.G. Ellis and W.A. Donahue, Hillsdale, New Jersey: Lawrence Erlbaum Associates, Inc., 1986. I am indebted to Dagmar Searle, Yoshiko Matsumoto, and Robin Lakoff for comments on the original transcript. I have made additions, revisions, and clarifications for this version, hence the change in the title.

Now the question naturally arises: Could we get an account of conversations parallel to our account of speech acts? Could we, for example, get an account that gave us constitutive rules for conversations in a way that we have constitutive rules of speech acts? My answer to that question is going to be "No." But we can say some things about conversations; we can get some sorts of interesting insights into the structure of conversations. So, before we conclude that we can't get an analysis of conversations parallel to our analysis of speech acts, let us see what sort of regularities and systematic principles we can find in the structure of conversations.

The first principle to recognize (and it's an obvious one) is that in a dialogue or a conversation, each speech act creates a space of possibilities of appropriate response speech acts. Just as a move in a game creates a space of possible and appropriate countermoves, so in a conversation, each speech act creates a space of possible and appropriate response speech acts. The beginnings of a theory of the conversational game might be a systematic attempt to account for how particular "moves," particular illocutionary acts, constrain the scope of possible appropriate responses. But when we investigate this approach, I believe we will see that we really do not get very far. To show this, let us first consider the most promising cases, so that we can see how special and unusual they are. Let us consider the cases where we do get systematic relationships between a speech act and the appropriate response speech act. The best cases are those that are misleadingly called "adjacency pairs," such as question/answer, greeting/greeting, offer/acceptance or rejection. If we consider question and answer sequences, we find that there are very tight sets of constraints on what constitutes an ideally appropriate answer, given a particular question. Indeed, the constraints are so tight that the semantic structure of the question determines and matches the semantic structure of an ideally appropriate answer. If, for example, I ask you a yes/no question, then your answer, if it's an answer to the question, has to count either as an affirmation or a denial of the propositional content presented in the original question. If I ask you a wh-question, I express a propositional function, and your appropriate response has to fill in the value of the free variable. For example, from an illocutionary point of view, the question "How many people were at the meeting?" is equivalent to "I request you: you tell me the value of X in 'X number of people were at the meeting.'" That is, genuine questions (as opposed to, e.g., rhetorical questions), in my taxonomy at least, are requests; they are directives; and they are in general requests for the performance of speech acts, where the form of the appropriate response speech act is already determined by the form of the question.

However, there are some interesting qualifications to be made to these points about questions. One is this: I said in *Speech Acts*[1] that questions were requests for *information*, and that suggests that every question is a request for an assertion. But that seems obviously wrong if you think about it. The point was brought home to me very forcefully when the book was in press, and one Friday afternoon a small boy said to me "Do you promise to take us skiing this weekend?" In this case, he was asking for a *promise*, not a piece of factual *information*. He was requesting me either to promise or refuse to promise and, of course, those are speech acts different from assertions.

A second qualification is this: I said that the structure of questions determines and matches the structure of answers. But an apparent counterexample can be found in the exasperating English modal auxiliary verbs. There are cases where the structure of the interrogative does not match that of the appropriate response. If I say to you "Shall I vote for the Republicans?" or "Shall I marry Sally?", the appropriate answer is not "Yes, you shall" or "No, you shall not." Nor even "Yes, you will" or "No, you won't." The appropriate answer is, oddly enough, imperative – "Yes, do" or "No, don't." That is, "Shall I?" doesn't invite a response using a modal auxiliary verb, rather it seems to require an imperative; and thus from an illocutionary point of view it requires a directive.[2]

A third qualification is this: Often a question can be answered by an indirect speech act. In such cases the answer may be semantically and pragmatically appropriate, even though the syntax of the answer does not reflect the syntax of the question. Thus, in an appropriate context, "How many people were at the meeting?" can be answered by any of the following:

> Everybody who was invited came.
> I counted 127.
> The auditorium was full.

even though none of these sentences matches the syntactical form of the propositional function expressed in the original question. They are answers in the way the following would not normally be:

[1] Searle, John R., *Speech Acts: An Essay in the Philosophy of Language*, Cambridge University Press, Cambridge, 1969, p. 66.

[2] I am indebted to Julian Boyd for discussion of this point.

None of your business.
How should I know?
Don't ask such dumb questions.

There are other classes of speech acts besides questions that serve to determine appropriate responses. An obvious case is direct requests to perform speech acts. Utterances such as "Say something in Portuguese" or "Tell me about last summer in Brazil" are straightforward, direct requests to perform speech acts, and they thus constrain the form of a possible appropriate reply.

The above are obviously two classes of speech acts in conversations where the dialogic sequence of initial utterance and subsequent response is internally related in the sense that the aim of the first speech act is only achieved if it elicits an appropriate speech act in response. How far can we get in discovering other such classes?

Well, a third – and rather large – class are those cases where the speaker performs a speech act that requires acceptance or rejection on the part of the hearer. For example, an offer, a proposal, a bet, or an invitation all invite a response on the part of the hearer. Their structure constrains the hearer to accept or reject them. Consider, for example, offers. An offer differs from an ordinary promise in that an offer is a conditional promise, and the form of the conditional is that the promise takes effect only if it is explicitly accepted by the hearer. Thus, I am obligated by my offer to you only if you accept the offer. Offers are commissives, but they are conditional commissives, and the condition is of a very special kind, namely, conditional on acceptance by the hearer. In the case of bets, the bet is not even fully made unless it is accepted by the hearer. If I say to you "I bet you five dollars that the Republicans will win the next election," that is not yet a completed bet. It only becomes a bet if you accept it. The bet has only been effectively made if you say "OK, you're on" or "I accept your bet" or some such.

If we consider cases such as offers, bets, and invitations, it looks as if we are at last getting a class of speech acts where we can extend the analysis beyond a single speech act, where we can discuss sequences. But it seems that this is a very restricted class. In assertions, there are no such constraints. There are indeed general conversational constraints of the Gricean sort and other kinds. For example, if I say to you "I think the Republicans will win the next election," and you say to me "I think the Brazilian government has devalued the Cruzeiro again," at least on the surface your remark is violating a certain principle of relevance. But notice, unlike the case of offers and bets, the illocutionary point of my speech act was nonetheless achieved. I did make an assertion, and my success in achieving that illocutionary point does not depend on your making an appropriate response. In such a case, you are just being rude, or changing the subject, or are being difficult to get on with, if you make such an irrelevant remark. But you do not violate a constitutive rule of a certain kind of speech act or of conversation just by changing the subject.

There are also certain kinds of formal or institutional speech act sequences where there are rules that constrain the sequencing. Think, for example, of courtrooms, formal debates, parliamentary procedures, and such like. In all of these cases, there are a set of extra-linguistic rules that impose a series of ceremonial or institutional constraints on the sequencing of utterances. The professionals are supposed to know exactly what to say and in what order, because the discourse is highly ritualized. The bailiff says "Everybody rise!" and then everybody rises. The bailiff then says "The Superior Court of the State of California, County of Alameda, is now in session, the Honorable J. B. Smitherby presiding." And then J. B. Smitherby comes and sits down. The bailiff says "Be seated and come to order," and then we can all sit down. The judge then starts conducting the proceedings in a highly ritualized fashion. Any incorrect speech act is subject to an "objection" which the judge is required to rule on. But that is hardly a good example of natural discourse. On the contrary, if you sit through a court hearing you are struck by its unnatural, highly structured and ceremonial character. Nonetheless there is something to be learned about the nature of conversation in general from this example, and that is that conversation only can proceed given a structure of expectations and presuppositions. I will come back to this point later.

II

So far it appears that traditional speech act theory will not go very far in giving us sequencing rules for discourse. So let us thrash around and see if we can find some other basis for a theoretical account. What I am going to conclude is that we will be able to get a theoretical account, but it won't be anything like our account of the constitutive rules of speech acts. I want to turn to two efforts or two approaches to giving a theoretical account and show in what ways I think they are inadequate. They both have advantages, but they also have certain inadequacies. First, Grice's approach with his maxims of conversation, and then some work in a subject that used to be called "ethno-methodology."

Let's start with Grice.[3] He has four maxims of quantity, quality, manner, and relation. (This terminology is, of course, ironically derived from Kant.) Quantity has to do with such things as that you shouldn't say too much or too little. Manner has to do with the fact that you should be clear; quality has to do with your utterances being true and supported by evidence; and relation has to do with the fact that your utterances should be relevant to the conversation at hand. I want to say that though I think these are valuable contributions to the analysis of language, they really are of limited usefulness in explaining the structure of conversation. Why? To begin with, the four are not on a par. For example, the requirement of truthfulness is indeed an *internal* constitutive rule of the notion of a statement. It is a constitutive rule of statement-making that the statement commits the speaker to the truth of the proposition expressed. There is no way to explain what a statement is without explaining what a true statement is, and without explaining that anybody who makes a statement is committed, other things being equal, to the truth of the proposition that he expressed in making the statement. It is the condition of satisfaction of a statement that it should be true, and it is an internal defect of a statement if it is false. But the other Gricean features are not like that. The standards of relevance, brevity, clarity, and so on, unlike truth, are not in that way internal to the notion of the speech act. They are all *external* constraints on the speech act, external constraints coming from general principles of rationality and cooperation. It is not a constitutive rule of statement-making that a statement should be relevant to the surrounding discourse. You can make a perfectly satisfactory statement, qua statement, and still change the subject of the conversation altogether. Notice in this connection that our response to the person who changes the subject in a conversation is quite different from our response to the person who, for example, lies.

Well, one might say "So much the better for Grice." After all, what we are trying to explain is how speech act *sequences* can satisfy conditions of being *de facto* internally related, in the way I was talking about earlier, without there being necessarily any internal requirement of that relation, that is, without there being any *de jure* requirement from inside the initial speech act, of the sort that we had for such pairs as are initiated by offers, invitations, and bets. One might say: what we want are not constitutive rules of particular speech acts but precisely maxims of the Gricean sort that will play the role for talk exchanges that constitutive rules play for individual utterances. To support

3 Grice, H.P., "Logic and Conversation," in *Syntax and Semantics, Volume 3, Speech Acts*, Peter Cole and J.L. Morgan (eds.), Academic Press, New York, 1975.

this we might point out that a series of random remarks between two or more speakers does not add up to a conversation. And this inclines us to think that relevance might be partly constitutive and hence explanatory of conversation in the same way that, for example, commitment to truth is partly constitutive and hence explanatory of statement-making.

The analogy is attractive, but in the end I think it fails. Given a speech act, we know what counts as meeting its conditions of success and nondefectiveness; but given a sequence of speech acts in a conversation, we don't yet know what counts as a relevant continuation until we know something which is still external to the sequence, namely, its purpose. But the fact that it is a conversation does not so far determine a purpose, because there is no purpose to conversations qua conversations in the way that there is a purpose to speech acts of a certain type qua speech acts of that type. Statements, questions, and commands, for example, each have purposes solely in virtue of being statements, questions and commands; and these purposes are built in by their essential conditions. But conversations do not in that way have an essential condition that determines a purpose. Relative to one conversational purpose an utterance in a sequence may be relevant, relative to another it may be irrelevant.

You can see this point if you think of examples. Think of what counts as relevance in a conversation involving a man trying to pick up a woman in a bar, where indirection is the norm, and contrast that with the case of a doctor interviewing a patient, where full explicitness is required. You might even imagine the same two people with the same background capacities and many of the same sentences, but the constraints of a relevant response are quite different. Thus, suppose the conversation has reached the following point:

A: How long have you lived in California?
B: Oh, about a year and a half.

One relevant response by A in the bar might be

A: I love living here myself, but I sure am getting sick of the smog in L.A.

That is not relevant in the clinic. On the other hand, a perfectly relevant move in the clinic, but probably not in the bar, might be:

A: And how often have you had diarrhoea during those eighteen months?

This variability is quite general. For example, in formal "conversations," such as in a courtroom, a statement may be stricken from the record as "irrelevant" or an answer as "nonresponsive." But in certain other formal conversations, such as in a linguistics seminar, similar "irrelevant" and "non-responsive" utterances would count as relevant and responsive. Still different standards would be applied in a casual conversation among friends.

The point I am making is: in the way that, for example, a commitment to truth is in part constitutive of statement-making, and therefore explanatory of statement-making, the way that relevance is "constitutive" of conversation is not similarly explanatory of conversation; because what constitutes relevance is relative to something that lies outside the fact that it is a conversation, namely, the purposes of the participants. Thus, you can't explain the general structure of conversation in terms of relevance, because what counts as relevance is not determined by the fact that it is a conversation. The fact that a sequence of utterances is a conversation, by itself, places no constraints whatever on what would count as a relevant continuation of the sequence.

We can now state this point more generally, that is, we can now make a general statement of the limitations of relevance to the analysis of conversational structure. Consider the syntax of "relevant." Superficially we might say: a speech act can be said to be relevant (or irrelevant) to a topic or issue or question. But once we see that, for example, a topic must be, as such, an object of interest to the speaker and hearer, we can now state a deeper syntax of "relevant." A speech act can be said to be relevant (or irrelevant) to a purpose, and a purpose is always someone's purpose. Thus, in a conversation, the general form would be: a speech act is relevant to the purpose P of a hearer H or a speaker S. Now, the problem is that there is no general purpose of conversations, qua conversations, so what will count as relevant will always have to be specified relative to a purpose of the participants, which may or may not be the purpose of the conversation up to that point. If we insist that it be relevant to the antecedently existing purpose of the conversation, then the account will be circular because the criteria of relevance are not independent of the criteria of identity of the particular conversation; and if we don't require relevance to the conversational purpose, then anything goes provided it is relevant to some purpose or other. That would put no constraints on the structure of actual talk exchanges.

Suppose, for example, I am having a conversation with my stock broker about whether or not to invest in IBM. Suppose he suddenly shouts, "Look out! The chandelier is going to fall on your head!" Now is his remark relevant? It is certainly not relevant to my purpose in investing in the stock market. But it certainly is relevant to my purpose of staying alive. So, if we think of this as one conversation, he has made an irrelevant remark. If we think of it as two conversations, the second one which he just initiated being about my safety, then he has made a relevant remark. But in neither case does relevance explain the general structure of conversations. Rather, the purpose of particular conversations explains what counts as relevant to that purpose, but it doesn't even explain what counts as relevant to that conversation, unless "that conversation" is defined in terms of that purpose.

Of the Gricean maxims, the most promising for explaining the structure of conversations seems to be relevance, and I have therefore spent some time discussing it. His maxims concerning quantity and manner don't seem to me plausible candidates for the job, so I will say nothing further about them. They both concern efficiency in communication, but they do not provide an adequate apparatus for getting at the details of conversational structure. Efficiency is only one among many constraints on talk sequences of the sort we have in conversation.

Though I think that the Gricean maxims are very useful in their own realm, they won't give us, for conversation, anything like what the rules of speech acts give us for individual speech acts.

Let us now turn then to the efforts of some sociolinguists who have studied the structure of conversation, as they would say, "empirically." One such effort at explaining the phenomenon of turn-taking in conversations is provided in an article by Sacks, Schegloff, and Jefferson.[4] They think that they have a set of rules, indeed, "recursive rules," for turn-taking in conversations. They say,

> The following seems to be a basic set of rules governing turn construction providing for the allocation of a next turn to one party and coordinating transfer so as to minimize gap and overlap. (1) For any turn at the initial transition relevance place of an initial turn construction unit: (a) If the turn so far is so constructed as to involve the use of a current speaker's select-next technique, then the party so selected has the right, and is obliged to take next turn to speak, no others have such rights or obligations and transfer occurs at that place. (b) If the turn so far is so constructed as not to involve the use of a current speaker's select-next technique, then self-selection for next speakership may, but need not be instituted. First speaker acquires rights to a turn and transfer occurs at that place. (c) If the turn so far is constructed as not to involve the use of a current speaker's select-next technique, then the current speaker may but need not continue unless another

[4] Sacks, H., Schegloff, E.A., and Jefferson, G., "A simplest systematics for the organization of turn-taking for conversation," *Language*, 1974, 50, pp. 696–735.

> self-selects. (2) If at the initial transition relevance place of an initial turn constructional unit neither 1a nor 1b is operated, and following the provision of 1c current speaker has continued, then the rule set a-c reapplies at the next transition relevance place, and recursively at each next transition relevance place until transfer is effected.

That is the rule for conversational turn-taking. Now, I have puzzled over this for a while, and my conclusion (though I am prepared to be corrected) is that that couldn't possibly be a rule for conversational turn-taking simply because nobody does or could follow it. The notion of a rule is, after all, rather closely connected with the notion of following a rule. And I want to argue that nobody does or could follow the turn-taking rule. Now what exactly does the rule say when it is stated in plain English? It seems to me Sacks, Schegloff, and Jefferson are saying the following: In a conversation a speaker can select who is going to be the next speaker, for example, by asking him a question. Or he can just shut up and let somebody else talk. Or he can keep on talking. Furthermore, if he decides to keep on talking, then next time there is a break in the conversation (that's called a "transition relevance place"), the same three options apply. And that makes the rule recursive, because once you have the possibility of continuing to talk, the rule can apply over and over.

Now, as a description of what actually happens in a normal conversation, that is, a conversation where not everybody talks at once, the rule could hardly fail to describe what goes on. But that is like saying that this is a rule for walking: If you go for a walk, you can keep walking in the same direction, or you can change directions, or you can sit down and stop walking altogether. Notice that the walking rule is also recursive, because if you keep on walking, then the next time you wonder what to do, the same three options apply – you can keep on walking in the same direction, you can change directions, or you can sit down and quit walking altogether. As a *description* of what happens when someone goes for a walk, that could hardly be false, but that doesn't make it a recursive *rule* for walking. The walking rule is like the Sacks, Schegloff, Jefferson rule in that it is almost tautological. It is not completely tautological because there are always other possibilities. When walking, you could start jumping up and down or do cartwheels. In talking, everybody might shut up and not say anything, or they might break into song, or they might all talk at once, or there might be a rigid hierarchical order in which they are required to talk.

But the real objection to the rule is not that it is nearly tautological; many rules are tautological and none the worse for that. For example, systems of constitutive rules define tautologically the activity of which the rules are constitutive. Thus, the rules of chess or football tautologically define chess or football; and similarly, the rules of speech acts tautologically define the various sorts of speech acts, such as making statements or promises. That is not my real objection. The objection to this kind of "rule" is that it is not really a rule and therefore has no explanatory power. The notion of a rule is logically connected to the notion of following a rule, and the notion of following a rule is connected to the notion of making one's behavior conform to the content of a rule because it is a rule. For example, when I drive in England, I follow the rule: Drive on the left-hand side of the road. Now that seems to me a genuine rule. Why is it a rule? Because the content of the rule plays a causal role in the production of my behavior. If another driver is coming directly toward me the other way, I swerve to the left, that is, I make my behavior conform to the content of the rule. In a theory of intentionality, we would say that the intentional content of the rule plays a causal role in bringing about the conditions of satisfaction. The rule has the world-to-rule direction of fit, that is, the point of the rule is to get the world, that is, my behavior, to match the content of the rule. And it has the rule-to-world direction of causation, that is, the rule achieves the fit by causing the appropriate behavior.[5] This is just a fancy way of saying that the purpose of the rule is to influence people's behavior in a certain way so that the behavior matches the content of the rule, and the rule functions as part of the cause of bringing that match about. I don't just *happen* to drive on the left-hand side of the road in England. I do it *because* that is the rule of the road.

Notice now a crucial fact for the discussion of the conversational turn-taking rule. There can be extensionally equivalent descriptions of my rule-governed behavior not all of which state the rules that I am following. Take the rule: Drive on the left-hand side of the road. We might describe my behavior either by saying that I drive on the left or, given the structure of English cars, by saying that I drive in such a way that on two-lane roads, while staying in one lane, I keep the steering wheel near the centerline and I keep the passenger side nearer to the curb. Now that actually happens in British cars when I drive on the left-hand side of the road. But that is not the rule that I am following. Both "rules" provide true descriptions of my behavior and both make accurate predictions, but only the first rule – the one about driving on the left – actually states a rule of my behavior, because it is the only one whose content plays a causal role in the production of the behavior. The

[5] For a further explanation of these notions, see Searle, John R., *Intentionality: An Essay in the Philosophy of Mind*, Cambridge University Press, Cambridge, 1983.

second, like the Sacks, Schegloff, Jefferson rule, describes a consequence of following the rule, given that the steering wheel is located on the right, but it doesn't state a rule. The so called rule for conversational turn-taking, like much similar research I have seen in this area, is like the second rule statement and not like the first. That is, it describes the phenomenon of turn-taking as if it were a rule; but it couldn't be a rule because no one actually follows that rule. The surface phenomenon of turn-taking is partly explicable in terms of deeper speech act sequencing rules having to do with internally related speech acts of the sort that we talked about before: but sometimes the phenomenon of turn-taking isn't a matter of rules at all.

Let us go through the cases. Case A: "Current speaker selects-next speaker." Well, speakers hardly ever directly select a subsequent speaker. People don't normally say in conversation "I select you to speak next" or "You talk next." Sometimes they do. If a master of ceremonies gets up and introduces you as the next speaker, then you are selected to talk next. He has certainly selected you to talk. But such cases are not very common. What normally happens, rather, is that the speaker asks somebody a question, or makes him an offer. The "rules" that determine that the second person is to speak aren't rules of "speaker selects-next technique," but they are consequences of rules governing questions or offers. The surface phenomenon of speaker selection is not the explanation; the explanation is in terms of the rules for performing the internally related speech act pairs. The "speaker selects-next" rule is not a rule; it is an extensionally equivalent description of a pattern of behavior which is also described, and more importantly explained, by a set of speech act rules.

Now consider the second case. Case B: Next speaker self selects. That just means that there is a break and somebody else starts talking. That "rule" says that when there is a break in the conversation anybody can start talking, and whoever starts talking gets to keep on talking. But I want to say that doesn't even have the appearance of being a rule since it doesn't specify the relevant sort of intentional content that plays a causal role in the production of the behavior. As we all know, the way it typically works in real life is this: Somebody else is talking and you want very much to say something. But you don't want to interrupt the speaker because (a) it's rude and (b) it's inefficient, since with two people talking at once it's hard to get your point across. So you wait till there is a chance to talk and then start talking fast before somebody else does. Now, where is the rule?

Case C is: Current speaker continues. Again, I want to say that is not a rule, and for the same reason. No one is following it. It just says that when you are talking, you can keep on talking. But you don't need a rule to do that.

Perhaps one more analogy will help to clarify the main point I am trying to make. Suppose that several researchers in ethnomethodology made empirical observations of an American football game and came up with the following recursive clustering rule: organisms in like-colored jerseys are obliged and have the right to cluster in circular groups at statistically regular intervals. (Call this the "law of periodic circular clustering.") Then at a "transition relevance place," organisms in like-colored jerseys cluster linearly (the law of linear clustering). Then linear clustering is followed by linear interpenetration (the law of linear interpenetration). Linear interpenetration is followed by circular clustering, and thus the entire system is recursive. The precise formalization of this recursion could also be stated with temporal parameters. The Sacks-Schegloff-Jefferson "rule" is like the "law" of clustering in that it finds regularities in phenomena that are explainable by other forms of intentionality. A statement of an observed regularity, even when predictive, is not necessarily a statement of a rule.

One final remark about the nature of "empirical" evidence before concluding this section. Many researchers feel that a serious study of conversation must proceed from transcriptions of real conversations that actually took place. And of course they are right in thinking that many things can be learned from studying actual events that cannot be learned from thinking up imaginary conversations alone. But it is also important to keep in mind that where theory is concerned the native speaker takes priority over the historical record. We are only willing to accept and use the transcriptions of conversations in our native culture to the extent that we find them acceptable or at least possible conversations. If some investigator came up with an impossible conversation we would reject it out of hand because we are masters of our language and its culture, and the fact that an impossible conversation might be historically actual is irrelevant. Thus the following is OK:

B: I don't know whether you have talked with Hilary about the diary situation.
A: WELL she has been EXPLAINING to me rather in rather more general TERMS . . . mmmm . . . what . . . you are sort of DOING and . . .
B: . . . what it was all . . . about . . . yes.
A: I gather you've been at it for nine YEARS.
B: . . . mmm . . . by golly that's true yes yes it's not a long time of course in the . . . uh . . . in this sort of . . . work . . . [6]

[6] From Svartvik, J., and R. Quirk (eds.), *A Corpus of English Conversation*, Lund; Gleerup, 1980, pp. 408–411, as cited in Wardhaugh, Ronald, *How Conversation Works*, Oxford: Basil Blackwell, 1985, pp. 202–203.

Because we recognize it as an intelligible fragment of a possible conversation. But if A had responded:

A: Whereof therefore maybe briny very was could of should to be.

or B had said:

B: UGGA BU BUBU UGGA

We would at the very least require some further explanation before taking the "data" seriously. The fact that the events had actually occurred would be by itself of no more theoretical interest than if one of the participants had just collapsed from a heart attack or the other had thrown up. To be of theoretical interest, the "empirical" facts have to accord with our inner abilities and not conversely.

III

Well then, if such "rules" are no help to us, let us go back to the beginning of our discussion. I said that it would be nice if we could get a theory of conversation that matches our theory of speech acts. I am not optimistic. I have examined two directions of investigation, but I think that neither gives us the sorts of results we wanted. The hypothesis that underlies my pessimism is this:

> *The reason that conversations do not have an inner structure in the sense that speech acts do is not (as is sometimes claimed) because conversations involve two or more people, but because conversations as such lack a particular purpose or point.*

Each illocutionary act has an illocutionary point, and it is in virtue of that point that it is an act of that type. Thus, the point of a promise is to undertake an obligation; the point of a statement is to represent how things are in the world; the point of an order is to try to get somebody to do something; and so forth. It is the existence of illocutionary points that enables us to get a well defined taxonomy of the different types of illocutionary acts.[7] But conversations don't in that way have an internal point simply in virtue of

7 Searle, John R., "A Taxonomy of Illocutionary Acts," in *Language, Mind and Knowledge*, Minnesota Studies in the Philosophy of Science, Vol. XI, K. Gunderson (ed.), University of Minnesota Press, 1975. Reprinted in *Expression and Meaning: Studies in the Theory of Speech Acts*, Cambridge University Press, 1979.

being conversations. Consider the similarities and differences between the following talk exchanges:

> A woman calling her dentist's office to arrange an appointment.
>
> Two casual acquaintances meeting each other on the street and stopping to have a brief chat in which they talk about a series of subjects (e.g., the weather, the latest football results, the president's speech last night).
>
> A philosophy seminar.
>
> A man trying to pick up a woman in a bar.
>
> A dinner party.
>
> A family spending a Sunday afternoon at home watching a football game on television and discussing the progress of the game among various other matters.
>
> A meeting of the board of directors of a small corporation.
>
> A doctor interviewing a patient.

Now, what are the chances of finding a well defined structure common to all of these? Are they all "conversations"?

Of course, they all have a beginning, a middle, and an end, but then, so does a glass of beer; that is not enough for an internal structure. The literature on this subject is partly skewed by the fact that the authors often pick telephone conversations, because they are easier to study. But telephone conversations are unusual in that most people, adolescents apart, have a fairly well defined objective when they pick up the phone, unlike two colleagues encountering each other in the hallway of a building, or two casual acquaintances bumping into each other on the street.

Though I am pessimistic about certain sorts of accounts of conversation, I am not saying that we cannot give theoretical accounts of the structure of conversation or that we cannot say important, insightful things about the structure of conversation. What sort of apparatus would we use to do that? Here I want to mention a couple of features that I think are crucial for understanding conversation, and, indeed, for understanding discourse generally.

One of the things we need to recognize about conversations is that they involve shared intentionality. Conversations are a paradigm of collective behavior. The shared intentionality in conversation is not to be confused with the kind of iterated intentionality discussed by Steven Schiffer[8] and David Lewis,[9] which involves what they call "mutual knowledge." In the case of mutual knowledge, I know that you know that I know that you know . . . that p. And you know that I know that you know that I know . . . that p. Schiffer and Lewis try to reduce the shared aspect to an iterated sequence, indeed, an infinite sequence of iterated cognitive states about the other partner. I think that their analysis distorts the facts. *Shared* intentionality is not just a matter of a conjunction of individual intentional states about the other person's intentional states. To illustrate this point I will give a rather crude example of shared intentionality. Suppose you and I are pushing a car. When we are pushing a car together, it isn't just the case that I am pushing the car and you are pushing the car. No, I am pushing the car as part of *our* pushing the car. So, if it turns out that you weren't pushing all along (you were just going along for a free ride and I was doing all the pushing), then I am not just mistaken about what you were doing, but I am also mistaken about what I was doing, because I thought not just that I was pushing (I was right about that) but that I was pushing as part of *our* pushing. And that doesn't reduce to a series of iterated claims about my belief concerning your belief about my belief about your belief, etcetera.

The phenomenon of shared collective behavior is a genuine social phenomenon and underlies much social behavior. We are blinded to this fact by the traditional analytic devices that treat all intentionality as strictly a matter of the individual person. I believe that a recognition of shared intentionality and its implications is one of the basic concepts we need in order to understand how conversations work. The idea that shared intentionality can be entirely reduced to complex beliefs and other intentional states leads to those incorrect accounts of meaning where it turns out you have to have a rather large number of intentions in order to perform such simple speech acts as saying "Good-bye," or asking for another drink, or saying "Hi" to someone when you meet him in the street. You do, of course, require some intentional states, but once you see that in collective behavior, such as conversations, the individual intentionality is derived from the collective intentionality, the account of the individual intentionality is much simpler. On the pattern of analysis I am proposing, when two people greet each other and begin a conversation, they are beginning a joint activity rather than two individual activities. If this conception

8 Schiffer, Steven, *Meaning*, Oxford: Clarendon Press, 1972.

9 Lewis, David, *Convention: A Philosophical Study*, Cambridge, MA: Harvard University Press, 1969.

is correct, then shared intentionality is a concept we will need for analyzing conversation.

Now, there is another concept I think we need for understanding conversation and, indeed, for understanding language generally, and that is the notion of what I call "the background." Now, let me work up to that briefly. Take any sentence, and ask yourself what you have to know in order to understand that sentence. Take the sentence "George Bush intends to run for president." In order fully to understand that sentence, and, consequently, in order to understand a speech act performed in the utterance of that sentence, it just isn't enough that you should have a lot of semantic contents that you glue together. Even if you make them into big semantic contents, it isn't going to be enough. What you have to know in order to understand that sentence are such things as that the United States is a republic, it has presidential elections every four years, in these elections there are candidates of the two major parties, and the person who gets the majority of the electoral votes becomes president. And so on. The list is indefinite, and you can't even say that all the members of the list are absolutely essential to understanding the original sentence, because, for example, you could understand the sentence very well even if you didn't understand about the electoral college. But there is no way to put all of this information into the meaning of the word "president." The word "president" means the same in "George Bush wants to run for president" as in "Mitterrand is the president of France." There is no lexical ambiguity over the word "president"; rather, the kind of knowledge you have to have to understand those two utterances doesn't coincide. I want to give a name to all of that network of knowledge or belief or opinion or presupposition: I call it "the network."

If you try to follow out the threads of the network, if you think of all the things you would have to know in order to understand the sentence "George Bush wants to run for president," you would eventually reach a kind of bedrock that would seem strange to think of as simply more knowledge or beliefs. For example, you would get to things like: people generally vote when conscious, or: there are human beings, or: elections are generally held at or near the surface of the earth. I want to suggest that these "propositions" are not like the genuine belief I have to the effect that larger states get more electoral votes than smaller states. In the way that I have a genuine *belief* about the number of electoral votes controlled by the state of Michigan, I don't in that way have a belief that elections go on at or near the surface of the earth. If I were writing a book about American electoral practices, I wouldn't put that proposition in. Why not? Well in a way, it is too fundamental to count as a belief. Rather it is a certain set of stances that

I take toward the world. There are sets of skills, ways of dealing with things, ways of behaving, cultural practices, and general know-how of both biological and cultural sorts. These form what I am calling "the background," and the fact that part of my background is that elections are held at or near the surface of the earth *manifests itself* in the fact that I walk to the nearest polling place and don't try and get aboard a rocket ship. Similarly, the fact that the table in front of me is a solid object is not manifested in any belief as such, but rather in the fact that I'm willing to put things on it, or that I pound on it, or I rest my books on it, or I lean on it. Those, I want to say, are stances, practices, ways of behaving. This then for our present purposes is the thesis of the background: all semantic interpretation, and indeed all intentionality, functions not only against a network of beliefs and other intentional states but also against a background that does not consist in a set of propositional contents, but rather in presuppositions that are, so to speak, preintentional or prepropositional.

To further illustrate the relevance of this point for semantic interpretation, consider the different interpretations given to verbs of action. Consider, for example, sentences of the form: "X cut Y." The interpretation that one attaches to "cut" alters radically in different sentences even though the semantic content doesn't alter. Consider the sentences:

(1) Sally cut the cake.
(2) Bill cut the grass.
(3) The barber cut Jim's hair.
(4) The tailor cut the cloth.
(5) I just cut my skin.

The interesting thing for our present discussion about these sentences is that the same semantic content occurs in each of them with the word "cut" but is interpreted differently in each case. In 1–5, the word "cut" is not used ambiguously. Its use in these cases contrasts with sentences where it is used with a genuinely different meaning such as "The president cut the salaries of the professors" or (one of Austin's favorites) "Cut the cackle!" or "He can't cut the mustard." In these cases, we are inclined to say that "cut" is used to mean something different from what it is used to mean in 1–5. But that it has the same meaning in sentences 1–5 is shown by the fact that the standard tests for univocality apply. So for example, you can have a conjunction reduction: for example, "General Electric has just invented a new device which can cut cakes, grass, hair, cloth, and skin." But if you then add "... and salaries, cackles, and mustard," it seems like a bad joke. But though "cut" means the same in 1–5, it is interpreted quite differently in each case. And thus, the semantic content by itself cannot account for the fact that we understand those sentences in radically different ways. We can see that we understand the occurrences in different ways if we consider analogous occurrences in directives. If I say "Bill, go cut the grass" and Bill goes out and stabs the grass with a knife, or attempts to slice it up the way one would a cake, or takes a pair of scissors to it, there is an important sense in which Bill did not do what I asked him to do. That is, he did not obey my literal and unambiguous request.

How is it that we are able to understand the word "cut" in sentences 1–5 so differently, given that it has the same semantic content in each occurrence? Someone might claim – indeed, I have heard it claimed – that it is part of the literal meaning of the verb that we interpret it differently in different verbal contexts. "Cut" with "grass" as direct object is interpreted differently from "cut" with "cake" as direct object, and thus the explanation would be given entirely in terms of the interaction of semantic contents.

But that explanation by itself won't do either, because if we alter the background in the right way, we could interpret the "cut" in "Cut the grass" as we interpret "cut" in "Cut the cake." For example, in California there are firms that sell instant lawns. They simply roll a lawn up and load it into your pickup truck. Now, suppose I am the manager of one of these sod farms and you order a half an acre of grass, and I tell my foreman "Go out and cut half an acre of grass for this customer." If he then gets out the lawnmower and starts mowing it, I'll fire him. Or imagine that we have a bakery where we have a super strain of yeast that causes our cakes to grow up all the way to the ceiling and for that reason we have to employ a man to chop the tops off the cakes. Suppose I tell him "Watch out – they are going toward the ceiling again. Start cutting the cakes!" If he then starts cutting the cakes in neat slices, I'm going to fire him as well. I want to say there is no obvious way that the traditional context free conception of semantic interpretation of sentences can account for the indefinite range of such facts.[10]

What then is different about these different sentences? What enables us to interpret them differently? Well, we have certain background practices. We know what it is to cut grass; we know what it is to cut cake; and we know that each is quite different from cutting a cloth. But those are human practices. The knowledge we have about such matters is either knowledge from the network or is so fundamental that it is not quite right to construe it as a propositional "knowing that . . . " at all. These are just ways we have of behaving.

[10] For more on this and other examples, see Searle, John R., "*The Background of Meaning*", in *Speech Act Theory and Pragmatics*, J.R. Searle, F. Kiefer, and M. Bierwisch (eds.), Dordrecht: D. Reidel, 1980, pp. 221–232. Also, *Intentionality: An Essay in the Philosophy of Mind*, Chapter 5.

Now notice a further point. There are many syntactically acceptable English sentences containing the word "cut" that we can't interpret at all. Suppose I say to you "Go cut that mountain!" or "Sally cut the coffee." In the sense in which we interpret 1–5 effortlessly, I don't know how to interpret these other examples. I can *invent* an interpretation for each of these, but when I do that, what I do is invent a background practice that fixes an interpretation. It doesn't take much imagination. Suppose we run a big freeway building crew and we are making interstate highways. We have two ways of dealing with mountains; we either level them or we cut right through them. So if I say to my foreman "Go cut that mountain," he just cuts a freeway right through it.

Many of my students immediately attach a metaphorical interpretation to "Cut the coffee." They interpret it as meaning: dilute the coffee in some way. But we could invent other interpretations. We could invent literal interpretations if we imagine ourselves engaging in certain sorts of practices. Notice that in the case of "The president cut the salaries," we immediately give it a metaphorical interpretation. But with a little ingenuity and an idiosyncratic president, we could give a literal interpretation. Suppose the salaries are always in the form of wads of dollar bills and an eccentric president insists on cutting the end off of each person's salary before handing it over. This would be an odd case, but we could in such a case imagine a literal interpretation of "cut." Now why is it that we so effortlessly attach a metaphorical interpretation as the normal case? The answer, I believe, is that we always interpret a sentence against a background of practices and within a network of other beliefs and assumptions which are not themselves part of the semantic content of the sentence. We assume that the speaker's utterance makes sense, but in order to make sense of it we have to fit it into the background. In this case, the metaphorical interpretation fits the background easily; the literal interpretation requires generating a new background.

One of the ways in which the background is crucial for understanding conversation is in the role that the background plays in determining conversational relevance. We saw earlier that relevance was in general relative to the purpose of the conversation; but we can now, I believe, deepen that point if we see that the purpose itself, and what constitutes relevance relative to that purpose, will depend on the shared backgrounds of the participants. One reason that we cannot get a non-circular account of "relevant" just by looking at a conversation is that what the participants in the conversation take as relevant, what counts as relevant, will always be relative to the cognitive apparatus they bring to bear on the conversation. That is to say, it will always be relative to their network and background.

In order to illustrate the operation of the background in the production and comprehension of conversation, I want to consider an example from real life. The following conversation took place on British television immediately after the conservative party victory that brought Mrs. Thatcher to power as prime minister for the first time.[11]

First Speaker: I think you know the question I'm going to ask you. What's the answer?
Second Speaker: We'll have to wait and see.
First Speaker: Would you like to?
Second Speaker: It all depends.

Two things are clear from this brief snatch of conversation. First, the amount of information contained in the lexical meanings, that is, in the semantic contents of the words and sentences uttered, is very minimal. Literally speaking, neither party says much of anything. Secondly, it is clear that the two participants understand each other perfectly well, and that a great deal is being conveyed. Now what is it that the two speakers have to know in order to understand each other so well on the basis of such minimal semantic content? And, what would we have to understand as spectators in order to understand what was being communicated in this conversation? Well, we might begin by listing the propositional contents which were known by British television viewers as well as by the two participants and which enabled them to understand the conversation. The list might begin as follows: The first speaker is Robin Day, a famous British television news broadcaster. The second speaker is Edward Heath, the former conservative prime minister. It is well known that Mr. Heath hates Mrs. Thatcher and Mrs. Thatcher hates Mr. Heath. Now, the question on everyone's mind at the time of this conversation was "Would Heath serve as a minister in a Thatcher cabinet?" It is obvious that the conversation construed simply as a set of utterances carrying literal semantic content is unintelligible. The natural temptation is to assume that it is made intelligible by the fact that these additional semantic contents are present in the minds of the speaker, the hearer, and the audience. What I am suggesting here is that they are still not enough. Or rather, that they are only enough because they themselves rest on a set of capacities that are not themselves semantic contents. Our ability to represent rests on a set of capacities which do not themselves consist in representations.

[11] My attention was called to this conversation by Philip Johnson-Laird.

In order to see how this works, let us imagine that we actually plugged in the semantic contents that we think would fix the interpretation of the conversation. Suppose we imagine the participants actually saying:

First Speaker: I am Robin Day, the famous British television news broadcaster.

Second Speaker: I am Edward Heath, the former British conservative prime minister, and I hate Mrs. Thatcher, the present British conservative prime minister. She hates me, too.

Now, if we plug in such semantic contents as these, it looks as if we have converted the conversation from something that is almost totally mysterious on the face to something that is completely intelligible on the face. But if you think about it for a moment, I think you will see that we have not overcome our original problem. The original conversation was intelligible only because the participants and the viewers had a lot of information that wasn't explicit in the conversation. But now this new conversation is similarly intelligible only because the participants and the observers still have a lot of information that is not explicit in the conversation. They understand the conversation as revised only because they understand what sorts of things are involved in being a prime minister, in hating other people, in winning elections, in serving in cabinets, and so on. Well, suppose we plugged all that information into the conversation. Suppose we imagine Heath actually stating a theory of the British government, and Day actually stating a theory of human hostilities and their role in personal relationships. So now we imagine the conversation enriched in something like the following fashion:

First Speaker: Hatred normally involves a reluctance to engage in close association with or appear to be accepting favors from the hated person.

Second Speaker: The authority of the prime minister in the British constitution has altered considerably since the days when the prime minister was considered *primus inter pares*, prior to the time of Walpole. The prime minister now has an authority which enables him or her to appoint and dismiss cabinet ministers almost at will, an authority tempered only by the independent popularity and political standing of other members of the party in the country at large.

Now that is the sort of thing people have to know in order to understand this conversation properly. But even if we plugged all of these propositions into the conversation, even if we filled in all of the information which we think would fix the right interpretation of the original utterances, it would still not be enough. We would still be left in our original position where the understanding of the conversation requires prior intellectual capacities, capacities which are still not represented in the conversation.

The picture we have is this. We think that since the original semantic contents encoded in the literal meaning of the sentences uttered are not at all sufficient to enable communication to take place, then communication takes place because of prior collateral information which speaker, hearer, and observer possess. This is true as far as it goes, but the problem still remains. The prior collateral information is no more self-interpreting than the original conversation. So it looks as though we are on the start of a regress, possibly infinite. The solution to our puzzle is this. Both the original utterances and the prior collateral information only function, that is, they only determine their conditions of satisfaction, against a background of capacities, stances, attitudes, presuppositions, ways of behaving, modes of sensibility, and so on, that are not themselves representational. All interpretation, understanding, and meaning, as well as intentionality in general, function against a background of mental capacities that are not themselves interpretations, meanings, understandings, or intentional states. The solution to our puzzle, in short, is to see that all meaning and understanding goes on against a background which is not itself meant or understood, but which forms the boundary conditions on meaning and understanding, whether in conversations or in isolated utterances. In the conversation we considered from British TV, the richness of the shared background enables a very minimal explicit semantic content to be informative and even satisfying to the participants and the audience. On the other hand some of the most frustrating and unsatisfying conversations occur between people of radically different backgrounds, who can speak at great length and achieve only mutual incomprehension.

12

ANALYTIC PHILOSOPHY AND MENTAL PHENOMENA

1. Introduction: The Behaviorist Background

Throughout most of its history analytic philosophy has exhibited a curious prejudice against the mental. Many, perhaps most, analytic philosophers have felt that there was something especially puzzling about mental processes, states, and events, and that we would be better off if they could be analyzed away or explained in terms of something else or somehow eliminated. One sees this attitude, for example, in the persistent use of pejorative adjectives, such as "mysterious" and "occult," that analytic philosophers from Ryle to Rorty use to characterize mental phenomena naively construed.

I first became aware of the pervasiveness of this attitude when I tried to extend my analysis of speech acts to intentional states. No one doubts the existence of promises, statements, apologies, and commands, but when the analysis is extended to beliefs, fears, hopes, desires, and visual experiences, suddenly philosophers raise a host of "ontological" doubts. I think that thinking and other mental processes and events, like linguistic processes and events, are biologically based and are as real as digestion, conversation, lactation, or any other of the familiar biologically based processes. This seems to me so obviously true as to be hardly worth arguing, but I am assured that it is a minority opinion in contemporary philosophy.

During the positivist and verificationist phase of analytic philosophy the reason for the urge to eliminate the mental was not difficult to see: if the meaning of a statement is its method of verification and if the only method of verification of statements about the mental is in the observations of behavior,

Reprinted by permission from *Midwest Studies in Philosophy*, vol. VI, 1981: 405–423.

at least where "other minds" are concerned, then it would appear that some sort of behaviorism is an immediate logical consequence of verificationism. Statements about the mental are equivalent in meaning to statements about behavior.

Most philosophers today regard behaviorism as dead; yet, as I shall argue, many of them hold views that suffer from the same sort of defects as behaviorism. So, let us begin by examining what is wrong with behaviorism. Sometimes in reading the literature on this subject one gets the impression that behaviorism is at fault because of some more or less technical reason: the behaviorists never quite got a satisfactory account of the notion of a disposition, or their analyses suffered from some sort of circularity, or they never could give a satisfactory formulation of the antecedent clauses in the analysanda, or they had weak answers to the "perfect actor" or simulation arguments. Or some such. I want to suggest that these defects are not the basic flaws in behaviorism; at most they are surface symptoms of the underlying problem. If we remember that in its material mode version, behaviorism is the view that mental phenomena just are patterns of the behavior, then it just seems obviously false. To me at least, its falsity seems clear as soon as I ask myself what it is like to have some conscious mental phenomenon such as a pain and contrast that with what it is like to engage in certain sorts of behavior appropriate to pains. For example, I now have a stomachache, not a violent one, but a nagging pain at the back of my stomach. The fact that I have this stomachache is quite a different fact, and indeed a different sort of fact altogether, from any facts, including conditional facts, about my behavior. Having a stomachache is one thing; engaging in various sorts of behavior appropriate to having a stomachache is something quite different.

I do not present this objection as an *argument* against behaviorism; if so, it would be question begging since the facts I am reminding myself of are stated in a way that simply asserts the falsity of behaviorism. What I want ultimately is not a refutation of behaviorism but an understanding of the underlying motives that gave rise to such an unplausible thesis in the first place.

Well, one might say, Rylean behaviorism was always troubled by the analysis of sensations such as pains. But it is much more satisfactory for beliefs and desires. It is not at all obvious that behavioristic analyses of beliefs and desires are false. Perhaps having beliefs and desires, especially in the right combination,[1] just is being disposed to behave in certain ways.

[1] It is sometimes correctly objected to behaviorism that in order to analyze desires one would have to assume fixed beliefs and conversely. But again, this is an "in house" objection that does not expose the underlying absurdity of the behaviorist approach.

Here again I want to argue that behaviorism is false, though its falsity is not as obvious in this case as in the case of sensations. Suppose I now have a desire to drive to my office; suppose I want to drive to my office, as they say, more than I want to do anything else right now. Suppose, furthermore, that I have a set of beliefs about my abilities to drive to my office, about my car and its functioning, about the proper route, and so on. Now, doesn't that all entail that I will, other things being equal, engage in certain sorts of behavior, namely behavior describable as driving to my office, or at least trying to drive to my office? And furthermore, doesn't the appropriate kind of behavior, such as driving to my office, itself manifest or express my beliefs and desires in such a way that given the appropriate formulations, we could say that the behavior is at least a sufficient condition of having a certain range of beliefs and desires? At this point another objection to behaviorism arises: If the project of behaviorism is to analyze mental notions in terms of behavioral notions, then the project fails because the notion of behavior in question, the kind of behavior described in the analysans of the behaviorists' analysis, is itself *intentional* behavior, and therefore the behavior in question is still, in the relevant sense, mental. If by "behavior" we mean human action, then behavior is more than a set of bodily movements or muscle contractions. The bodily movements count as actions only if they are caused by intentions, and the intentions in question are as much mental as the beliefs and desires that they are being invoked to analyze.[2] Rylean behaviorism about beliefs and desires is therefore confronted with a dilemma: either the behavior in question is full-blown human behavior, that is to say, human actions performed intentionally, or it is not. If the former, then the analysis of the mental into the behavioristic is the analysis of the mental into the mental, and we are still left with the mental component in the notion of behavior. If the latter, then we have to construe behavior as bodily movements described solely as bodily movements; and no analysis of statements about beliefs and desires and intentions into statements about bodily movements will ever be adequate because the movements are not yet human actions, and the notion of a bodily movement by itself is inadequate for any analysis of mental states. A human body, for example, might be wired up in such a way that it would undergo all the bodily movements characteristic of driving a car to an office even though it was totally unconscious or even dead. If, in short, "behavior" means action, then behavior is mental. If it means bodily movements, then it is not behavior, and the analysis

[2] For a discussion of the mental element in actions, see Searle (1979).

fails. At this point, the objection to analyzing beliefs and desires in terms of bodily movements (including dispositions to bodily movements) is much like the objection to analyzing sensations such as pain in terms of behavior (including dispositions to behavior): the distinction between mental states and sheer physical bodily movements is as stark as the distinction between pain and behavior.

I want to keep in mind these two objections to behaviorism – the non-identity of sensations and behavior and the mentalistic element in human actions – in what follows. I now want to introduce a distinction between what I will call ascriptions of *intrinsic mental phenomena* on the one hand and *observer relative mental ascriptions* on the other hand. This distinction can be made clear using unproblematic and uncontroversial examples. Suppose I now say that I have a stomachache or that Reagan believes he can win the election. When I make such statements I am ascribing intrinsic mental phenomena to myself and Reagan. But suppose I say that the expression "il pleut" in French means it is raining or that my pocket calculator adds and subtracts but does not divide. In such cases I am not ascribing any intrinsic mental phenomena to the expression "il pleut" or to my pocket calculator. Such statements are in part shorthand statements for the intrinsic mental phenomena of French speakers or users of pocket calculators. They are, roughly speaking, shorthand for saying such things as that by convention people who speak French use the sentence "il pleut" to mean "it is raining" and that I am able to use my calculator for addition and subtraction but not division. There are not two kinds of mental phenomena, intrinsic mental phenomena and observer relative mental phenomena; rather, there are ascriptions of mental predicates where the ascription does not ascribe an intrinsic mental phenomenon to the subject of the ascription. In such cases the only mental phenomena in question are in the minds of the observers (or users), not in the subject of the ascription. Thus there are two kinds of *ascriptions* but only one kind of mental phenomena.

2. Carburetor Functionalism

I want now to turn to functionalism, the most influential of the current forms of the rejection of the mental. I will argue that functionalism suffers from very much the same sort of difficulties as behaviorism and that, in addition, it rests on a confusion between observer relative and intrinsic mental ascriptions.

First, a few words about the recent history of the philosophy of mind to explain how functionalism evolved out of physicalism. In the early days of physicalism, there were a series of objections from more or less dualistically inclined philosophers to the physicalists' view that mental states were identical with brain states. Most of these objections were versions of the argument from Leibniz's Law (e.g., my stomachache is in my stomach but my brain state is in my head, so my stomachache cannot be identical with my brain state), and Smart[3] and his colleagues justifiably felt that they could answer them (e.g., it is not my stomachache, but my experience of having a stomachache, which is identical with a state of my central nervous system). But there were two classes of arguments that were more troublesome.

First Objection. Suppose physicalism is true as a contingent identity thesis. Then all mental states are identical with some physical states of the brain. But then some physical states of the brain are also mental states, and some other states of the brain are not mental states. What is the difference between them? Well, the obvious difference is that the physical states that are mental states have mental properties and the others do not. But now we seem to be left with a dualism of properties in place of our original dualism of entities; so physicalism is a species of the very dualism it was designed to replace. In place of "mysterious," "occult" mental entities, we are left with "mysterious," "occult" mental properties.

Smart answered this objection by saying that it was possible to describe these entities in a language that did not mention any mental properties, in a language that was "topic neutral." For example, instead of saying, "I am having an orange afterimage" one could say, "Something is going on in me which is like what goes on when I see an orange." But that is no answer. The fact that one can mention an object that has mental properties without mentioning that it has those properties is as irrelevant to its possession of those properties as the fact that one can mention a locomotive without mentioning the fact that it is a locomotive is irrelevant to the fact that it is a locomotive. One could refer to a locomotive in a "topic neutral" way, as, for example, "a certain item belonging to the Southern Pacific Railroad." But that does not make it any less of a locomotive, and the fact that one can talk of mental states in a veiled topic neutral vocabulary does not make them any less mental. This, by the way, is a recurring fallacy in analytic philosophy, the confusion between features of the language we use to describe a phenomenon and features of the phenomenon.

3 For a discussion of these issues see the articles by Smart, Shaffer, and Cornman in Rosenthal, ed. (1971).

Second Objection. Early physicalists believed that if two people were in the same type of mental state, they must be in the same type of corresponding neurophysiological state, that, for example, if you and I both now believe that it is snowing, we must both have the same type of neurophysiological state which realizes that belief. But for a variety of reasons it seems most implausible to suppose that this is true. Even if mental states are physical states, it can hardly be true that type identical mental states can be identified with type identical neurophysiological states.

The way out of this objection is to notice that many sorts of things can be type identical at one level of description even though each instance is token identical with some object at a lower level of description and those objects at the lower level of description are not type identical. Clocks are the same type of thing at the level of description "clock," even though each clock is token identical with some physical realization, say, a set of mechanically powered gears and wheels, or a set of electrically operated quartz oscillators; and those physical realizations may be type different. And if this works for clocks and carburetors, why not for mental states as well? Thus, you and I can each have the same belief that it is snowing, even though our neurophysiologies may not be type identical, just as your car and my car can each have a carburetor, even though mine is steel and yours is brass. But what is it then that the mental states have in common that makes them type identical? I believe the obvious answer is that mental states are type identical because of their common mental features, whether features of consciousness or of intentionality or both or some further sorts of mental features. But such is the reluctance of many analytic philosophers to take mental phenomena at their face value that this common sense answer was not the one proposed.

According to the functionalists, just as clocks and carburetors are identified by their functions, not by how those functions are realized in the physical structure, so mental states are identified by their functions, and not by how those functions are realized in the brain. Mental states are functional states in a sense that is supposed to be made clear by analogy with clocks and carburetors, and so on. And now the answer to the second objection has, *en passant,* also answered the first. For the "mysterious," "occult" mental properties turn out to be metaphysically harmless functional properties. In a word, type-type identity theories gave way to token-token theories and with them came carburetor functionalism. Functional materialism turned out, more or less inadvertently, to be a kind of eliminative materialism because the functional analysis eliminated any problems about irreducibly mental properties.

An immediate and obvious objection to functionalism is that it seems it could not be right because the mental states in question are intrinsic and functions are always observer relative. The ascription of a function to a system or to an element of a system is always made relative to some goal, purpose, or objective; functions are never just causes, they are causes relative to a teleology. My carburetor intrinsically causes many things, only some of which are its functions; for example, it exerts pressure on the engine block, it makes a hissing sound, it supports the air cleaner, it accumulates dirt, and it mixes air and gasoline. When we say that its *function* is to mix air and gasoline, we are saying more than that it causes the mixing of air and gasoline; we are also saying that *its purpose* is to mix air and gasoline relative to the overall purposes of the system. But such purposes are never intrinsic; they are assigned by us. If I decide to use my carburetor solely for supporting my air cleaner, then its function changes even though there are no changes in any of the intrinsic causal features of the system. The observer relativity of functions, by the way, is also true of systems that are not artifacts. For example, the heart causes the circulation of the blood, a thumping noise in the chest, and pressure on the lung. To say that *its function* is to pump blood is to assign observer relative intentionality to it. A linguistic clue to these facts is that as soon as we assign a function to some causal element, a whole intentionalistic vocabulary becomes appropriate which is inappropriate for causal relations *tout court*; thus we can speak of "malfunction," "breakdown," "functioning properly," and so on.

Now because mental states are intrinsic and functional states are observer relative, it can never be constitutive of mental states that they are functional states. Even if mental (= brain) states always had the same causal relations and even if we always assigned the same functions to these states; still, the features of these states that make them *mental* states are intrinsic and so could not be constituted by any observer relative stance we might take. To put the same point differently, if we try to define mental states in terms of their functions, then something else might serve just those functions, even though it lacked the intrinsic features we were trying to define. The very feature that made carburetor functionalism so appealing, namely, the analogy between the functional level and the physical level of description of carburetors, and so forth, on the one hand, and the mental and physical level of descriptions of beliefs, and so forth, on the other hand, is fatal in the end to carburetor functionalism; because the mental level of description is intrinsic and not functional.

I believe that most contemporary functionalists would feel that this is not a serious objection to their view because, so they might argue, the notion of a function is not really essential to functionalism. Ultimately they want to define mental states in terms of their *causal* relations where the causes are intrinsic, even if the functions are not. The argument would then turn on whether the causal features are sufficient to define intrinsic mental features. And I will come to this point shortly.

3. Turing Machine or Organizational Functionalism: Putnam and Dennett

Let us continue with our story. Carburetor functionalism was soon replaced by Turing machine functionalism. On this view, mental states are indeed functional states, but not just any kind of functional state; rather, they are logical states of a computer, and thus they are *intrinsic* states at least at the level of description of the computer program. Turing machine functionalism is also superior to carburetor functionalism in that it seems to promise a richer theory of the mind, according to which mental processes are computational processes; and this theory seems to be consistent with and supported by current work in cognitive psychology and artificial intelligence. I will consider the work of two authors in this tradition, Hilary Putnam and Daniel Dennett.

I begin with Putnam even though he claims to have abandoned Turing machine functionalism at least in its cruder forms (Putnam, 1975, pp. 298–99). I believe he abandoned it for the wrong reasons. The two reasons he gives for abandoning it are first, that a Turing machine can only be in one state at a time whereas a human can be in many psychological states at the same time, and second, some psychological states such as jealousy are related to other psychological states in a holistic fashion that is unlike the relations among Turing machine states. But this would still permit him to hold that psychological states are matters of functional organization, and it is this aspect of Turing machine functionalism that I want to discuss, not the specific limitations of the computer analogy that have to do with the scope and discreteness of machine states. So perhaps "organizational functionalism" would be a better term than "Turing Machine functionalism" for the view I am criticizing.

Putnam introduces the notion of a "Description" of a system, where a "Description" is defined as a specification of the states and input-output relations of the system as determined by the machine table (the computer program) for that system. He then states a version of organizational functionalism about conscious mental states such as pains.

The hypothesis that "being in pain is a functional state of the organism" may now be spelled out more exactly as follows:

(1) All organisms capable of feeling pain are Probabilistic Automata.
(2) Every organism capable of feeling pain possesses at least one Description of a certain kind (i.e., being capable of feeling pain *is* possessing an appropriate kind of Functional Organization).
(3) No organism capable of feeling pain possesses a decomposition into parts which separately possess Descriptions of the kind referred to in (2).
(4) For every Description of the kind referred to in (2), there exists a subset of the sensory inputs such that an organism with that Description is in pain when and only when some of its sensory inputs are in that subset (Putnam, 1975, p. 434).

It seems to me that this analysis suffers from the same sort of defects as classical behaviorism: being in pain is one thing; satisfying all these conditions or anything like these conditions is something quite different. I will argue for that conclusion by showing that a system could satisfy all these conditions and not feel anything at all, that these conditions are not constitutive of nor sufficient for having sensations such as pains. Since (2) and (4) are the heart of the analysis, I will dispose of (1) and (3) briefly.

(1) "All organisms capable of feeling pain are Probabilistic Automata."

Since everything is a probabilistic automaton under some description or other, as Putnam concedes, this statement is not much help. It does not serve to discriminate organisms capable of feeling pain from anything else. Furthermore, it is important to emphasize that "organism" in the statement does not mean organism in any biological sense. It just means system. It is essential to functionalism of the sort that both Putnam and Dennett adhere to that any system at all capable of having the right functional organization is capable of pain. It need not be an organism in the sense that plants and animals are organisms. Indeed, as we noted earlier, one of the original motivations for functionalism was the recognition that an indefinite number of different types of system could be functionally isomorphic. Robots, for example, could count as "organisms" for Putnam's purposes. So, in what follows, I will use the word "system" since systems are what is being talked about.

(3) "No system capable of feeling pain possesses a decomposition into parts which separately possess Descriptions of the kind referred to in (2)."

The reason for putting in this condition is that many systems can consist of sub-systems and the sub-system may be capable of feeling pain even when the system is not capable of feeling pain. Suppose, for example, we have a system composed of many people working together in a large bureaucracy. Such a system can realize a certain machine table without it being the case that the system suffered any pain in addition to the pain suffered by the individual people, and in order to eliminate these sorts of counterexamples Putnam has inserted condition (3). The elimination of a class of potential counterexamples by simple fiat is generally the sign of a theoretical weakness, and we will shortly see that Putnam's analysis is still subject to related counterexamples.

(2)

and

(4) "Every system capable of feeling pain possesses at least one Description of a certain kind (being capable of feeling pain *is* possessing an appropriate kind of Functional Organization). For every Description of this kind there exists a subset of the sensory inputs such that a system with that Description is in pain when and only when some of its sensory inputs are in that subset."

What (2) and (4) together amount to is this: Beings capable of pain are those and only those that instantiate a certain computer program; the computer program specifies a set of transition probabilities between input, output, and internal states, and the system will actually be in pain when the right input activates the system according to the program.

There is a way of trivializing Putnam's view so that it implies that a system is in pain if and only if it is in pain. That, I take it, is not his intent. His idea is rather that just as there are specific machine tables for pain, so there are specific inputs for pain. We do not need to know exactly *what they are* but simply *that there are some,* and we can define functionalism in terms of them whatever they are. Furthermore, the use of the expression "sensory" in "sensory input" is as potentially misleading as the use of the term "organism." "Sensory" in this context does not mean sensory in the biological sense, since any system such as, for example, a robot could have all sorts of sensory inputs without having any of the familiar biological apparatus for the senses. Otherwise, it is impossible to interpret Putnam's various remarks about robots.

Now once you lay bare the real character of the claims made in (2) and (4), you can easily see that it is possible for systems or organisms to satisfy the conditions and not have any pains. I think the claim is as obviously false as behaviorism, and I will present two related arguments to try to make its falsity apparent.

The Argument from Anesthesia. Let the system in question be me. By hypothesis I am capable of feeling pain because I instantiate a certain machine table. Let us suppose that the machine table is upset and that this is done by anesthetizing the relevant portion of my central nervous system, so that I cannot feel any pains. I now no longer instantiate the machine table. But suppose further that I make up for this by simply memorizing the steps in the machine table, so that I can now go through the steps in my mind. On Putnam's account there is no reason why my own mind could not be the element of the system that instantiates the machine table. Whenever somebody gives me the relevant sensory input, say, he punches me in the nose, I do not feel anything because I am anesthetized, but I "look up" in the machine table what I am supposed to do next, and I follow through all the steps until I reach the output and then I say or print out, "Ouch!" I cannot feel anything, but I still have the relevant sensory inputs; I still instantiate the machine table and I still have the right input-output "transition probabilities." I satisfy all of Putnam's conditions (1)–(4), but I do not feel any pains at all.

This argument may seem rather swift, but I think in fact the counterexample is decisive. Machine table plus inputs could not be constitutive of nor sufficient for pain because a human agent could in his own mental processes instantiate any machine table you like and could have any inputs you care to induce in him and still not feel the relevant sensations if his specific neurophysiological states are not appropriate. This suggests that functional organization is not the feature of the neurophysiology that really matters, and this suggestion will be pursued in the next objection. It is also important to emphasize that though this objection is stated in terms of machine tables, it would apply to other sorts of functional organization. It is directed at organizational functionalism and not just at the Turing machine version of organizational functionalism.

The Argument from Biology. Insofar as we know anything about the causal basis of pains and other sensations, we know that they are specific to quite definite sorts of animal and human nervous systems. Humans and many species of animal are capable of suffering pains; but trees, shrubs, and flowers are not, much less stones, waterfalls, and mountains. It is an amazing consequence of the claims of Turing machine functionalism that *any sort of substance whatever* is capable of feeling pain, provided only that it instantiates the machine table of principle (2) and has the sort of receptors described in principle (4). Though functionalists recognize and even embrace this consequence, its implausibility is masked from us by the fact that they seldom go through any detailed examples, so let us now try such an example. In my office is a computer console hooked up to a routine garden-variety computer called a PDP-10. Now let us suppose, in line with Putnam's number (2), there is a quite specific machine table which human beings instantiate and which enables them to feel pain. I know of no reason at all to suppose it is true, but let us give it to Putnam for the sake of the argument. Let us now program the PDP-10 with exactly this machine table. Notice that the machine table is purely formal; it has nothing to do with the specific material in which it is instantiated. As Putnam repeatedly insists, two systems can have the same Functional Organization, while having quite different constitutions, and to repeat, "Being capable of feeling pain *is* possessing a certain kind of Functional Organization" (*ibid.*, p. 434). So on Putnam's definition, the PDP-10 is now capable of pain, presumably all the way from mild discomfort to the most frightful agony. We now add a "sensory input." We introduce a transducer which is such that whenever I slam the door of my office or hit the console with my fist this produces an input to the computer as programmed for pain, and the "transition probabilities" are such that on my automatic typewriter the machine prints out, "Ouch!" "You are giving me a terrible stomachache!" "Please stop!" and so on.

We have now satisfied all of Putnam's conditions. We have a probabilistic automation; by fiat we can give it any machine table or other sort of functional organization that you like; it has no subsystems with the same Description; and it has sensory inputs that trigger the appropriate pain-responses. (And if I have chosen the wrong inputs, it does not matter because the argument remains the same no matter what sensory inputs you put in it.) Now is there any reason at all to suppose that the computer is in pain? Real intrinsic pain? Notice that the functionalist thesis is not that for all we know the computer *might* be in pain, but that the computer *must* be in pain because it is in a functional state equivalent to the functional state that human beings are in when they are in pain; and that is all that pain is: a functional state. I think it is obviously empirically false that the computer is in pain, because, to put it as an understatement, it is made of the wrong kind of material and is the wrong sort of system altogether to have pains. To have pains it would have to have a nervous system with neurons, biologically specific pain receptors, and so forth, or at least it would have to have something that was *causally* and not merely *formally* equivalent to an animal nervous system.

Some other sort of system besides animal nervous systems might be capable of having pains, that is an empirical question; but in order to be capable of having pains the system would have to have the relevant causal powers equal to the causal powers of animal nervous systems, and merely instantiating the same program would never be sufficient to guarantee that. Suppose by some incredible miracle my PDP-10 were in frightful agony. Even if that were true, it would still be no help to Turing machine functionalism, because if it were true it would have to be because the specific causal structure of the hardware somehow duplicated the causal powers of animal nervous systems, and that, as far as functionalism is concerned, is quite accidental. Even if my PDP-10 had, unknown to us, an electrochemical structure capable of feeling pains, the thesis of functionalism is that structure does not matter; what matters is functional organization, and that is defined by purely formal considerations quite independently of the structure. Even if the PDP-10 is in pain, we can then put the same program in a set of water pipes, wind machines, or any crazy Rube Goldberg apparatus you might care to construct, provided only that it is stable and enduring enough to carry the program. We could, for example, make the system out of windmills, old beer cans, and paper clips, and, according to organizational functionalism, any such system must be in pain. Against this I am arguing that from everything we know about physiology, it seems incredible to suppose that these other systems *could be* in pain, much less that they *must be* in pain.

If we put these two arguments together, we get a sequence of steps to show that both the main claims of organizational functionalism are false. Anybody who wanted to defend this sort of functionalism would have to show that something is wrong with this argument.

The two claims are:

a. For a human to be in pain or some other mental state is just to instantiate a certain sort of functional organization (such as a computer program) with the right inputs and outputs;
b. Any system such as a robot that was functionally equivalent to a human, that is, that had the right organization and the right input and output relations, would also have to be in pain in virtue of those facts.

Against these I argue:

1. Humans and at least some animals have nervous systems that are causally sufficient to enable them to feel pains and have other sorts of mental states (this is an empirical assumption, shared by both sides in the dispute, about the causal basis of mental phenomena).

2. Any system capable of having pains and other mental states must have the relevant causal powers equivalent to human and animal nervous systems (this is a trivial consequence of 1).
3. Instantiating a certain functional organization such as a program could never by itself be sufficient for mental states, because it would be possible for an agent to instantiate the program and not have the relevant mental states (by the argument from anesthesia). This entails the negation of a.
4. Therefore, a system could not have the relevant causal powers described in 2 solely in virtue of instantiating a certain organization with certain input-output relations (by 2 and 3).
5. Human and animal nervous systems have a causal capacity to produce mental states which is *not* constituted by their having a certain functional organization with certain input-output relations (this is a consequence of 1 and 3).
6. Other systems such as robots could not have mental states solely in virtue of having a functional organization with the right input-output relations but would have to have other causal powers equivalent to those of the brain (a consequence of 2 and 4). This entails the negation of b.

Throughout both these arguments I have been supposing, as a concession for the sake of argument, that my machine table must have some relevant role to play in my feeling of pains, and that might even be true, but there is so far not the slightest reason to suppose it is true. What I am doing here is arguing against the view that organizational functionalism gives us a sufficient condition for the mental. I am conceding for the sake of argument that it might give us a necessary condition, though I do not believe there is any argument for that view, and once you see that it does not give a sufficient condition, most of the motivation for supposing it might give a necessary condition is removed.

I now turn to Dennett, whose opposition to the mental is even more explicit than Putnam's. Typical of Dennett's remarks about mental phenomena is the claim that "beliefs, desires, pains, mental images, experiences – as all these are *ordinarily* understood" are not "good theoretical entities" (Dennett, 1978, p. xx). The difficulty with this claim is that there are quite different ways in which something can fail to be a "good theoretical entity." Witches and goblins fail to be good theoretical entities because such things do not exist; but tables and chairs, and mountains and beaches, fail to be good theoretical entities not because such things do not exist, but because the laws that describe the course of nature do not use these terms; they do not mention objects under the description "chair," "table," "mountain," or "beach." In that sense, these sorts of things are not good theoretical entities, but so what? At most, that is a remark about which sorts of terms figure in the construction of scientific theories and not about the *existence* of chairs, tables, mountains, and beaches. Now, does Dennett think mental phenomena are like witches or like mountains? Can it be that Dennett really thinks pains and beliefs are like witches and goblins in that they do not exist at all "as ordinarily understood"? (How many non-ordinary ways are there to understand, say, the stomachache I referred to earlier?) He discusses how difficult it is to "convince someone that there are no pains or beliefs" (*ibid.*, p. xx), and he declares that it will have to be done piecemeal. He concludes one such effort with the sentence "Then, since I am denying that any entity could have the features of a pain or a thought, so much the worse for the ontological status of such things" (*ibid.*, p. 38). And in a subsequent discussion (Dennett, 1980, p. 76) he says he is indeed "claiming that there are no such things as pains, although people do feel pain." He does not find this view self contradictory (I do), but for present purposes our concern is not with its consistency but with the argument that "strictly speaking there could be no such things as pain" (*ibid.*, p. 76). The argument is as follows:

> But if, as I have claimed, the intuitions we would have to honor were we to honor them all do not form a consistent set, there can be no true theory of pain, and so no computer or robot could instantiate the true theory of pain which it would have to do to feel real pain. Human beings and animals could no more instantiate the true theory of pain, (there being none), which lands us with the outrageous conclusion that no one ever feels pain (Dennett, 1978, p. 228).

This argument contains, in my view, something more outrageous than the conclusion, and that is its logic. From the fact that the set of intuitions we have about a class of objects is inconsistent, and therefore the class is such that none of the objects could satisfy *all* of the intuitions, it simply does not follow that no such objects exist. Compare: the intuitions we have about chairs do not form a consistent set; therefore, there is no true theory of chairs; therefore, chairs do not exist. Or compare: the set of intuitions people have about Jimmy Carter do not form a consistent set; therefore, there is no true theory of Jimmy Carter; therefore, Jimmy Carter does not exist. With the best will in the world there is simply no way you can rescue the formal structure of Dennett's argument that "strictly speaking" pains do not exist, and the objections I am making to it are at least as old as Wittgenstein's discussion of "game" and other family resemblance notions.

But even assuming that Dennett's arguments against the existence of mental phenomena such as pains are inadequate, what about his positive thesis concerning the mental, about those states which presumably are left over after the nonexistent ones are eliminated? I now turn to his "Cognitive Theory of Consciousness" (*ibid.*, pp. 149–73).

He describes, in some detail, a flow chart for a system that has consciousness. He then asks (Thomas Nagel's question), "What is it like to be an entity that instantiates the flow chart?" His supposition is that there is something it is like if the entity is conscious, and if not, not. Here is the answer: "Suppose I put forward the bold hypothesis that you are a realization of the flow chart and that it is in virtue of this fact that it seems to us – and to you – that there is something it is like to be you" (*ibid.*, p. 165). Having consciousness is thus on his account "a matter of having a certain sort of functional organization." He then challenges us, "Can you give good grounds for denying the hypothesis and if so, what are they? What personal access do you have and to what?" (*ibid.*, p. 165).

One feels one must be misunderstanding the questions because the answer seems too obvious. Yes, one can give good grounds for denying the hypothesis. Indeed, taken quite literally, it seems obviously false and false for the same sort of reason that old-fashioned logical behaviorism is false. Having conscious states such as bodily sensations and visual experiences is one thing, and instantiating the flow chart is something quite different. Bodily sensations such as tickles and itches are constituted by the way they intrinsically feel and are realized in nervous systems. Flow charts are constituted by satisfying certain functional descriptions and can be realized in any substance you like. They have no essential connection with either feelings or nervous systems. If it is not obvious on the face of it that instantiating the flow chart is neither constitutive of nor sufficient for the possession of the relevant conscious states, the same two arguments I marshaled against Putnam can again be invoked here. First, the flow chart is totally independent of the forms of its realization. This means that all sorts of substances can instantiate the flow chart even though they are inappropriate for having visual experience, tickles, itches, and so on. The flow chart can be instantiated by our fancy Rube Goldberg machine made entirely of beer cans, paper clips, and windmills.

And second, the argument from anesthesia that we used against Putnam also applies to Dennett, though in a slightly modified form. The flow chart will have to have variations for different sorts of conscious states, say, itches, visual experiences, and so on. Let a person whose eyes are closed go through the steps in the flow chart that are specific to vision. He can use braille or any other method to get through the flow chart. He will indeed have conscious states, he is conscious of going through the flow chart, but he has the wrong conscious states since he has his eyes closed and has no visual experiences. He cannot see anything, even though the flow chart in question is specific for vision.

I said earlier that functionalists showed a tendency to confuse intrinsic mental states with the causal features that might warrant observer relative ascriptions of mental states. In Dennett's case this shift from intrinsic to observer relative ascriptions of mental phenomena is made a matter of principle with his introduction of the notion of "intentional systems" and "the intentional stance." On his account both humans and computers with certain sorts of program are "intentional systems," and an intentional system is just one where we find it appropriate to adopt "the intentional stance." In the adoption of the intentional stance, "One predicts behavior . . . by ascribing to the system *the possession of certain information,* and supposing it to be *directed by certain goals* and then working out the most reasonable or appropriate action on the basis of these ascriptions and suppositions" (*ibid.*, p. 6). It is then, he says, but a small step to describe this information and goals as beliefs and desires. But we must not ask if these really are beliefs and desires because "the definition of intentional systems I have given does not say that intentional systems really have beliefs and desires but that one can explain and predict their behavior by ascribing beliefs and desires to them, and the decision to adopt this strategy is pragmatic and is not intrinsically right or wrong" (*ibid.*, p. 7).

Well, one can agree that it is open to anybody to adopt any strategy he finds useful, but the question remains, what is the status of the ascription of the mental states, whether the ascription is of information and goals, or beliefs and desires? Assuming we do find it useful, how are we supposed to interpret this usefulness? Even if we have not defined intentional systems in such a way that we say that they really have beliefs and desires, there will still be a difference between those intentional systems that really have beliefs and desires and those that do not, and in the case of those that do, the ascriptions have entirely different interpretations from the case of those that do not. For example, in the case of those that do, the beliefs and desires play causal roles determined by their specific intrinsic features. Dennett thinks the case of the computer and the human being are the same; in both cases we find it useful to adopt the intentional stance, and it is up to anybody to adopt some other strategy if he finds it more useful. But there is an enormous difference between my attributing a "desire" to a chess-playing computer to castle on the strong side and my saying I have a desire to drink a glass of cold beer. In the computer case, it is just a useful shorthand for describing how the system functions. There are no intrinsic mental phenomena in question at all. But in my own case I do not attribute to myself a desire for a beer because I find it useful in predicting my behavior, but because I want a beer. In my own case, I am stating facts about intrinsic mental phenomena, and whether or not people find it useful to adopt "the intentional stance" toward me is quite irrelevant to what the facts really are. In short, whether a system really has beliefs and desires is quite independent of whether or not we find it useful to make observer relative ascriptions of beliefs and desires. Furthermore, we only understand the observer relative attributions in a way that is parasitic on the use of the same expressions to specify intrinsic mental states. We understand the metaphorical non-literal use of "belief" and "desire" as applied to computers because we see these attributions as based on an analogy with systems such as human beings who literally have intrinsic beliefs and desires.[4]

I think I can make clear my sense of the strangeness of Dennett's project and of functionalism in general with the following analogy. Suppose that there were a group of philosophers who were puzzled by the existence of hands; suppose there was a long tradition of being worried about the ontological status of hands. And suppose that a functionalist view of hands became fashionable. On one version of this view, we are told that we do not have to worry about the existence of hands because it is all a matter of adopting the "manual stance" toward certain systems which we will describe as "manual systems." To paraphrase Dennett: "the definition of a manual system does not say that manual systems really have hands but that one can explain and predict their behavior by attributing hands to them, and the decision to adopt this strategy is pragmatic and not intrinsically right or wrong." I think that the intentional stance approach to understanding beliefs and desires is about as useful as the manual stance approach would be to understanding hands. In each case the question of analyzing the intrinsic features of mental states (or hands) gets replaced by a different question: under what conditions do we find it useful to talk *as if* a system had mental states (or hands)? And to ask that question amounts to changing the subject

[4] Also, when I adopt the intentional stance is that supposed to be intrinsic or not? Do I really have an intentional stance or is it just a case of adopting an intentional stance to my intentional stance? If the former, we are left with intrinsic intentionality; if the latter, it looks like we are in a vicious regress.

while still deluding ourselves into thinking we are addressing the original philosophical issues.

In sum, I have made three objections to Dennett's account: first, that the argument to show that pains, and so forth, do not really exist is invalid; second, that the cognitive theory of consciousness is subject to counterexamples; and third, that the notion of the intentional stance conceals but does not get rid of the crucial distinction between observer relative mental attributions and attributions of intrinsic mental phenomena.

Most of my discussion of functionalism has been addressed to organizational functionalism because it seems to me the richest and most interesting of the versions I have seen, but I want to conclude this part of the argument by showing how some of the same worries apply quite generally to other sorts of functionalist accounts. Consider the following functional definition from Grice which he calls a "first shot" at a definition of belief. "X believes that p just in case x is disposed, whenever x wants (desires) some end E, to act in ways which will realize E given that p is true rather than in ways which will realize E given that p is false" (Grice, 1975, p. 24). Now compare that with an analogous definition of hands: "X has a hand just in case x is disposed whenever x wants (desires) some graspable and retrievable object O_{gr} to act in such a way that will bring it about that x grasps and retrieves O_{gr} rather than that he does not grasp and retrieve O_{gr}."

The problem I have with such definitions is not just that one can always think up counterexamples, but that the enterprise of this sort of definition seems so dubious in the first place. Shoemaker (unpublished) tells us that on his version of functionalism it is the view that "mental states can be defined in terms of their relations, primarily their causal relations, to sensory inputs, behavioral outputs and other mental states." Analogously, a functionalist view of hands would be that "hands can be defined in terms of their relations, primarily their causal relations, to manual inputs, behavioral outputs and other features of the body including mental states." Now let us suppose that after years of ingenious philosophical effort the functionalist dream of satisfactory definitions was realized for both hands and mental states; suppose we had such definitions and nobody could think up a good counterexample. What would we have achieved? In the case of our definition of hands, not very much; because our definitions still leave out the intrinsic properties of hands, all they tell us about is the functional role of hands. Analogously, our definitions of mental states do not tell us the intrinsic properties of mental states, only their functional role. But it might be replied that the very thesis of functionalism is that mental states do not have any intrinsic properties except their functional role, so that is hardly an objection. But now I want to pick up the thread of our earlier discussion of the intrinsic-observer relative distinction. We left off where the question was: are the acknowledged causal properties of mental states sufficient to define their intrinsic mental properties? And by now it should be clear that my answer to that question is no, and for the same sorts of reasons that the acknowledged behavioral manifestations of pains are not sufficient to define pains and the acknowledged causal features of hands are not sufficient to define hands. Indeed, all the arguments I have presented so far are just ways of trying to exhibit this basic intuition. The intrinsic features of, for example, beliefs, pains, and desires are just that: intrinsic features; the strategy of the functionalist, like that of the behaviorist, is to get us to take a third person observer relative stance, in which we agree that mental states do indeed stand in causal relations; just as we agree with the behaviorist that they have behavioral manifestations. But the arguments that I have presented, such as the argument from anesthesia and the argument from biology, are designed to remind us that something could have all the right causal relations and still not have the right mental properties.

4. Diagnosis and Conclusion

I believe that functionalism, like the behaviorism which preceded it, requires not so much refutation as diagnosis. Why would anyone hold such an unplausible view? Why would anyone believe, for example, that one's own pains, tickles, and itches, as well as one's beliefs, fears, hopes, and desires, were constituted by the fact that one was the instantiation of a flow chart or a computer program? And more generally, why does this phase of analytic philosophy seem to exemplify a longer-term reluctance to take mental phenomena at their face value?

I believe, in fact, that there are many reasons, more than I can hope to discuss in this article, and some of those that I will not be discussing should be mentioned at least in passing. There are arguments, such as those of Quine on indeterminacy, to show that where intentional states are concerned there are no facts of the matter beyond certain dispositions to behavior. And there are a series of confusions about the relations between intentionality with-a-t and intensionality with-an-s. Many philosophers believe that the propositional contents of beliefs and desires belong to a class of mysterious entities, called intensions, and that we would be better off to avoid believing in such entities. But I think these are not the arguments that have really mattered in the long run. On my diagnosis there are three major reasons for the appeal of such views as functionalism and for the long-run prejudice against the mental in analytic philosophy.

1. *Verificationism.* Positivism and verificationism are officially dead, but they live on in certain verificationist tendencies that one finds in functionalist authors. In analyzing pains and beliefs Putnam and Dennett do not try to describe the intrinsic properties of such mental phenomena; rather, they are concerned with such questions as "When would we attribute such mental states to a system? What is the explanatory role of such attributions to a system? Under what conditions do we think ourselves justified or not justified in making such intentionalistic attributions?" But these questions are not the same as "What are the intrinsic properties of mental states?" Notice that in both authors the approach is almost entirely from a third-person point of view, and indeed the confusion between observer relative and intrinsic attributions of the mental derives largely from this third-person approach. As long as we think of mental states as something to be ascribed from outside, it can be made to seem as if what matters is the adoption of an "intentional stance" and the "pragmatic" usefulness of treating something as an "intentional system." No one would think it of much use in the philosophy of mind to worry about these "stances" if he were concentrating on his own mental states. Think what it is actually like to have a pain in the stomach or a passionate desire for a cold beer and ask yourself if you are talking about real mental phenomena or just adopting a stance. The cure, in short, for the verificationism of Putnam, Dennett, and others and for their persistent confusion of the question "What is it to have mental states?" with such questions as "What is the functional role of the ascription of mental states?" is to insist at least at some point on the first-person point of view. It reveals a fundamental confusion to suppose that we can get clear about mental states entirely by examining the functioning of third-person attributions of the mental.

2. *Cognitive Science.* The second reason is peculiar to functionalism, but I think it is important. Many philosophers have the conviction that they are utilizing the results of something called "cognitive science" and that somehow the computer has given us remarkable new insights into the operation of the mind. On the surface, this manifests itself in a great deal of more or less intimidating technical jargon. There is much talk about Turing machines, finite state automata, analog and digital computers, machine tables, flow charts, transducers, and so on. The illusion is thus conveyed that philosophical problems about the mental have been converted into technical questions in automata theory capable of solution by the cooperative efforts of philosophers and cognitive scientists, including both psychologists and computer scientists. Underlying this surface appearance is a fairly serious fallacy. From the fact that at some level of description the brain is a digital

computer (or, if you like, a set of digital computers) together with the fact that the programs of the brain can be instantiated by any other sort of computer sufficiently rich and complex to carry the program, the fallacious inference is drawn that what the brain does in producing mental phenomena is nothing more than what these other sorts of computers would be doing if they instantiated the program. And this fallacious inference leads naturally to the thesis of Turing machine functionalism. Being in a certain mental state just is instantiating a certain sort of computer program. To put it another way, the fallacy is in moving from the true premise that the brain is a computer, in the sense that it instantiates computer programs, to the false conclusion that all that the brain does which is relevant to the production of the mental is to instantiate computer programs, that the only psychologically relevant feature of brain states is that they are logical states of a computer. The premise could hardly be false: since everything is a digital computer at some level of description, brains are too. But the conclusion is obviously false, as I have claimed in both the argument from biology and the argument from anesthesia. It is false both because no program by itself guarantees the causal powers that are specific to the biochemistry of the brain, and because a system such as a human agent could instantiate the program and still not have the relevant mental states.

3. *Fear of Cartesianism.* I believe that the deepest source of the prejudice against the mental is the fear that to admit mental entities at their face value would necessarily involve us in the worst excesses of Cartesianism, that we will be postulating a class of mysterious and occult entities, inhabiting another metaphysical realm beyond the reach of scientific investigation, that we will be left with the self or the soul, with privileged access and incorrigibility, and all the rest of it. Or, perhaps worst of all, that we will be left with a "mind-body problem."

Indeed it is a curious fact about the history of behaviorism and functionalism that neither was *independently* motivated. No one examined his own pains and discovered them to be patterns of behavior or Turing machine states; rather, these theories were proposed as solutions to other problems in philosophy, such as the problem of other minds and especially the "mind-body problem." But suppose there is not any such problem as the "mind-body problem" anymore than there is such a problem as the "digestion-stomach problem." Suppose that, as I believe to be the case, thinking and perceiving are as much natural and biological phenomena as digestion or the circulation of the blood. Suppose that mental phenomena are both caused by and realized in the structure of the brain. If so, we can give up not only dualism but "monism" and "physicalism" as well, for the antidualist jargon only has a point if we accept the dualist categories, such categories as kinds of substance and relations between kinds of substances. No one feels that he has to choose between monism and dualism where digestion is concerned; nor does he have to choose between epiphenomenalism, interactionism, and so forth, nor to postulate the existence of a metaphysical self or a transcendental ego that digests. Why should cognition be treated any less naturalistically? The most effective way to answer behaviorism and functionalism is not, as I have done, by making "objections" to them, but by removing the philosophical picture that motivated them in the first place.

References

Dennett, Daniel C., *Brainstorms, Philosophical Essays on Mind and Psychology* (Montgomery, Vt., 1978).

———, "Reply to Professor Stich," *Philosophical Books* 21, no. 2 (1980): 73–76.

Grice, H. P., "Method in Philosophical Psychology," *Proceedings and Addresses of the American Philosophical Association*, vol. 48 (Newark, Del., 1974–75).

Putnam, H., *Mind, Language, and Reality; Philosophical Papers*, vol. 2 (Cambridge, 1975).

Rosenthal, David M., ed. *Materialism and the Mind-Body Problem* (Englewood Cliffs, N. J., 1971):

Cornman, James W., "The Identity of Mind and Body," pp. 73–79: Shaffer, Jerome, "Mental Events and the Brain," pp. 67–72; Smart, J. J. C., "Sensations and Brain Processes," pp. 53–56.

Searle, John R., "The Intentionality of Intention and Action," *Inquiry* 22 (1979): 253–80.

Shoemaker, Sydney, "The Missing Absent Qualia Argument," unpublished.

13

INDETERMINACY, EMPIRICISM, AND THE FIRST PERSON

The aim of this essay is to assess the significance of W. V. Quine's indeterminacy thesis. If Quine is right, the thesis has vast ramifications for the philosophy of language and mind; if he is wrong, we ought to be able to say exactly how and why.

I

Let us begin by stating the behaviorist assumptions from which Quine originally proceeds. For the sake of developing an empirical theory of meaning, he confines his analysis to correlations between external stimuli and dispositions to verbal behavior. In thus limiting the analysis, he does not claim to capture all the intuitions we have about the pretheoretical notion, but rather the "objective reality"[1] that is left over if we strip away the confusions and incoherencies in the pretheoretical "meaning." The point of the "behavioristic ersatz" is to give us a scientific, empirical account of the objective reality of meaning. On this view, the objective reality is simply a matter of being disposed to produce utterances in response to external stimuli. The stimuli are defined entirely in terms of patterns of stimulations of the nerve endings, and the responses entirely in terms of sounds and sound patterns that the speaker is disposed to emit. But we are not supposed to think that

Reprinted by permission from *Journal of Philosophy*, vol. LXXXIV, no. 3 (March 1987): 123–147.

I am indebted to a large number of people for comments and criticism of earlier drafts of this paper. I especially want to thank Noam Chomsky, Dagfinn Føllesdal, Ernest Lepore, Brian McLaughlin, George Myro, Dagmar Searle, and Bruce Vermazen.

[1] *Word and Object* (Cambridge, Mass.: MIT Press; New York: Wiley, 1960), p. 39.

between the stimulus and the verbal response there are any mental entities. We are not supposed to think that there is any consciousness, intentionality, thoughts, or any internal "meanings" connecting the stimuli to the noises. There is just the pattern of stimulus and the pattern of learned response. There will, of course, be neurophysiological mechanisms mediating the input and the output, but the details of their structure do not matter to a theory of meaning, since any mechanism whatever that systematically associated stimulus and response would do the job as well. For example, any computer or piece of machinery that could emit the right sounds in response to the right stimuli would have "mastered" a language as well as any other speaker, because that is all there is to the mastery of a language. Quine, I take it, does not deny the existence of inner mental states and processes; he just thinks they are useless and irrelevant to developing an empirical theory of language.

Such a view is linguistic behaviorism with a vengeance. It has often been criticized and, in my view, often refuted, for example, by Noam Chomsky in his review of B. F. Skinner.[2] On one construal, my Chinese room argument can also be interpreted as a refutation.[3] One way to refute this version of extreme linguistic behaviorism (let us call it "behaviorism" for short) would be to offer a reductio ad absurdum of its basic premises; and, indeed, it seems to me that Quine has offered us one such famous reductio (*op. cit.*, ch. 2). If behaviorism were true, then certain distinctions known independently to be valid would be lost. For example, we all know that, when a speaker utters an expression, there is a distinction between his meaning rabbit and his meaning rabbit stage or undetached rabbit part. But, if we actually applied the assumptions of behaviorism to interpreting the language of an alien tribe, we would find there was no way of making these distinctions as plain facts of the matter about the language used by the native speakers. Suppose, for example, the natives shouted "Gavagai!" whenever a rabbit ran past, and suppose we tried to translate this into our English as "There's a rabbit!" or simply, "Rabbit!" The stimulus – which, remember, is defined entirely in terms of stimulations of nerve endings – is equally appropriate for

2 "Review of B. F. Skinner's *Verbal Behavior*," in Jerry Fodor and Jerrold Katz, eds., *The Structure of Language* (Englewood Cliffs, N. J.: Prentice-Hall, 1964), pp. 547–578.

3 In the Chinese room argument, the man in the room follows a computer program that makes his verbal behavior indistinguishable from that of a Chinese speaker, but he still does not understand Chinese. He satisfies the behavioral criterion for understanding without actually understanding. Thus, the refutation of strong AI is a fortiori a refutation of behaviorism. [See my "Minds, Brains, and Programs," *Behavioral and Brain Sciences*, III (1980): 417–457; and *Minds, Brains, and Science* (Cambridge, Mass.: Harvard, 1984).]

translating "Gavagai!" as "There's a stage in the life history of a rabbit!" or "There's an undetached part of a rabbit!" The same pattern of stimulation of the photoreceptor cells does duty for all three translations. So, if all there were to meaning were patterns of stimulus and response, then it would be impossible to discriminate meanings, which are in fact discriminable. That is the reductio ad absurdum.

It is crucial to this argument to see that, even if we got more patterns of stimulus and response for our tribe, that still would not enable us to make the discriminations we need to make. Suppose we learned their expression for 'is the same as' and tried to use it to enable us to tell whether they meant rabbit or rabbit stage or undetached rabbit part. We could get the rabbit to run past again, and if they said "Same gavagai," we would have at least pretty good evidence that they did not mean, for example, rabbit stage by 'gavagai'. But this would be no help to us at all, because exactly the same sorts of doubt that we had about 'gavagai' in the first place would now apply to the expression for 'is the same as'. As far as matching stimuli and responses is concerned, we could equally well translate it as 'is a part of' or 'belongs with'. The conclusion we are forced to is this: assuming linguistic behaviorism, there will be endlessly different and inconsistent translations, all of which can be made consistent with all actual and possible evidence concerning the totality of the speech dispositions of the native speakers. As far as the behavioral evidence is concerned, there is nothing to choose between one translation and another even though the two are inconsistent.[4]

On Quine's view, the unit of analysis for empirically testing translations is not words or individual expressions but whole sentences. The only direct empirical checks we have on translations are for those sentences which are associated directly with stimulus conditions, the "observation sentences." On this view, 'Gavagai!', 'Rabbit!', 'Rabbit stage!', 'Undetached rabbit part!' all have the same determinate stimulus meaning; they have "stimulus synonymy," since the same stimulus conditions would prompt assent to or dissent from them. The indeterminacy arises when we attempt to form "analytical hypotheses" that state the meanings of particular words or other elements of the sentence. The indeterminacy that attaches to the elements of observation sentences is at least constrained by the stimulus conditions that prompt

[4] In what sense exactly can two translations be inconsistent? We cannot simply say that they have different *meanings*, for that would seem to imply the existence of determinate meanings. Rather, we must say that they are inconsistent in the sense that one system of translation will accept translations that the other system would reject [Quine, "Reply to Harman," *Synthese*, XIX, 1/2 (December 1968): 267–269; also, *Word and Object*, pp. 73/4.]

assent to or dissent from those sentences. The determinate stimulus meaning that attaches to observation sentences should at least seem puzzling to us, however, since sentences that have the same stimulus meaning do not in any ordinary sense of 'meaning' have the same meaning. By any reasonable standard of objective reality, it is a matter of objective reality that "There's a rabbit" and "There's an undetached rabbit part" just do not mean the same things. The significance of this point for the overall theory will emerge later.

Now, why exactly is Quine's argument a reductio ad absurdum of extreme linguistic behaviorism? There are two positions which are inconsistent:

(1) The thesis of behaviorism: The objective reality of meaning consists entirely of correlations between external stimuli and dispositions to verbal behavior.[5]

(2) In a given case of speech behavior, there can be a plain fact of the matter about whether a native speaker meant, for example, rabbit, as opposed to rabbit stage, or undetached rabbit part, by the utterance of an expression.

If alternative and inconsistent translation schemes can all be made consistent with the same patterns of stimulus and response, then there cannot be any fact of the matter about which is right, because, according to (1), there isn't anything else to be right about. But this is inconsistent with (2); so if we accept (2), (1) must be false.

I think it is clear which of (1) or (2) we have to give up. Quine has simply refuted extreme linguistic behaviorism. But why am I so confident about that? Why not give up (2)? The answer is the obvious one: if behaviorism were correct, it would have to be correct for us as speakers of English as well as for speakers of Gavagai-talk. And we know from our own case that we do mean by 'rabbit' something different from 'rabbit stage' or 'undetached rabbit part'. If my English-speaking neighbor, having read Quine, decides that he can't tell whether by 'rabbit' I mean rabbit, undetached rabbit part, or rabbit stage, then so much the worse for him. When I saw a rabbit recently, as I did in fact, and I called it a rabbit, I meant rabbit. In all discussions in the philosophy of language and the philosophy of mind, it is absolutely essential at some point to remind oneself of the first-person case. No one, for example, can convince us by argument, however ingenious, that pains do not exist if in fact we have them, and similar considerations apply to Quine's example. If somebody has a theory according to which there isn't

[5] Sometimes Quine talks about behavior *simpliciter*, sometimes about *dispositions* to behavior. I think the notion of dispositions to behavior is the one he prefers.

any difference between my meaning rabbit and my meaning rabbit part, then I know that his theory is simply mistaken; and the only interest his theory can have for me is in trying to discover where he went wrong. I want to emphasize this point, since it is often regarded as somehow against the rules in these discussions to raise the first-person case.

In a different philosophical environment from the one we live in, this might well be the end of the discussion. Linguistic behaviorism was tried and refuted by Quine using reductio ad absurdum arguments. But, interestingly, he does not regard it as having been refuted. He wants to hold behaviorism, together with the conclusion that, where analytical hypotheses about meaning are concerned, there simply are no facts of the matter, together with a revised version of (2), the thesis that we can in fact make valid distinctions between different translations. And some authors, such as Donald Davidson[6] and John Wallace,[7] who reject behaviorism, nonetheless accept a version of the indeterminacy thesis. Davidson, in fact, considers and rejects my appeal to the first-person case. Why does the thesis of the indeterminacy of translation continue to be accepted? And what larger issues are raised by the dispute? I now turn to these questions.

II

We need to consider three theses:

(A) The indeterminacy of translation
(B) The inscrutability of reference
(C) The relativity of ontology

In this section, I will first explain the relations between (A) and (B), and then try to say more about the character of the thesis Quine is advancing. In the next section, I will try to show that (C) is best construed as an unsuccessful maneuver to rescue the theory from the apparently absurd consequences of (A) and (B).

The thesis of the indeterminacy of translation is that, where questions of translation and, therefore, of meaning are concerned, there is no such

6 "The Inscrutability of Reference," *Southwestern Journal of Philosophy,* X (1979): 7–19, reprinted in *Inquiries into Truth and Interpretation* (New York: Oxford, 1984), pp. 227–241; page references are to this version.

7 "Only in the Context of a Sentence Do Words Have Any Meaning," *Midwest Studies in Philosophy,* II: *Studies in the Philosophy of Language* (1977).

thing as getting it right or wrong. This is not because of an epistemic gulf between evidence and conclusion, but because there is no fact of the matter to be right or wrong about.

From (A), so stated, (B) follows immediately. For if there is no fact of the matter about whether or not a speaker *meant* rabbit as opposed to rabbit stage, then equally, there is no fact of the matter about whether or not he is *referring* to a rabbit or a rabbit stage. In Fregean terminology, indeterminacy of sense entails inscrutability of reference.

Now, if we were to construe (A) as just the claim that there are no psychological facts of the matter about meanings in addition to facts about correlations of stimulus and response, then it would seem puzzling that we didn't derive that conclusion immediately from extreme linguistic behaviorism. It would seem puzzling that there is so much heavy going about 'gavagai', and so forth. But thesis (A) is stronger than just the thesis of behaviorism; that is, it is stronger than the claim that there isn't any meaning in addition to correlations of stimulus and response. It says further that there are an indefinite number of equally valid but inconsistent ways of correlating stimulus and verbal response in the vocabulary of an alien language with that of our language. The thesis that there are no objectively real meanings in addition to dispositions to verbal behavior was already assumed at the beginning of the discussion. Quine rejected any appeal to meanings, in any psychological sense, from the start. That was never at issue. What was at issue was the possibility of empirically motivated correct translations from one language to another, *given behaviorism;* the issue was whether or not there is an empirically motivated notion of sameness of meaning left over after we have adopted extreme linguistic behaviorism.

We will see the importance of this consideration when we see why several criticisms that are made of Quine miss the mark. Chomsky, for example, has repeatedly claimed that Quine's thesis of indeterminacy is simply the familiar underdetermination of hypothesis by empirical evidence.[8] Because any empirical hypothesis makes a claim that goes beyond the evidence, there will always be inconsistent hypotheses that are consistent with any actual or possible evidence. But underdetermination, so construed, does not entail that there is "no fact of the matter." Now Quine's response to Chomsky's objection seems at first sight puzzling. He grants that indeterminacy is underdetermination, but claims that it is underdetermination at one remove and, therefore, that there is no fact of the matter. He claims that, even if we

[8] Cf., for example, his "Quine's Empirical Assumptions," *Synthese,* XIX, 1/2 (December 1968): 53–68.

have established all the facts about physics, semantics is still indeterminate. He writes:

> Then when I say there is no fact of the matter, as regards, say, the two rival manuals of translation, what I mean is that both manuals are compatible with all the same distributions of states and relations over elementary particles. In a word, they are physically equivalent.[9]

But this answer seems inadequate to Chomsky and at one time seemed inadequate to me, because underdetermination at one remove is still just underdetermination. It wouldn't be sufficient to show that there is no fact of the matter. The objection to Quine that Chomsky makes (and that I used to make) is simply this: for any given higher-level "emergent" or "supervenient" property, there will be (at least) two levels of underdetermination. There will be a level of the underdetermination of the underlying physical theory, but there will also be a theory at the higher level, for example, at the level of psychology; and information at the level of microphysics is, by itself, not sufficient to determine the level of psychology. As Chomsky once put it, if you fix the physics, the psychology is still open; but equally, if you fix the psychology, the physics is still open. For example, the theory of all the dispositions of physical particles that go to make up my body, by itself, would leave open the question of whether or not I am in pain. The thesis that I am in pain is underdetermined at one remove. Now why is it supposed to be any different with meaning? Of course, there are two levels of underdetermination, but in both cases there are facts of the matter – in one case, facts of psychology, and in the other case, facts of physics. I now believe that this answer misses Quine's point altogether because it fails to see that he is assuming from the start that there is no psychologically real level of meaning beyond simple physical dispositions to respond to verbal stimuli. To repeat, Quine assumes from the very start the nonexistence of (objectively real) meanings in any psychological sense. If you assume that they are so much as possible, his argument fails. But now it begins to look as though the real issue is not about indeterminacy at all; it is about extreme linguistic behaviorism.

Many philosophers assume that Quine's discussion is sufficient to refute any sort of mentalistic or intentionalistic theory of meaning. But what our discussion of Chomsky's objections suggests is that this misconstrues the nature of the discussion altogether. It is only *assuming* the nonexistence of intentionalistic meanings that the argument for indeterminacy succeeds at all.

9 *Theories and Things* (Cambridge, Mass.: Harvard, 1981), p. 23.

Once that assumption is abandoned, that is, once we stop begging the question against mentalism, it seems to me that Chomsky's objection is completely valid. Where meanings psychologically construed are concerned, there is the familiar underdetermination of hypothesis by evidence, and that underdetermination is in addition to the underdetermination at the level of physical particles or brute physical behavior. So what? These are familiar points about any psychological theory. There is nothing special about meaning and nothing to show that where meaning is concerned there is no fact of the matter.

To deepen our understanding of these points, we must now turn to the thesis of the relativity of ontology.

III

Quine recognizes that the proofs of the indeterminacy of translation and of the inscrutability of reference seem to be leading to absurd consequences. He writes:

> We seem to be maneuvering ourselves into the absurd position that there is no difference on any terms, interlinguistic or intralinguistic, objective or subjective, between referring to rabbits and referring to rabbit parts or stages; or between referring to formulas and referring to their Gödel numbers. Surely this is absurd, for it would imply that there is no difference between the rabbit and each of its parts or stages, and no difference between a formula and its Gödel number. Reference would seem now to become nonsense not just in radical translation but at home.[10]

The indeterminacy thesis seems to have the absurd consequence that indeterminacy and inscrutability apply to the first-person case, to oneself: "If it is to make sense to say even of oneself that one is referring to rabbits and formulas and not to rabbit stages and Gödel numbers, then it should make sense equally to say it of someone else" (*ibid.*, 47).

Quine recognizes something that many of his critics have missed, and that is the real absurdity of the indeterminacy argument once you follow out its logical consequences: followed to its conclusion, the argument has nothing essentially to do with translating from one language to another or even understanding another speaker of one's own language. If the argument is valid, then it must have the result that there isn't any difference *for me*

[10] *Ontological Relativity and Other Essays* (New York: Columbia, 1969), pp. 47/8.

between *meaning* rabbit or rabbit stage, and that has the further result that there isn't any difference for me between *referring to* a rabbit and referring to a rabbit stage, and there isn't any difference for me between something's *being* a rabbit and its *being* a rabbit stage. And all of this is a consequence of the behaviorist assumption that there isn't any meaning beyond behaviorist meaning. Once we concede that as far as behaviorist "stimulus meaning" is concerned, 'There's a rabbit' and 'There's a rabbit stage' are "stimulus synonymous," then the rest follows, because on the behaviorist hypothesis there isn't any other kind of objectively real meaning or synonymy. I think, with Quine, that these consequences are absurd on their face, but if there is any doubt about their absurdity, recall that the whole argument about 'Gavagai' was understood by me (or you) only because we know the difference for our own case between meaning rabbit, rabbit stage, rabbit part, etcetera.

I said in the last section that the thesis of indeterminacy is the thesis that there cannot be empirically well-motivated translations of the words of one language into those of another, given behaviorism. But if this thesis is correct, then there cannot even be "correct" translations from a language into itself. By observing my idiolect of English, I can't tell whether by 'rabbit' I mean rabbit stage, rabbit part, or whatnot. Quine need not have considered Gavagai speakers. He could have simply observed in his own case that there was no "empirical" difference between his meaning one thing or the other and, therefore, that there was no real difference at all. And that result, as he correctly sees, is absurd. *If the indeterminacy thesis were really true, we would not even be able to understand its formulation; for when we were told there was no "fact of the matter" about the correctness of the translation between rabbit and rabbit stage, we would not have been able to hear any (objectively real) difference between the two English expressions to start with.*

Here is Quine's picture: I am a machine capable of receiving "nerve hits" and capable of emitting sounds. I am disposed to emit certain sounds in response to certain nerve hits; and, objectively speaking, that is all there is to meaning. Now the stimulus meaning of "There's a rabbit stage" is the same as that of "There's a rabbit," since the sounds are caused by the same nerve hits. It isn't just that Quine has a technical notion of "stimulus meaning" which he wants to add to our common-sense notion of meaning. No, he thinks that, as far as objective reality is concerned, stimulus meaning is all the meaning there is. And it is his notion of stimulus meaning which generates the absurdity.

The resolution of this "quandary," according to Quine, lies in perceiving the *relativity* of reference and ontology. "Reference *is* nonsense except relative to a coordinate system" (*ibid.*, 47), and the coordinate system is provided by a background language. The question for me of whether I am referring to a rabbit by 'rabbit' is answered by simply taking the English background language for granted, by "acquiescing in our mother tongue and taking its words at face value" (49). Just as in physics it makes sense to speak of the position and velocity of an object only relative to a coordinate system, so analogously it makes sense to talk of the reference of an expression only relative to some background language. Indeed, where translation from another language is concerned, reference is doubly relative: relative first to the selection of a background language into which to translate the target language, and relative second to the arbitrary selection of a translation manual for translating words of the target into the background.

Now, does this answer remove the apparent absurdity? I do not see how it does; indeed I shall argue that it simply repeats the problem without solving it.

I believe that with the thesis of relativity we have reached the crux of the indeterminacy argument. For this issue we can forget all about 'gavagai' and radical translation; they were merely picturesque illustrations of the consequences of behaviorism. The crucial thesis can be exemplified as follows:

> There is no empirical difference between the claim that I meant rabbit by 'rabbit' and the claim that I meant, for example, rabbit stage by 'rabbit'.

This is a consequence of the original thesis of *Word and Object*, and it is now admitted to be absurd. So to get out of the absurdity we substitute a revised relativity thesis:

> Relative to one arbitrarily selected translation scheme we can truly say that I meant rabbit, relative to another scheme, equally arbitrary, that I meant, for example, rabbit stage, *and there is no empirical difference between the two schemes.*

But the revised thesis is just as absurd as – and indeed expresses the same absurdity as – the first. And this should not surprise us, because the original absurdity arose in a discourse that already was relativized; it arose relative to my idiolect of English. The absurdity is that, if I assume my idiolect is a fixed set of dispositions to verbal behavior, then any translation of one word into itself or another of my idiolect is absolutely arbitrary and without empirical content. There is no way for me to tell whether by 'rabbit' I mean rabbit, rabbit stage, rabbit part, and so forth. This applies even to simple disquotation: there is no way even to justify the claim that by 'rabbit' I mean rabbit. Now, it does not meet this difficulty to say that we can fix meaning and reference by making an arbitrary selection of a translation manual. The arbitrariness of the selection of the translation manual is precisely the problem, since it is a reflection of the arbitrariness of the selection from among the original range of alternative analytical hypotheses. Quine's thesis of relativity does not remove the absurdity; it simply restates it.

When Quine advises us to acquiesce in our mother tongue and take words at their face value, we have to remind ourselves that, on his account, our mother tongue consists entirely of a set of dispositions to verbal behavior in response to sensory stimuli, and, so construed, the empirical face value of 'rabbit' and that of 'rabbit stage' are indistinguishable. We really cannot have it both ways. We cannot, on the one hand, insist on a rigorous behaviorism that implies that there is no fact of the matter and then, when we get in trouble, appeal to a naive notion of a mother tongue or home language with words having a face value in excess of their empirical behavioral content. If we are serious about our behaviorism, the mother tongue is the mother of indeterminacy, and the face value is counterfeit if it suggests that there are empirical differences when in fact there are none.

But what about the analogy with physics? Will that rescue us from the absurdity? One of the peculiar features of this entire discussion is the speed with which breathtaking conclusions are drawn on the basis of a few sketchy remarks and underdescribed examples. To try to get at least a little bit clearer about what is going on, let us try to state this particular issue a little more carefully. To begin, I want to state some more of the common-sense, pre-Quinean intuitions that lead me, and to a certain extent Quine himself, to think that the theses of indeterminacy and inscrutability lead or threaten to lead to absurd results. To make it intuitively easier, let us consider the case of translation from one language to another, though it is important to remember that any difficulty we find with translation from one language to another we will also find with the case of one language alone. Let us suppose that, as I am out driving with two French friends, Henri and Pierre, a rabbit suddenly crosses in front of the car, and I declare "There's a rabbit." Let us suppose further that Henri and Pierre do not know the meaning of the English 'rabbit', so each tries to translate it in a way that is consistent with my dispositions to verbal behavior. Henri, we may suppose, concludes that 'rabbit' means *stade de lapin.* Pierre, on the basis of the same evidence, decides it means *parti non-détachée d'un lapin.* Now according to our pre-Quinean intuitions, the problem for both Henri and Pierre is quite simple: they both got it wrong. It is just a plain fact about me that when I said "rabbit," I did not mean *stade de lapin* or *partie non-détachée d'un lapin.* Those are just bad translations. Of course, when I say that, I am making certain assumptions about the meanings of these expressions in French and, therefore, about the meanings that Henri and Pierre attach to these expressions. And these assumptions, like any other empirical assumptions, are subject to the usual underdetermination of hypotheses by evidence. Assuming that I got the assumptions right, Henri and Pierre are just mistaken. But even assuming that I got my assumptions wrong, if they are wrong in a certain specific way, then Henri and Pierre are just right. That is, if, for example, Henri means by *stade de lapin* what I mean by *lapin,* then he understands me perfectly; he simply has an eccentric way of expressing this understanding. The important thing to notice is that, in either case, whether they are right about my original meaning or I am right in thinking that they are wrong, there is a plain fact of the matter to be right or wrong about.[11]

These are some of the common-sense intuitions that we need to answer. Does the analogy with the relativity of motion get us out of this quandary? Let's take the idea seriously and try it out. Suppose that in the car during our rabbit conversation Henri expresses the view that we are going 60 miles an hour, while Pierre on the other hand insists we are going only 5 miles an hour. Later it turns out that Pierre was observing a large truck we were passing and was estimating our speed relative to it, while Henri was talking about our speed relative to the road surface. Once these relativities are identified there is no longer even the appearance of paradox or disagreement. Pierre and Henri are both right. But are they analogously both right about the translation of 'rabbit' once the coordinate systems have been identified? Is it a case of moving at different semantic speeds relative to different linguistic coordinate systems? It seems to me that these absurdities are just as absurd when relativized.

[11] One of the most puzzling aspects of this whole literature is the remarks people make about the ability to speak two or more languages and to translate from one to the other. Quine speaks of the "traditional equations" (*Word and Object,* p. 28) for translating from one language into another. But, except for a few odd locutions, tradition has nothing to do with it. (It is a tradition, I guess, to translate Frege's *Bedeutung* as 'reference', even though it doesn't really mean that in German.) When I translate 'butterfly' as *papillon,* for example, there is no tradition involved at all; or, if there is, I certainly know nothing of it. I translate 'butterfly' as *papillon* because that is what 'butterfly' means in French. Similarly, Michael Dummett speaks of "conventions" for translating from one language to another [see "The Significance of Quine's Indeterminacy Thesis," *Synthese,* XXVII, 3/4 (July/August 1974): 351–397]. But the point is that, if you know what the words mean, there isn't any room for further conventions. By convention, the numeral '2' stands for the number two in the Arabic notation, 'II' stands for the same number in the Roman notation. But, for these very reasons, we don't need a further convention that '2' can be translated as 'II'.

On Quine's view, I am right relative to English in thinking that I meant rabbit, Pierre is right relative to French in thinking that I meant *partie non-détachée d'un lapin*, and Henri is also right relative to French in thinking that I meant *stade de lapin – even though Henri and Pierre are inconsistent with each other, and both are inconsistent with the translation I would give.* And it is not an answer to this point to maintain that the appearance of inconsistency derives from the fact that we each have different translation manuals, because the problem we are trying to deal with is that we know independently that both of their translation manuals are just plain wrong. It was the apparent wrongness of the translation manuals that we were trying to account for. To put the point more generally, the aim of the analogy with physics was to show how we could remove the apparent paradoxes and absurdities by showing that they were just as apparent but as unreal as in the physics case. We see that there is no absurdity in supposing that we can be going both 5 and 60 miles an hour at the same time, once we see that our speed is relative to different coordinate systems. But the analogy between physics and meaning fails. Even after we have relativized meaning, we are still left with the same absurdities we had before.

Why does the analogy break down? In physics the position and motion of a body consist entirely in its relations to some coordinate system; but there is more to meaning than just the relations that a word has to the language of which it is a part; otherwise the question of translation could never arise in the first place. We can't detach the specific motion or position of an object from a reference to a specific coordinate system and translate it into another system in the way we can detach a specific meaning from a specific linguistic system and find an expression that has that very meaning in another linguistic system. Of course, a word means what it does only relative[12] to a language of which it is a part, but the very relativity of the *possession* of meaning presupposes the nonrelativity of the *meaning* possessed. This has no analogue in the relativity of physical position and motion.

Someone might object that I seem to be assuming the very "myth of the museum" that Quine is challenging, the view that there exists a class of mental entities called "meanings." But my point is neutral between the various

[12] I argue elsewhere that the functioning of a speaker's meaning is also relative to a whole Network of intentional states and a Background of preintentional capacities. I believe that this relativity is vastly more radical than has been generally appreciated and, indeed, more radical than Quine's indeterminacy thesis, but it is irrelevant to this part of the indeterminacy dispute. [See my *Intentionality: An Essay in the Philosophy of Mind* (New York: Cambridge, 1983), chaps. 1 and 5.]

theories of meaning. Let meaning be a matter of ideas in the head à la Hume, dispositions to behavior à la Quine, uses of words à la Wittgenstein, or intentional capacities à la me. It doesn't matter for this point. Whatever meaning is, we need to distinguish the true thesis that a word has the particular meaning it has only relative to a language from the false thesis that the meaning itself is relative to a language. Indeed, we are now in a position to state the argument in a way that is independent of any particular theory of meaning: grant me that there is a distinction between meaningful and meaningless phonetic sequences (words). Thus, in English, 'rabbit' is meaningful, 'flurg' is meaningless. Such remarks are always made relative to a language. Perhaps in some other language 'flurg' is meaningful and 'rabbit' is meaningless. But if 'rabbit' is meaningful in English and 'flurg' is meaningless, there must be some feature that 'rabbit' has in English which 'flurg' lacks. Let's call that feature its *meaning*, and the class of such features of words we can call *meanings*. Now, from the fact that 'rabbit' has the particular feature it has relative to English, it does not follow that the feature, its meaning, can exist only relative to English. Indeed, the question whether 'rabbit' has a translation into another language is precisely the question whether in the other language there is an expression with that very feature. The analogy between relativity in physics and semantics breaks down because there are no features of position and motion except relations to coordinate systems. And Quine's argument is a reductio ad absurdum because it shows that the totality of dispositions to speech behavior is unable to account for distinctions concerning the feature, meaning, which we know independently to exist, the distinction between the meaning of 'rabbit' and that of 'rabbit stage', for example. You cannot avoid the reductio by calling attention to the fact that 'rabbit' has the feature, its meaning, only relative to English, because the reductio is about the feature itself, and the feature itself is not relative to English.

My aim so far has not been to refute extreme linguistic behaviorism, but to show:

> First, the thesis of the indeterminacy of translation is just as well (indeed, I think better) construed as a reductio ad absurdum of the premises from which it was derived as it is construed as a surprising result from established premises.
>
> Second, the theory of the relativity of ontology does not succeed in answering the apparent absurdities that the thesis of indeterminacy and inscrutability leads us into.

What about refuting linguistic behaviorism on its own terms? There have been so many refutations of behaviorism in its various forms that it seems otiose to repeat any of them here. But it is worth pointing out that Quine's argument has the form of standard and traditional refutations of behaviorism. We know from our own case, from the first-person case, that behaviorism is wrong, because we know that our own mental phenomena are not equivalent to dispositions to behavior. Having the pain is one thing, being disposed to exhibit pain behavior is another. Pain behavior is insufficient to account for pain, because one might exhibit the behavior and not have the pain, and one might have the pain and not exhibit it. Analogously, on Quine's argument, dispositions to verbal behavior are not sufficient to account for meanings, because one might exhibit behavior appropriate for a certain meaning, but that still might not be what one meant.

If someone has a new theory of the foundations of mathematics and from his new axioms he can derive that $2 + 2 = 5$, what are we to say? Do we say that he has made an important new discovery? Or do we say, rather, that he has disproved his axioms by a reductio ad absurdum? I find it hard to imagine a more powerful reductio ad absurdum argument against behaviorism than Quine's indeterminacy argument, because it denies the existence of distinctions that we know from our own case are valid.

IV

I have tried to show how the doctrines of indeterminacy and inscrutability depend on the special assumptions of behaviorism and that, consequently, the results can equally be taken as a refutation of that view. But now an interesting question arises. Why do philosophers who have no commitment to behaviorism accept these views? I will consider Donald Davidson, because he accepts the doctrine of indeterminacy while explicitly denying behaviorism. Davidson takes the frankly intentionalistic notion of "holding a sentence true" (i.e., believing that it is true) as the basis on which to build a theory of meaning. What then is the area of agreement between him and Quine which generates the indeterminacy? And what does he have to say about the "quandary" that Quine faces? How does he deal with the first-person case? Davidson answers the first question this way:

> The crucial point on which I am with Quine might be put: all the evidence for or against a theory of truth (interpretation, translation) comes in the form of facts about what events or situations in the world cause, or would cause, speakers to assent to, or dissent from, each sentence in the speakers' repertoire (*op. cit.*, 230).

That is, as long as the unit of analysis is a whole sentence and as long as what causes the speaker's response is an objective state of affairs in the world – whether the response is assent and dissent, as in Quine, or holding a sentence true, as in Davidson – Davidson agrees with Quine about the indeterminacy thesis. (There are some differences about the extent of its application.)

But how exactly does the argument work for Davidson? How does Davidson, who rejects behaviorism, get the result that reference is inscrutable? I believe a close look at the texts suggests that he does accept a modified version of Quine's conception of an empirical theory of language. Though he accepts an intentionalistic psychology, he insists that semantic facts about the meanings of utterances must be equally accessible to all the participants in the speech situation, and thus for him the first-person case has no special status.

Quine grants us an apparatus of stimuli and dispositions to verbal response. Davidson grants us conditions in the world (corresponding to Quine's stimuli), utterances, and the psychological attitude of "holding true," directed at sentences. But, since the unit of empirical test is still the sentence, as opposed to parts of the sentence, and since different schemes of interpreting sentences in terms of parts of sentences can be made consistent with the same facts about which sentences a speaker holds true and under what conditions the speaker holds those sentences true, Davidson claims we still get inscrutability. The basic idea is that there will be different ways of matching up objects with words, any number of which could equally well figure in a truth theory that explained why a speaker held a sentence true.

The puzzle about Davidson is that, if you set out the argument as a series of steps, it doesn't follow that there is inscrutability *unless* you add an extra premise concerning the nature of an empirical theory of language. Here are the steps:

(1) The unit of empirical analysis in radical interpretation is the sentence (as opposed to subsentential elements).
(2) The only empirical evidence for radical interpretation is the fact that speakers "hold true" certain sentences in certain situations.
(3) There are alternative ways of matching words with objects which are inconsistent, but any number of which could equally well explain why a speaker held a sentence true.

But these three do not entail any inscrutability or indeterminacy about what the speaker actually meant and what he is referring to. For that you need an extra premise. What is it? I believe that it amounts to the following:

(4) All semantic facts must be publicly available to both speaker and hearer. If the interpreter cannot make a distinction on the basis of *public*, empirical evidence, then there is no distinction to be made.

Here is one of his examples: if everything has a shadow, then in a circumstance in which a speaker holds true the sentence 'Wilt is tall', we can take 'Wilt' to refer to Wilt and 'is tall' to refer to tall things, or we can with equal empirical justification take 'Wilt' to refer to the shadow of Wilt and 'is tall' to refer to the shadows of tall things. The first theory tells us that 'Wilt is tall' is true iff Wilt is tall. The second theory tells us that 'Wilt is tall' is true iff the shadow of Wilt is the shadow of a tall thing.

Davidson summarizes the argument thus:

> The argument for the inscrutability of reference has two steps. In the first step we recognize the empirical equivalence of alternative reference schemes. In the second step we show that, although an interpreter of the schemer can distinguish between the schemer's schemes, the existence of alternative schemes for interpreting the schemer prevents the interpreter from uniquely identifying the reference of the schemer's predicates, in particular his predicate 'refers' (whether or not indexed or relativized). *What an interpreter cannot on empirical grounds decide about the reference of a schemer's words cannot be an empirical feature of those words.* So those words do not, even when chosen from among arbitrary alternatives, uniquely determine a reference scheme (235; my italics).

In order to understand this argument it is crucial to see that it rests on the special assumption I mentioned about the nature of an empirical account of language and about the public character of semantics. From the mere fact that alternative reference schemes are consistent with all the *public* empirical data it simply doesn't follow by itself that there is any indeterminacy or inscrutability. Indeed, this is simply the familiar underdetermination thesis all over again: different hypotheses will account equally for the speaker's "hold true" attitudes, but, all the same, one of the hypotheses may be right about exactly what he meant by his words while another hypothesis may be wrong. In order to get the result of inscrutability, an additional premise is needed: since language is a public matter, all the facts about meaning must be public facts. Meaning is an "empirical" matter, and what is empirical about language must be equally accessible to all interpreters. Only given this assumption, this special conception of what constitutes the "empirical" and "public" character of language, can the argument be made to go through.

In order to deepen our understanding of what is going on here, let us contrast the common-sense account of the speech situation with Davidson's account. On the common-sense account, when I make the assertion, "Wilt is tall," by 'Wilt' I refer to Wilt, and by 'is tall' I mean: is tall. When I say "Wilt," I make no reference explicitly or implicitly to shadows, and, similarly, when I say "is tall," I make no reference to shadows. Now these are just plain facts about me. They are not theoretical hypotheses designed to account for my behavior or my "hold-true" attitudes. On the contrary, any such theory has to start with facts such as these. But, on Davidson's view, there is no empirical basis for attributing these different intentional states to me. Since all the empirical facts we are allowed to use are facts about what sentences I hold true and under what (publicly observable) conditions, there is no way to make the distinctions that our common-sense intuitions insist on. As with behaviorism, different and inconsistent interpretations at the subsentence level, at the level of words and phrases, will all be consistent with all the facts about what sentences I hold true under what conditions. But now it begins to look as if Davidson's version of inscrutability might also be a reductio ad absurdum of his premises, just as Quine's account was a reductio ad absurdum of behaviorism.

Before we draw any such conclusion, let us first see how Davidson deals with the obvious objection that is suggested by the common-sense account: since we do know in our *own* use of language that we are referring to Wilt, for example, and not to Wilt's shadow, and since what we seek in understanding another person is precisely what we already have in our own case, namely (more or less) determinate senses with determinate references, why should anyone else's references and senses be any less determinate than our own? Of course, in any given case I might get it wrong. I might suppose someone was referring to Wilt when really it was the shadow he was talking about. But that is the usual underdetermination of hypotheses about other minds from publicly available evidence. It does not show any form of inscrutability. What, in short, does Davidson say about the "quandary" that Quine faces, the first-person case?

> Perhaps someone (not Quine) will be tempted to say, 'But at least the speaker knows what he is referring to.' One should stand firm against this thought. The semantic features of language are public features. What no one can in the nature of the case figure out from the totality of the relevant evidence cannot be a part of meaning. And since every speaker must, in some dim sense at least, know this, *he cannot even intend to use his words with a unique reference for he knows that there is no way for his words to convey the reference to another* (235; my italics).

Quine tries to avoid the quandary by an appeal to relativity, but on Davidson's view there really isn't any quandary in the first place. Semantic features are public features, and since the public features are subject to the indeterminacy, *there is no such thing as unique reference.* Furthermore, "in some dim sense" I must know this; so *I can't even intend to refer to rabbits as opposed to rabbit parts, and I can't intend to refer to Wilt as opposed to Wilt's shadow.*[13]

Now, I believe this is a very strange view to hold, and I propose to examine it a bit further. First of all, let us grant that, for "public" languages such as French and English, there is at least one clear sense in which semantic features are, indeed, public features. I take it all that means is that different people can understand the same expressions in the same way in French and English. Furthermore, let us grant, at least for the sake of argument, that the public features are subject to underdetermination in at least this sense: I could give different but inconsistent interpretations of someone's words, all of which would be consistent with all of the actual and possible evidence I had about which sentences he held true. Now what follows? In our discussion of Quine's view we saw that indeterminacy, as opposed to underdetermination, is a consequence only if we deny mentalism from the start; it is not a consequence of underdetermination by itself. But, similarly, on Davidson's view the indeterminacy follows only if we assume from the start that different semantic facts must necessarily produce different "publicly observable" consequences. Only given this assumption can we derive the conclusion that speaker's meaning and reference are indeterminate and inscrutable. But, I submit, we know quite independently that this conclusion is false, and, therefore, the premises from which it is derived cannot all be true. How do we know the conclusion is false? We know it because in our own case we know that we mean, for example, Wilt as opposed to Wilt's shadow, rabbit as opposed to rabbit stage. When I seek to understand another speaker, I seek to acquire in his case what I already have for my own case. Now, in my own case, when I understand myself, I know a great deal more than just under what external conditions I hold what sentences true. To put it crudely: in addition, I know what I mean. Furthermore, if another person understands me fully, he will know what I mean, and this goes far beyond just knowing under what conditions I hold what sentences true. So, if his understanding me requires much more than just knowing what sentences I hold true under what conditions, then my understanding him requires much more than

[13] Kirk Ludwig has pointed out to me that this seems to lead to a pragmatic paradox, since it looks as if, in order to state the thesis, we have to specify distinctions that, the thesis says, cannot be specified.

knowing what sentences he holds true under what conditions. Just knowing his "hold true" attitudes will never be enough for me fully to understand him. Why should it be? It would not be enough for me to understand me; and since, to repeat, what I need to acquire in his case is what I already have in my own case, I will need more than just these attitudes.

But what about Davidson's claim that what an interpreter cannot figure out from the totality of the relevant evidence cannot be part of meaning? Well, it all depends on what we are allowed to count as "figuring out from the totality of the relevant evidence." On the common-sense account, I do figure out from the relevant "evidence" that by 'Wilt' you mean Wilt and not Wilt's shadow, and the "evidence" is quite conclusive. How does it work? In real life I understand the speech of another not only within a Network of shared assumptions, but more importantly against a Background of nonrepresentational mental capacities – ways of being and behaving in the world which are both culturally and biologically shaped and which are so basic to our whole mode of existence that it is hard even to become aware of them (see my *Intentionality, op. cit.*, ch. 5). Now, given the Background, it will, in general, be quite out of the question that, when you say in English, "Wilt is tall" or "There goes a rabbit," you could with equal justification be taken to be talking about Wilt's shadow or rabbit stages. We get that surprising result only if we forget about real life and imagine that we are trying to understand the speech of another by constructing a "theory," using as "evidence" only his "hold true" attitudes directed toward sentences or his dispositions to make noises under stimulus conditions. Language is indeed a public matter, and, in general, we can tell what a person means if we know what he says and under what conditions he says it. But this certainty derives not from the supposition that the claim about what he means must be just a summary of the (publicly available) evidence; it is rather the same sort of certainty we have about what a man's intentions are from watching what he is doing. In both cases we know what is going on because we know how to interpret the "evidence." And in both cases the claims we make go beyond being mere summaries of the evidence, in a way that any claim about "other minds" goes beyond being a summary of the "public" evidence. But the fact that the interpretation of the speech of another is subject to the same sort of underdetermination[14] as any other claim about

[14] Here is an example of such underdetermination from real life. Until he was in middle age, a friend of mine thought that the Greek expression *hoi polloi* as used in English meant the elite of rich people, but that it was characteristically used ironically. Thus, if he saw a friend in a low-class bar he might say, "I see you have been hobnobbing with the hoi pol-

other minds does not show either that there is any indeterminacy or that we cannot, in general, figure out exactly what other people mean from what they say.

I conclude that our reaction to Davidson's version should be the same as our reaction to Quine's: in each case the conclusion of the argument is best construed as a reductio ad absurdum of the premises. Davidson's view is in a way more extreme than Quine's because he holds a view which is, I believe, literally incredible. Plugging in the first-person example to what he literally says, Davidson holds that what no external observer can decide from external evidence cannot be part of what I mean. Since such observers can't decide between inconsistent interpretations, and since I must, in some dim sense at least, know this, I cannot even intend to use 'rabbit' to mean rabbit as opposed to rabbit stage or undetached rabbit part, for I know there is no way for my words to convey this reference to another. This does not seem to me even remotely plausible. I know exactly which I mean, and though someone might get it wrong about me, just as I might get it wrong about him, the difficulty is the usual "other-minds problem" applied to semantics.

V

In any discussion like this there are bound to be issues much deeper than those which surface in the actual arguments of the philosophers involved. I believe that the deepest issue between me on the one hand and Davidson and Quine on the other concerns the nature of an empirical theory of language.

Both Quine and Davidson adopt the thought experiment of "radical translation" as a model for building an account of meaning. In radical translation an interpreter or translator tries to understand speakers of a language of which he has no prior knowledge whatever. On Davidson's view, "all understanding of the speech of another involves radical interpretation."[15] But the model of an unknown foreign language enables us to make more precise what sorts of assumptions and evidence we need to interpret someone else's speech.

loi." Since he spoke ironically and interpreted other people as speaking ironically, there were no behavioral differences between his use and the standard use. Indeed, he might have gone his whole life with this semantic eccentricity undetected. All the same, there are very definite facts about what he meant.

[15] "Radical Interpretation," *Dialectica*, XXVII (1973): 313–328, reprinted in *Inquiries into Truth and Interpretation*, pp. 125–139.

Notice that the model of radical translation already invites us, indeed forces us, to adopt a third-person point of view. The question now becomes, How would *we* know the meaning of the utterances of some *other* person? And the immediate difficulty with that way of posing the question is that it invites confusion between the epistemic and the semantic; it invites confusion between the question, *How* do you know? and the question, *What* is it that you know *when* you know? But the linguistically relevant facts must be the same in the questions, What is it for me to understand another person when he says "It's raining"? and What is it for me to understand myself when I say "It's raining"? since, to repeat, what I have when I understand him is exactly what he has when he understands me. But then I already understand me; so anything I can learn from studying his case I could learn from studying my case.

Still, the thought experiment of radical translation can be very useful in semantic theory because it focuses the question of how we communicate meaning from one speaker to another. The difficulty is that both Quine and Davidson set further constraints on the task of radical translation than those which any field linguist would in fact employ. I have twice watched the linguist Kenneth L. Pike[16] perform the "monolingual demonstration" where he begins to construct a translation of a totally alien language into English. And it seems quite clear to any observer of Pike that he does not confine his conception of translation to that described by Davidson and Quine. For example, Pike does not confine his investigation to matching verbal behavior and sensory stimuli in the manner of Quine, nor does he confine it to hold-true attitudes in the manner of Davidson. Rather, he tries to figure out what is going on in the mind of the native speaker, even at the level of particular words. And he can do this because he presupposes that he shares with the speaker of the exotic language a substantial amount of Network and Background (see fn 12 above).

Now granted that the thought experiment of radical interpretation is useful in understanding the notion of communication, why shouldn't the problem of radical interpretation be posed in common-sense mentalistic terms? Why should we place on it the further behavioristic or "empirical" constraints that Quine and Davidson so obviously do? Quine's writings contain scattered remarks of the following sort: "Our talk of external things, our very notion of things, is just a conceptual apparatus that helps us to foresee and control the triggering of our sensory receptors in the light of previous

[16] Pike's work appears to be the original inspiration for the idea of radical translation (see Quine, *Word and Object*, p. 28).

triggering of our sensory receptors. The triggering, first and last, is all we have to go on."[17]

Such a remark has the air of discovery, but I believe it simply expresses a preference for adopting a certain level of description. Suppose one substituted for the phrase "triggering of our sensory receptors" in this paragraph, the phrase "the movement of molecules." One could then argue that the movement of molecules, first and last, is all we have to go on. Both the "movement of molecules" version and the "sensory receptors" version are equally true and equally arbitrary. In a different philosophical tradition, one might also say that all we have to go on, first and last, is the thrownness (*Geworfenheit*) and the foundedness (*Befindlichkeit*) of Dasein in the lifeworld (*Lebenswelt*). Such remarks are characteristic of philosophy, but it is important to see that what looks like a discovery can equally be interpreted as simply the expression of preference for a certain level of description over others. The three choices I gave are all equally interpretable as equally true. How do we choose among them? I believe that all three – sensory receptors, molecules, and Dasein – are insufficient levels of description for getting at certain fundamental questions of semantics. Why? Because the level of semantics that we need to analyze also involves a level of intentionality. Semantics includes the level at which we express beliefs and desires in our intentional utterances, at which we mean things by sentences and mean quite specific things by certain words inside of sentences. Indeed, I believe that the intentionalistic level is already implicit in the quotation from Quine when he uses the expressions 'foresee' and 'control'. These convey intentionalistic notions, and, on Quine's own version of referential opacity, they create referentially opaque contexts. No one, with the possible exception of a few neurophysiologists working in laboratories, tries to foresee and control anything at the level of sensory receptors. Even if we wanted to, we simply don't know enough about this level. Why then in Quine do we get this round declaration that all we have to go on is the stimulation of the sensory receptors? I think it rests on a resolute rejection of mentalism in linguistic analysis, with a consequent insistence on having a third-person point of view. Once you grant that a fundamental unit of analysis is intentionality, then it seems you are forced to accept the first-person point of view as in some sense epistemically different from the point of view of the third-person observer. It is part of the persistent objectivizing tendency of philosophy and science since the seventeenth century that we regard the third-person objective point of

[17] *Theories and Things*, p. 1.

view as preferable to, as somehow more "empirical" than, the first-person, "subjective" point of view. What looks then like a simple declaration of scientific fact – that language is a matter of stimulations of nerve endings – turns out on examination to be the expression of a metaphysical preference and, I believe, a preference that is unwarranted by the facts. The crucial fact in question is that performing speech acts – and meaning things by utterances – goes on at a level of intrinsic first-person intentionality. Quine's behaviorism is motivated by a deep antimentalistic metaphysics which makes the behaviorist analysis seem the only analysis that is scientifically respectable.

A similar though more subtle form of rejection of the first-person point of view emerges in Davidson's writings in a number of places. Davidson tacitly supposes that what is empirical must be equally and publicly accessible to any competent observer. But why should it be? It is, for example, a plain empirical fact that I now have a pain, but that fact is not equally accessible to any observer. In Davidson, the crucial claims in the passages I quoted are where he says, "What an interpreter cannot on empirical grounds decide about the reference of a schemer's words cannot be an empirical feature of those words"; and prior to that where he claims, "What no one can in the nature of the case figure out from the totality of the relevant evidence cannot be a part of meaning." Both of these have an air of truism, but in actual usage they express a metaphysical preference for the third-person point of view, a preference which is assumed and not argued for; because, as in Quine's case, it seems part of the very notion of an empirical theory of language, an obvious consequence of the fact that language is a public phenomenon. What Davidson says looks like a tautology: What can't be decided empirically isn't empirical. But the way he uses this is not as a tautology. What he means is: What can't be conclusively settled on third-person objective tests cannot be an actual feature of language as far as semantics is concerned. On one use "empirical" means: subject to objective third-person tests. On the other use it means: actual or factual. There are then two different senses of "empirical"; and the argument against the first-person case succeeds only if we assume, falsely, that what isn't conclusively testable by third-person means isn't actual. On the other hand, once we grant that there is a distinction between the public evidence available about what a person means and the claim that he means such and such – that is, once we grant that the familiar underdetermination of evidence about other minds applies to semantic interpretation – there is no argument left for inscrutability.

The rival view that is implicit in my argument in this. Language is indeed public; and it is not a matter of meanings-as-introspectable-entities, private objects, privileged access, or any of the Cartesian paraphernalia. The point, however, is that, when we understand someone else or ourselves, what we require – among other things – is a knowledge of intentional contents. Knowledge of those contents is not equivalent to knowledge of the matching of public behavior with stimuli nor to the matching of utterances with conditions in the world. We see this most obviously in the first-person case, and our neglect of the first-person case leads us to have a false model of the understanding of language. We think, mistakenly, that understanding a speaker is a matter of constructing a "theory," that the theory is based on "evidence," and that the evidence must be "empirical."

14

SKEPTICISM ABOUT RULES AND INTENTIONALITY

In his book *Wittgenstein on Rules and Private Language*, Saul Kripke[1] presents a "skeptical paradox" which he attributes to Wittgenstein. I think, in fact, that his presentation involves a misinterpretation of Wittgenstein, but for most of the purposes of the present discussion, that doesn't matter. As Kripke says, he is primarily discussing "Wittgenstein's argument as it struck Kripke, as it presented a problem for him" (p. 5). Until further notice when I say, for example, "Wittgenstein claims that..." I mean: according to Kripke, Wittgenstein claims that....

I will begin by setting out the paradox and the solution that Kripke proposes. Given any symbol or word, there is nothing in my past history, including my past mental states, that would both explain and justify my current application of the word or symbol. So, for example, suppose I am given the expression "68 + 57," and suppose that this is a computation I have never performed before and, indeed, that I have never before computed with numbers as large as 57. There is no fact about my past history that makes it the case that by correctly computing "57 + 68" I must come up with the result "125" instead of the result "5." There is nothing about my past history that determines that the expression "+" shouldn't be interpreted as standing for the quus function, where 'quus' is symbolized by '@' and is defined as:

$$\begin{aligned} x @ y &= x + y, \text{ if } x, y < 57 \\ &= 5 \text{ otherwise.} \end{aligned}$$

"Now," asks the Kripkean skeptic, "what fact about me makes it the case that by '+' in the past I meant plus rather than quus?" And his skeptical

[1] Cambridge, Massachusetts: Harvard University Press, 1982.

answer is, "There isn't any fact about me." It follows from this that any new application of the expression "+" is a total leap in the dark. For if I might equally well have meant quus, then I might equally well have meant anything at all or nothing at all. There is no fact about me, no fact about my past history, that makes it the case that my present usage will only accord with my past usage if I give the answer "125." No instructions that I gave myself or that I was given in the past compel or justify the answer "125" rather than "5." For no fact about me makes it the case that when I used the term "+" in the past, I meant plus rather than quus.

Notice that on this form of skepticism, it would not be sufficient to answer it for me merely to explain the *causes* which incline me to answer "125" instead of "5"; rather it is a condition of adequacy on the answer that it must show how I am *justified* in answering "125" rather than "5." Kripke writes,

> An answer to the skeptic must satisfy two conditions. First, it must give an account of what fact it is (about my mental state) that constitutes my meaning plus, not quus. But further, there is a condition that any putative candidate for such a fact must satisfy. It must in some sense show how I am justified in giving the answer "125" to "68 + 57." (p. 11)

The skeptical solution to the paradox, which Kripke attributes to Wittgenstein, is to call attention to the role of community, the role of other people in my application of words and symbols. Wittgenstein holds, with the skeptic, that there is no fact as to whether I mean plus or quus. But Wittgenstein then says there are "assertability conditions" (Kripke's term, not Wittgenstein's) which allow us to attribute to people an understanding of the meaning of expressions. And these assertability conditions depend on public agreement. Any application of a word or symbol necessarily involves reference to a community and depends on there being general agreement within the community about the correct use of the word or symbol. Such attributions are simply inapplicable to a single person considered in isolation, and it is for this reason that Wittgenstein rejects the possibility of a "private language." Wittgenstein concedes to the skeptic that there are no truth conditions, no facts corresponding to the statement "I meant plus rather than quus," and which make the statement true. Rather, he says, we have to look at how such statements are used. And their use depends on there being a community. There is a language game played by the community of attributing to one of its members the grasping of a certain concept. But when we play this game, we are not attributing any special states of mind. On this view, Wittgenstein is claiming that we should not say that people agree on the results of addition because they have all grasped the concept or rule for addition; rather, we are entitled to say that they grasp the concept of addition because they agree on the results of addition problems. The attribution of grasping the concept does not explain the results; rather a certain consistency in the results makes it possible to play the language game of attributing the grasp of concepts. Kripke calls this move "the inversion of (the) conditional" (p. 93ff).

I want to save my criticisms for later, but it is important to point out now that there is an oscillation, indeed, I think an inconsistency, in the way that Kripke characterizes Wittgenstein's position. Sometimes he talks as if Wittgenstein were presenting a form of skepticism about rules, concepts, meanings, and so forth. But in fact the argument as we have stated it so far has no skeptical implications at all about either the existence or the explanatory power of these entities. The skepticism is entirely about words and symbols and has no implications whatever about rules or concepts. This oscillation comes out in the discussion of the inversion of the conditional. Sometimes he characterizes Wittgenstein's views in terms of words and symbols, sometimes in terms of concepts. Thus, he writes (p. 95), "If Jones does not come out with '125' when asked about '68 + 57,' we cannot assert that he means addition by '+.'" But he also writes (pp. 93–94n), "We do not say 12 + 7 = 19 and the like because we all grasp the concept of addition; we say we all grasp the concept of addition because we all say 12 + 7 = 19 and the like." But the second formulation, which makes reference to concepts but not to words and symbols, is simply not justifed by Kripke's argument. What the argument shows – if valid – is entirely about words and symbols and not about concepts and rules at all. The skepticism is entirely about the presence of mental phenomena sufficient to mediate the relation between expressions on the one hand and concepts on the other. But the most naive Fregean view about the explanatory power of concepts (meanings, rules, functions, etc.) is left entirely untouched by the argument as presented. As far as the argument goes, it would be perfectly OK to say:

> The concept of addition explains the results of addition.

Indeed, there is even no skepticism about the following sort of claim:

> Jones's grasp of the concept of addition explains his results in adding.

The skepticism in question is entirely about the quite distinct claim:

> Jones's meaning addition by "+" explains his results in addition.

It is about the latter sort of claim that the argument – if valid – would force us to invert the conditional and say, rather,

> The fact that Jones gets certain results enables us to say of him that he means addition by "+."

Because Jones gets the same sort of results as the community at large we can say that he means the concept of addition by the word "plus" and the expression "+." I will later on suggest that Wittgenstein's primary argument is about rules, meanings, concepts, and so forth; but at this point it is essential only to call attention to the distinction.

To help us understand this argument and its solution better, Kripke compares it with Hume's famous skeptical argument regarding causation and necessary connection. Hume argues that there is no fact of the matter about necessary connection. When we say that A caused B, the word "cause" does not correspond to any connection between A and B. Hume's skeptical solution to the problem is to discover another relation, namely, constant conjunction, and then claim that we are justified in attributing causal relations, not on the basis of a relation actually corresponding to the word "cause" in each individual instance, but rather to a general feature, namely, that causal relations always instantiate regularities. Just as it would make no sense for Hume to say that one event of a certain type caused another event of a certain type only one time in the entire history of the universe, so it makes no sense for Wittgenstein to say that a man used a word in accordance with a rule only one time in the history of the universe. Rather, the notion of using a word or symbol in accordance with a rule presupposes a community. However, there is a disanalogy between Hume and Wittgenstein which Kripke does not remark on. Hume actually gives us truth conditions for the word "cause." He actually provides a new definition of "cause" in terms of priority, contiguity, and constant conjuction that provides well-defined truth conditions, facts that the attribution of causal relations correspond to. But Kripke's Wittgenstein does not provide us with truth conditions for the attribution of the understanding of words and symbols. Rather, he provides assertability conditions within the language game.

Now what are we to make of this skeptical paradox and its alleged solution? I find it very puzzling. Suppose we try to take it naively and ask, "What, in fact, about my past history makes it the case that, if I am to be consistent with that history, by '+' I now mean plus and not quus?" The answer seems obvious. It is a fact about my past history that I have been trained to do arithmetic in a certain way, and as part of that training I learned to use the "+" sign for addition and not for some other function. According to that training, if I now compute "57 + 68" and get anything other than "125," I have made a mistake. Indeed, since we are assuming perfect memories, I can say that here is how it went: At Montclair School in Denver, Colorado, I learned how to add and I learned to use the "+" sign for addition. The way it went in a case like this is as follows:

> When you see a problem like "57 + 68," first you add the 7 and the 8 and get 15; then you write down the "5" and carry the 1. Then you add the 5 and the 6 and get 11 and you then add the 1 you just carried, and then you write the "12" that you get as a result. It comes out "125."

These are just plain and simple facts about the way I have learned arithmetic and the way I have learned to use the "+" symbol when doing arithmetic. Later on I will argue that this is exactly the right sort of answer to give to Kripke's skeptic, but not yet. But it is clear that the skeptic will not accept this line of argument. He will ask, "In what does this training consist? What fact about the mental processes induced in you by the training makes it the case that the right answer is '125' and not '5'? Won't all of the steps you described admit of the introduction of quus like forms of skepticism?"

What is especially puzzling about this form of skepticism is that in ways that are not entirely clear the common-sense answer has been ruled out of court as illegitimate. We will understand this better if we compare it with a similar form of skepticism. I think the argument Kripke attributes to Wittgenstein is less like Hume on causation than it is like Russell's paradox about the existence of the world in the past. How, asks Russell, do we know that the world didn't come into existence thirty seconds ago with all of our fossils, memories, libraries, and photographs intact? This is usually taken as an epistemic problem, but it can equally well be interpreted as an ontological problem: What fact about the world as it is right now, at present, makes it the case that it existed in the past? In this form the question is not epistemic because, like Kripke's skeptical paradox about meanings, it allows us to have perfect knowledge. In the Kripke paradox, we assume that we have perfect memories about the past, and then ask ourselves what fact about the past makes it the case that I meant plus rather than quus. And on the Russellian version of the skeptical paradox, we can ask what fact about the present makes it the case that present objects existed in the past. The only answers one could give to such questions would be commonsensical answers. Objects must have existed in the past, for example, because I bought this watch five years ago in Geneva, or I had Chinese food for lunch earlier today. But notice that in posing the skeptical problem, we have somehow or other ruled these common-sense answers out of court. This is characteristic of a certain kind of philosophical skepticism: the common-sense, Moore-type answers have been ruled out as illegitimate in advance. So the only possible answers are now treated as unacceptable answers. In this case, the standard things in which age consists are not now allowed to count. And similarly, in ways we have not yet made clear, in Kripke's example the standard ways in which one has knowledge of how words relate to rules or concepts, which then one can apply to new cases, are simply not allowed to count. The form of the question "What fact about you in the past makes it the case that . . . ?" has now been subtly reinterpreted in a way that precludes us from giving the common-sense answers, the only answers that could possibly answer the questions. The correct answer would be, for example, "I learned addition; and when I did, I learned to use the '+' sign for addition." And this knowledge gives me both a causal account of why I give the answer "125" and a normative account of why that answer is correct and other answers are not correct. Now why is it that this answer is not allowed to count, and what exactly is the metaphysical picture that seems to block this answer?

Before trying to answer that, let us go the next step in the argument. We were making certain assumptions in the presentation of the original Wittgensteinian paradox, and Kripke is quite explicit about these assumptions. We were assuming that in the past we had never actually added numbers larger than 57, and therefore we were also assuming that we never actually added these two numbers, 68 and 57. However, the skeptical paradox is meant to be completely general. In order to get the discussion started, Kripke has to state the problem as if it were about how facts about the past justify my present behavior, but the argument is meant to apply quite independently of these past-present considerations. He simply has to use this as an expository device in order to state the argument at all. But once stated, we are supposed to be able to see that it is completely general and applies to every application of a word or symbol. So let us go to the next step and ask, "How would the problem be affected if we abandoned these assumptions?" Suppose I said that I actually was given this very problem in addition by an arithmetic teacher on February 27, 1938: "68 + 57," and I was told that the correct answer was "125." But here, even if I say that I remember the answer to this particular problem and the correct answer is "125," that response will not be regarded as an appropriate response to this form of skepticism. Similarly, if I say, "I do remember, in fact, that we did work with the '+' sign for numbers greater than 57, and the result was not calculated according to the quus function, but according to the plus function." That is, the two assumptions that we made in order to get the argument going are not supposed to be essential to the argument. But what is the response that the skeptic makes when we tell him that we actually do remember this particular addition and we do remember that we proceeded according to the plus function with numbers greater than 57?

In order to answer this it seems to me that Kripke has to rely on a second argument. He seems to think that the two arguments are the same, but it seems to me that they are not exactly equivalent. The second argument is that even if you are given an intentional content, even if you are given a "fact of the matter," it is still subject to different interpretations. Even if you remember that the correct answer to the problem "68 + 57" is "125," that remark is still subject to different interpretations. For example, how do you know that the "+" in "68 + 57 equals 125" should not be interpreted as the schmuss function, according to which 68 + 57 = 125 on Wednesday afternoon, February 27, 1938, but otherwise = 5? In short, any fact of the matter that we are able to introduce about me to answer the skeptical problem will always be subject to reinterpretation, and that reinterpretation will be sufficient to reintroduce the skeptical problem that the fact-of-the-matter was supposed to answer.

Kripke makes it clear that the paradox is not just about the relation between the past and the present, but is intended to be completely general. However, the way that it becomes general is not made completely explicit in the text. In order to make the problem completely general, Kripke has to rely on a new concept, the concept of interpretation. Here the thesis is that intentional phenomena – rules, meanings, etcetera – are not self-interpreting. The same intentional phenomenon is subject to different interpretations. This seems to me a quite different argument. Kripke's original argument is that there simply are no mental facts of the matter which constrain our uses of words and symbols at all. Wittgenstein's argument, I believe, is there are facts of the matter, but any facts of the matter about meanings are subject to alternative interpretations. Now we see the importance of the objection I made earlier:

Kripke's argument is entirely about words and symbols. For Kripke the addition function (the rule for addition, the concept of addition) is absolutely clear, unambiguous, and unproblematic. The only skeptical problem is about whether or not the contents of the mind are sufficient to guarantee that in my usage the symbol "+" and the word "plus" stand for that function or for something else. On my reading, Wittgenstein's discussion, unlike Kripke's, is only incidentally about words and symbols. It is primarlily about the traditional notions of rules, concepts, meanings, and mental states. Wittgenstein's actual examples seem to me to support my understanding of his texts rather than Kripke's. So, for example, consider a typical case that

Wittgenstein gives. A child is taught to continue the series 2, 4, 6, 8 . . . , and then when he gets to 1000, he continues it 1004, 1008, 1012. . . . Now here, we think of the child as simply offering a different interpretation for a rule, a different way of applying a function, a different way of understanding a procedure. He thinks that when the numbers get big enough, then you have to "do the same thing," but doing the same thing here counts as putting down 1000, 1004, 1008, 1012. . . . Or consider Wittgenstein's example of adding 3 plus 4. If you put three dots in a circle and four dots in another circle, then 3 plus 4 equals 7 (Fig. 1).

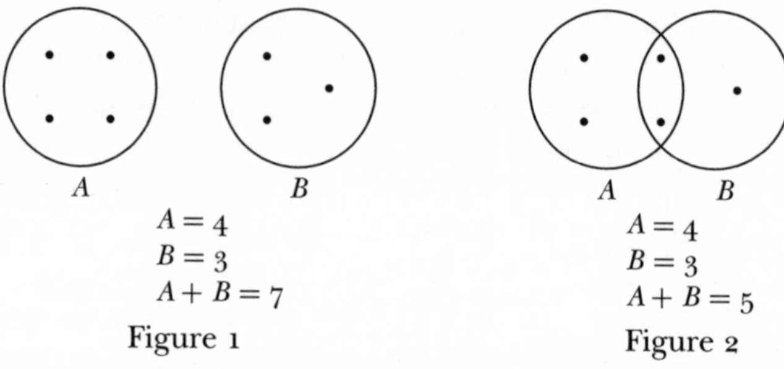

Figure 1

Figure 2

But if the two circles overlap in such a way that two of the dots are shared by both circles, then though *A* equals 3 and *B* equals 4, *A* plus *B* only equals 5 (Fig. 2). Now that is a possible interpretation of the rule for arithmetic. Indeed, that is an interpretation that we actually follow in certain cases. If I ask you to add the number of people in the class who can speak French to the number of the people in the class who can speak Spanish, do you count the French-speaking Spanish speakers once or twice? Most of us, I think, would just count people, that is to say, a French-speaking Spanish speaker would count as one and not as two. But the rules for addition don't fix that interpretation in advance. Well, what does fix that interpretation?

I will get to that in a minute. At present I just want to insist on this distinction:

> Kripke's problem is: Assuming a world of fixed and unproblematic rules, concepts, functions, etcetera, what mental facts about me make it the case that my words stand for one of these entities, for example, addition, rather than another, for example, quaddition.
>
> And his answer is: There are no such mental facts of the matter. Every new step is a leap in the dark.

Kripke then supplements this style of skepticism with another that I believe is closer to Wittgenstein:

> There are psychological facts of the matter about our use of words but they are not by themselves sufficent to determine the use of the words, since they are subject to different interpretations. Indeed the whole apparatus of rules, meanings, concepts, functions, and so forth, is problematic in precisely this way.

I will argue that Wittgenstein's solution to his problem – which is not Kripke's problem – appeals to what I call "the Background." In particular, Wittgenstein is anxious to insist that not every application of the rule should properly be described as an interpretation. The crucial paragraph here is #201.

> This was our paradox: no course of action could be determined by a rule, because every course of action can be made out to accord with the rule. The answer was: if everything can be made out to accord with the rule, then it can also be made out to conflict with it. And so there would be neither accord not conflict here.
>
> It can be seen that there is a misunderstanding here from the mere fact that in the course of our argument we give one interpretation after another; as if each one contented us at least for a moment, until we thought of yet another standing behind it. What this shews is that there is a way of grasping a rule which is *not* an *interpretation*, but which is exhibited in what we call "obeying the rule" and "going against it" in actual cases.
>
> Hence there is an inclination to say: every action according to the rule is an interpretation. But we ought to restrict the term "interpretation" to the substitution of one expression of the rule for another.

Part of the point, I take it, of these passages is to insist that it is wrong to suppose that every application of a rule requires a new act of interpretation. Skepticism about the possibility of alternative interpretations is blocked by the fact we are just trained to act in certain ways. No further or subsequent "interpretation" is necessary. But how exactly does this answer the skepticism? I will come back to this question later.

However, whether or not I am right in my interpretation of Wittgenstein is really irrelevant to the present dispute. The present dispute is: How shall we answer the style of skepticism that Kripke presents? In order to answer it, we have to understand its form. And I am claiming that, in fact, there are two independent arguments: one Kripke's and one Wittgenstein's.

It is hard to see how the solution that Kripke gives to the skeptical paradox in any way solves the paradox. If we are to think of the paradox from the first person point of view (as Kripke insists we should) – that is, if we are to think of the paradox as a paradox of the form, What fact about me makes it the case that I meant plus rather than quus in the past when I used the "+" sign? – then equally, the problem would arise for my perception of the agreement of other people. If there is a problem about what fact about me makes it the case that by "+" I meant plus in the past, then equally, there will be a problem about what fact about me makes it the case that by "agreement" I meant agreement rather than, say, quagreement in the past? What fact about my past makes me correct in describing these people's behavior as in "agreement." That is, if I am in doubt as to what fact about my past behavior and my past mental states makes for the validity of the present application of a word, then the words "agreement" and "disagreement," both of which concepts are necessary for my application of the solution to the skeptical paradox that Kripke provides, are equally in doubt.

Oddly enough, Kripke seems to recognize this very difficulty, but it is hard to see how he says anything to solve it. On the very last page of the book in a footnote added in the proof, he writes:

> If Wittgenstein had been attempting to give a necessary and sufficient condition to show that '125', not '5', is the 'right' response to '68 + 57', he might be charged with circularity. For he might be taken to say that my response is correct if and only if it agrees with that of others. But even if the sceptic and I both accept this criterion in advance, might not the sceptic maintain that just as I was wrong about what '+' meant in the past, so I was wrong about 'agree'? Indeed, to attempt to reduce the rule for addition to another rule – "Respond to an addition problem exactly as others do!" – falls afoul of Wittgenstein's strictures on 'a rule for interpreting a rule' just as much as any other such attempted reduction....
>
> What Wittgenstein *is* doing is describing the utility in our lives of a certain practice. Necessarily he must give this description in our own language. As in the case of any such use of our language, a participant in another form of life might apply various terms in the description (such as "agreement") in a non-standard 'quus-like' way. Indeed, we may judge that those in a given community 'agree', while someone in another form of life would judge that they do not. This cannot be an

objection to Wittgenstein's solution unless he is to be prohibited from any use of language at all. (p. 146)

It is hard to see how this is an adequate reply, because the skeptical solution is supposed to be a *solution.* That is, on the model of Hume's skeptical solution to the problem of causation it was supposed to show how I can be justified in my use of a word, even while accepting the original skeptical argument, just as Hume shows how we can be justified in using the word "cause," even while accepting the original skepticism about necessary connection. But Kripke's solution fails to show that; it fails to show that we have any genuine assertibility conditions, because the arguments for the original skeptical position in the first place are equally arguments against any assertibility conditions. The problem is not, as Kripke suggests, a difficulty in the attempt to get truth conditions as opposed to assertibility conditions. The problem is to get any rational constraint at all on our use of words, and Kripke's proposed solution does not show how this is possible.

It is time to try to make a fresh start. As I remarked before, we could give a nonepistemic version of Russell's skepticism about the past, but it seems we could give a nonepistemic version of just about any form of skepticism. And once we do that it looks like Kripke's is not a new form of skepticism at all. Consider:

What fact about this very experience makes it an experience of an object in the external world?
What fact about this very experience makes it not a hallucination?
What fact about the present makes it the case that the world existed in the past?
What fact about my present self makes me identical with a person who existed in the past?
What fact about your present behavior makes it the case that you are now in pain?
What fact about any two events considered in isolation makes it the case that the first caused the second?

and finally:

What fact about my past experiences makes it the case that I meant plus and not quus?

All of these are nonepistemic in the sense that a perfect knower, say, God, would not be able to solve the skeptical problem for any of them *given the way the problem was structured.* So, for example, if God knew all there was to know about my *present* experience, He still would not know whether or not it was veridical, whether it was an experience of an independently existing object in the world. And so on through all of the other sorts of examples. Notice furthermore that in order to make the skepticism work we have to hear these questions in a very special way, a way that makes the common-sense answer inappropriate. So, for example, the common-sense answer to the first question is: This experience of seeming to see a table in front of me will actually be one of seeing a table in front of me, if there really is a table in front of me and the fact that there is a table there is in a certain sort of a way causing me to have this very visual experience. But then why isn't this sort of answer sufficient to deal with Kripke's as well as all the other forms of skepticisms? To put it generally, skepticism of this form gets going by restricting the range of admissible answers to the questions to an area that is too small to account for the questions being asked. There isn't any fact about the present that makes it the case that present objects existed in the past other than the fact that many of them did exist in the past. This sounds circular but it isn't really. The circularity is removed when you consider individual cases. The facts about this watch that makes it the case that it existed in the past are such things as that it was manufactured in Switzerland about forty-five years ago; I bought it in a store in Geneva in 1960; I have owned it since; and so forth. Any one of these truths is sufficient to entail that it existed in the past. Of course these answers are "question begging" in the sense that they appeal to a kind of fact which it was the aim of the skepticism to rule out. But why should we allow it to be ruled out? As long as we only scrutinize the watch as we have it now, we find no fact about it that makes it the case that it existed before. But why should we? Similarly, when we are asked what fact about my past makes it the case that I meant plus rather than quus, we find nothing either in my brain or in my introspectible mental states which is sufficient by itself to guarantee that I meant one rather than the other. But, again, why should we? Notice that the skepticism in question works only because we tacitly accept a certain interpretation of the crucial question, "What fact about x makes it the case that p?" And on this interpretation the fact that x is such that p is the case is not regarded as an acceptable answer. But if we take seriously the question "What fact about me makes it the case that by '+' I mean addition and not quaddition?" we would get facts like the following: I was taught to use the "+" sign for addition in school; and finally I got the hang of it. I simply learned addition. There was never any possibility of quaddition, it was never even in question. In fact, I never heard of quaddition until I heard Kripke talk about it. The fact about my past that makes it the case that I meant addition and not quaddition is that I learned to use "+" for addition and not for quaddition. Period. And the fact about my present that makes it the case that I now mean addition and not quaddition is simply the fact that I mean addition and not quaddition. Period. Of course, this fact will have further consequences. It will have the consequence that I will be able to see that certain sorts of answers are mistaken and others correct, for example.

Now it is at this point that Kripke's second argument comes into play and it is at this point that we get to what I believe is the real Wittgensteinian argument. From now on when I say "Wittgenstein claims that . . . " I don't mean Wittgenstein according to Kripke claims that, though to avoid squabbles about exegesis I must insist that I am explaining Wittgenstein's argument as it struck Searle, as it presented a problem for him; and I am not confident about the historical Wittgenstein, about whom it is always difficult to be confident anyhow. It seems to me that at this point Wittgenstein would say: Yes, of course you were taught to do it this way, but wouldn't it have been possible to interpret the teaching in some other way? What about the teaching guarantees that "125" is the right answer? "No course of action could be determined by a rule because every course of action can be made out to accord with the rule." In short, what I learn from the teaching need not be automatically self-interpeting. I could always give it some other interpretation. Even if I am endowed with the richest set of concepts, rules, meanings, functions, and so forth, they are still not self-interpreting.

I think the examples that Wittgenstein gives are really rather unlike the examples that Kripke gives. The Kripke examples are all cases where it appears there is no fact of the matter at all that makes it the case that I meant one thing as opposed to something else by a word. But the Wittgenstein examples, like the example of continuing the series 2, 4, 6, 8 . . . by going on 1004, 1008, 1012 . . . , are all cases where it does seem that there is a fact of the matter, but that the fact is subject to different interpretations. It seems that the intentional contents are not self-interpreting in a way that would block the possibility of what any normal person would call a "misinterpretation." To repeat, it seems to me that Wittgenstein's problem is not a "no fact of the matter" form of skepticism (indeed, it seems to me misleading to call Wittgenstein's argument a form of skepticism at all), but it is a puzzle in which he calls attention to the possibility of always raising alternative *interpretations* of the facts of the matter. It seems to me Wittgenstein's actual solution to this form of skepticism is rather swift. "What this shews is that there is a way of grasping a rule which is *not an interpretation*, but which is exhibited in what we call 'obeying the rule' and 'going against it' in actual cases. Hence there is an inclination to say: Every action according to the rule is an interpretation. But we ought to restrict the term 'interpretation' to the substitution of one expression of the rule for another" (para 201).

But the passage I have quoted still leaves open the question, "What makes it the case that there are ways of grasping a rule which are not interpretations, where we just act, where we just act in a way that we would call 'obeying the rule' and 'going against it' in actual cases?" I am not really sure what Wittgenstein's answer to this question would be. But I know the answer that I would give to the question, and I think that my giving this answer has been heavily influenced by Wittgenstein. In any case, whether or not it is Wittgenstein's answer, here is the answer I would give: It is just a fact about our practices, about the way we were brought up to behave, that we count certain sorts of things as correctly applying a rule and others not, that we count certain sorts of things as correctly doing addition and others not. True, the rules of addition, like any rule, are subject to alternative interpretations. Indeed, this phenomenon is true of all intentionality. It is always possible to offer alternative interpretations of any intentional content. But what fixes the interpretation in actual practice, in real life, is what I have elsewhere called "the Background."[2] We have Background ways of behaving, and our understanding of any rule or of any intentional content is always against such a Background. Just as any intentional content only fixes conditions of satisfaction relative to a Background, and just as any intentional content is relative in the sense that alternative sets of truth conditions would be determined by the same intentional content given different Backgrounds, the same applies to Wittgenstein's examples of obeying rules and following rules and going against rules. In any given case of applying the rule, my behavior is fixed by the fact that I have the rule and I apply the rule only against a set of Background practices and capacities. I don't have to offer a new interpretation for the rule, indeed, I am with Wittgenstein in thinking that in the ordinary sense, I don't have to offer an interpretation of the rule at all. I simply act and I simply act on the rule when I am obeying the rule. As Wittgenstein says, "'Obeying a rule' is a practice."[3]

[2] John Searle, *Intentionality, An Essay in the Philosophy of Mind*, Cambridge: Cambridge University Press, 1983.

[3] *Philosophical Investigations*, para 202.

NAME INDEX

The author wishes to thank Josef Moural for preparing the indexes.

SUBJECT INDEX